Transcultural Literary Studies: Politics, Theory, and Literary Analysis

Special Issue Editor
Bernd Fischer

Special Issue Editor
Bernd Fischer
The Ohio State University
USA

Editorial Office
MDPI AG
St. Alban-Anlage 66
Basel, Switzerland

This edition is a reprint of the Special Issue published online in the open access journal *Humanities* (ISSN 2076-0787) in 2016 (available at:
http://www.mdpi.com/journal/humanities/special_issues/transcultural_literary_studies).

For citation purposes, cite each article independently as indicated on the article page online and as indicated below:

Author 1; Author 2; Author 3 etc. Article title. *Journal Name*. **Year**. Article number/page range.

ISBN 978-3-03842-394-2 (Pbk)
ISBN 978-3-03842-395-9 (PDF)

Table of Contents

About the Guest Editor

Bernd Fischer, Dr. phil., Universität Siegen, 1982; Professor of German at The Ohio State University since 1982; Department Chair, 1996–2008 and 2012–2014; Visiting appointments at Essen, Hamburg, Siegen, and Case Western Reserve University; Alexander von Humboldt Fellow, 1994, 2005, and 2016; Editor, *The German Quarterly*, 1997–1999; Books (selection): *Ein anderer Blick—Saul Aschers politische Schriften* (2016); *Heinrich von Kleist and Modernity* (2011, with Tim Mehigan); *Cultural Politics and the Politics of Culture* (2007, with Helen Fehervary); *A Companion to the Works of Heinrich von Kleist* (2003); *Das Eigene und das Eigentliche: Klopstock, Herder, Fichte, Kleist. Episoden aus der Konstruktionsgeschichte nationaler Intentionalitäten* (1996); *Christoph Hein: Drama und Prosa im letzten Jahrzehnt der DDR* (1990); *Ironische Metaphysik: Die Erzählungen Heinrich von Kleists* (1988); *Kabale und Liebe: Skepsis und Melodrama in Schillers bürgerlichem Trauerspiel* (1987); *Literatur und Politik: Die `Novellensammlung von 1812' und das 'Landhausleben' von Achim von Arnim* (1983).

Editorial

Special Issue Introduction "Transcultural Literary Studies: Politics, Theory, and Literary Analysis"

Bernd Fischer

Department of Germanic Languages and Literatures, The Ohio State University, Hagerty Hall,
1775 College Road Columbus, OH 43210, USA; fischer.5@osu.edu; Tel.: +1-614-292-6985; Fax: +1-614-292-8510

Academic Editor: Albrecht Classen
Received: 2 November 2016; Accepted: 21 November 2016; Published: 21 December 2016

As we witness the rise of intemperate nationalism, self-indulgent nativism, and aggressive xenophobia in many countries, multi- and intercultural studies and initiatives have come under considerable pressure. At least for now, it seems that they have not been able to offer satisfactory alternatives for populations that suffer under the ill effects of globalization or believe so. Theories of transculturalism arose out of the concern that part of the blame can be attributed to an underlying identity model that has not been able to set itself sufficiently apart from its own origins in culturalist traditions, leaving the door open for strong nationalistic and ethnocentric orientations. But how can we imagine transcultural communities? It seems sensible to examine whether transculturalism—with its questioning of the dominance of group identity and its return to the individual as privileged site for cultural multiplicity—can offer guideposts for conceptualizing 'individual' diversity without underplaying the role of class, religion, and community. To my mind, the question has not yet been answered. Some features of transculturalism, especially those that adhere to central propositions of the Enlightenment and Modernism, should be viewed cautiously with political and historical awareness. Among those, I would count elitist individualism and utopianism, teleologically structured conceptualizations of humanism, and an indiscriminating belief in the ascendency of human universals, most recently appropriated from 'hard' human sciences such as evolutionary anthropology. Highlighting transcultural interpretations (in critical tension with ideas of national or sub-national cultures) is, by no small measure, a political decision that has often been prompted by a search for commonalities as a basis for the design of universal human rights, international law, transnational structures, and global education. At the same time, transcultural approaches are, *prima fasciae*, rooted in the ethos and tradition of the natural sciences, numerous social sciences, and even some areas within the humanities (e.g., philosophy). In short, transcultural studies cannot escape operating in the midst of ideological and political minefields. All the more, I would like to thank the contributors to this issue of *Humanities*, who did not shy away from taking risks in order to expound upon their particular understandings of transculturalism in interpretations of significant literary texts from the Middle Ages all the way to the 21st century.

As I discuss in my introductory essay, I don't consider it an accident that several contributions highlight the impact of the emergence of enlightened cultural cosmopolitanism in the long 18th century. But the transcultural story of the post-Roman period did certainly not start there. One of the most impressive illustrations of the link between philosophical advances and transcultural identity is, to my mind, the first post-classical Enlightenment at the height of the Middle Ages, perhaps best exemplified by the Sephardic Jewish philosopher and scientist Maimonides, who, born in Cordova, traveled through much of North Africa and immersed himself deeply into the study of the Arab Enlightenment, served as Saladin's personal physician, became a revered teacher in the Jewish communities of Morocco and Egypt and wrote his famous *Guide for the Perplexed* in Arabic. In the arts, we can find some reflection of this early episode of transculturality at the Sicilian royal court in *Palermo* of Frederick II of Hohenstaufen, e.g., the *Sicilian School* of poetry.

Albrecht Classen shows in his contribution that the late medieval Mediterranean world continued to inspire a transculturally enriched literature. Furthermore, the impact of the cultural encounters between the different religions, languages, and populations on the shores of the Mediterranean Sea reached far into its hinterlands, from the Middle East and the kingdoms of Niger and Mali to the world north of the Alps. The prose novels Classen discusses demonstrate how 'German' writers engaged the Mediterranean horizon. To what extent these late medieval novels comprise traits of transcultural aesthetics is indeed a fascinating question. At the center of Classen's study are Elisabeth von Nassau-Saarbrücken's *Königin Sibille* (1437), Thüring von Ringoltingen's *Melusine* (1456), the Scottish Princess Eleonor's novel *Pontus und Sidonia* (between 1440 and 1460), and the anonymously published *Fortunatus* (1509), which Classen calls the ultimate departure toward the transcultural in the Mediterranean context. It is Cyprus, the novel's quintessential international location, to which Fortunatus returns after his grand tour through much of the known world; in Classen's words: it is there where the Mediterranean and the transcultural meet and form a significant union. Classen concludes that specific foundations for a transcultural world emerge in the novels he examined, because their protagonists travel through concretely identifiable spaces, reflecting what Classen calls a significant "spatial turn" towards specific geographic terms and the assumption of an accessible multi-religious and multi-ethnic Mediterranean region.

Claudia Nitschke's reading of Joachim Heinrich Campe's *Robinson der Jüngere* (1779/80; *Robinson the Younger*) examines how Campe's adaptation of Defoe's novel explores the reconstruction of civilization for a commentary on contemporary social reality by offering (at the same time affirmative and challenging) transcultural perspectives on the most basic roots of civilized society. Campe's novel is pedagogical and sets the story in a frame narrative that allows for it being reflected and discussed by the family's children, in particular. Nitschke zeros in on the narrative evaluation of the emerging rules and norms and discusses the novel's reflections on 'innate' and taught values to an extent within the context of Georg Lakoff's and Mark Johnson's 'philosophy in the flesh'; i.e., the idea that basic moral metaphors root in bodily experience and social interactions that expose a high level of commonality over history and across cultures. Nitschke finds that "what bestows legitimacy on Robinson's actions is the fact that they coincide with 'values' that are indeed shared (or are potentially shareable) by everyone, even the 'savages'. Only when Robinson meets this very premise, is learning and readapting possible. He can influence the process of valuing and its evaluative results, but he cannot interfere with the 'blueprint' that is shared by all human beings." Thus Campe's novel provides the kind of 'first draft' that Moral Foundation Theory emphasizes as a transcultural basis for experiential revisions and developments. One of the subliminal outcomes (as Nitschke carefully puts it) of Campe's narration of his social experiment is that the basic interactive emergence of morality includes potentially all of God's children and serves in this sense as a core position for universal human rights.

Steven D. Martinson introduces his literary analysis with a brief discussion of a number of theoretical approaches—e.g., Chladenius, Herder, Alois Wierlacher, and Wolfgang Welsch—that speak to conceptual distinctions between inter- and trans-culturalism. In Martinson's assessment, the most striking distinction has been nicely condensed in Friedrich Schulze-Engler's suggestion that "transcultural studies do not focus on what culture does with human beings but what different human beings do with culture." Martinson then offers condensed readings of Lessing's dramas *Die Juden* and *Nathan der Weise* and Goethe's drama *Iphigenie auf Tauris* that focus on intercultural and transcultural dimensions. The basic underlying precept is that "the transcultural dimensions of literary texts cultivate transcultural mentalities".

James F. Howell investigates the launch of a transcultural memory site: the place of Alexander von Humboldt in US history. To Howell's mind, Humboldt's brief visits to Philadelphia and Washington, D.C. in 1804, as well as his relations with the founding fathers were hardly as significant as current US and European historians claim. Why then, Howell asks, do we witness such emphatic appeals to reintroduce Humboldt into the functional memory (in the sense of Aleida Assmann) of the US? For Howell, this advocacy offers a peek into the potential of a transcultural fashioning of cultural memory in a contemporary context. "The depictions of Humboldt in North America and Europe, and more importantly, the cultural motivations and aspirations behind those depictions, have aligned to such an extent that a transcultural space has been created in which multiple cultures can communicate about pressing needs and concerns while drawing on common points of reference." The concerns that Howell isolates in recent US and European studies have shifted away from the 19th-century appreciation of Humboldt's *Kosmos* into the political realm: Humboldt as "a climate change activist *avant-la-lettre*" or as "an embodiment of Enlightenment ideals and their potential".

Arianna Dagnino offers the volume's most comprehensive definition of the transcultural in the context of literary analysis. Here are some of the elements she includes: (a) Transculture denotes a person's "freedom to live on the border of her 'inborn' culture or beyond it"; (b) The transcultural (or "transplace") describes "an all-inclusive space of subjective consciousness and cultural possibilities which does not deny the formative importance of native cultures—and, to some extent, their accompanying worldviews—but at the same time allows an openness to the reception, integration, and negotiation of other cultures"; (c) The transplace usually depends upon a 'transpatriation' process, which "facilitates the development of a transcultural lens", a decentering of all cultures in relation to all other cultures; (d) Transpatriation emphasizes the importance of "unlearning" identity formation strongly dependent on ethnicity, nationality, locality, or religious affiliation; (e) Transculture/ality carries an anti-ideological stance, a kind of ethical orientation on cultural overlap, exchange, fluidity and movement, rather than the dominance of difference; (f) "Though individualist in perspective, transculture/ality should not, however, be seen as a (somewhat natural) extension of the traditional liberal understanding of the individual. [...] As Epstein claims, in relation to our present, transculture 'differs from both leveling globalism and isolating pluralism'." As a case in point, Dagnino illustrates the development of a transcultural disposition and "its re-enactment in the form of transcultural narratives" in the novel *The Young Maronite* by the Libyan/Italian author Alessandro Spina.

Dagnino sorts out the novel's transnational locales (Benghazi, Italy, Istanbul, and Sicily), its political setting (the beginnings of Italy's colonial enterprise in Africa), its cross-cultural figurations, its proliferation of points of view, and the complexity of its linguistic codes and narrative genres. Dagnino describes the novel's core "the art of unbelonging" as a "transcultural desire" (Maurizio Ascari), which takes the form of cultural translation. Regarding Spina's narrative style, she distinguishes him as a transcultural writer from his "cousin species (migrant/diasporic/exile/postcolonial writers)" by emphasizing "his relaxed attitude when facing issues linked to identity, nationality, rootlessness and dislocation.

Eleonora Rao discusses Alice Kaplan's fascinating 'language memoir' *French Lessons* (1993) as an autobiographical story of entering into the space of a second self via a linguistic order. Rao interjects Derrida's caution that we are ultimately alienated from all linguistic orders, as all languages we know are not ours, but always the language of the other. The space of the self (the language we speak) is always somewhere else. Nevertheless Rao maintains that Kaplan's 'language memory' (supported by her theoretical reflections on language) suggests at least this much: a preference for a language over another depending on the context and the emotion in question. Thus, French could, for instance, become Kaplan's verbal safe-house, an instant refuge, and hiding place. Still, maintaining or regaining contact with the language of affect is vital. "Even though French had a salvific role in a phase of Kaplan's life, as it was responsible for her 'resurrection,' for her 'new skin', English remains the language of [in Kristeva's words] 'the body's nocturnal memory' the language of 'the bittersweet slumber of childhood'". But this does not mean that in Kaplan's story an 'authentic' American self is lurking under a French one. Rather Kaplan confesses that she is grateful to her adapted languages "for teaching me that there is more than one way to speak, for giving me a role, for being the home I've made from my own will and my own imagination".

Valérie K. Orlando's article analyzes *Le Retour de l'Éléphant* (The Return of the Elephant, 2003) by the Tunisian author Abdelaziz Belkhodja and *Aux Etats-Unis d'Afrique* (African USA, 2006) by the Djiboutian author Abdourahman A. Waberi as exemplary cosmopolitan narratives that demonstrate a transnational turn in African literature in the modus of 'what-ifs'. These "hypothetical narratives" imagine a futuristic utopia/dystopia, where the world order has been reversed—failed, impoverished, and backward Western states that are confronted with an advanced, highly educated, and prosperous African continent; a constellation that allows for unique explorations of the potentials and drawbacks of globalization, migration, and other global trials of the 21st century. Orlando's analysis highlights two postcolonial concepts: Abdelkébir Khatibi's *une pensée-autre*—an emphatic postcolonial *being-in-the-world*, rather than being uniquely defined by tribe, nation or race—and Achille Mbembe's theory of *Afropolitanism*—a global aesthetic *creolization* or *pluralization* of African modes of being-in-the-world. Although Orlando observes that the two dystopic utopian narratives remain "caught in a 'double attachment', in the middle of what Khatibi defines as 'the constantly reemerging world of the colonizer' and the 'tribal Makhzen [state power] of the postcolonial nation'," they, nevertheless, force Africa to confront its failings; and the West, "as it looks in the mirror and sees its image reflected back, is compelled to consider the potential that the African continent could offer if the tables were turned." Furthermore, Orlando concludes that these Afropolitan novels partake in cosmopolitan ideals "that ground Africans' being-in-the-world" and embrace a world citizenship that has left colonialism and post-colonialism behind.

James Tartaglia tries his hands on a philosophical approach to what he calls the transculturalist standoff, basically the Herderian paradox that humanism's and, for that matter, transculturalism's aim to transcend cultural baggage is itself rooted in a specific historical and geographical culture. Tartaglia stresses the difference between evaluative and descriptive judgments about the meaning of life or the lack of it and discusses two traditions: (a) "post-Nietzschean" philosophers and their reaction to Nihilism (Rorty is seen as the "clearest writer from this tradition"); and (b) the recent meaning-of-life debate, in particular, the attempts to circumvent the metaphysical aspects of the meaning-of-life question by posing it as a meaning-in-life question, which purportedly then could be judged according to objective (or subjective criteria) for a meaningful life. Tartaglia engages extensively in this debate (which is the topic of his most recent book), and argues that all its proponents ultimately fail, and so does the post-Nietzschean philosophy. Both continue to argue within a culturalist context and do not acknowledge that the life-is-meaningless position (nihilism) is not merely an evaluative, but rather a descriptive judgment. As soon as this is understood, Tartaglia believes, new avenues for a more productive approach to the transcultural standoff open up. The conflict of two humanistic thoughts (universal human values and the value of particularities) would no longer be "metaphysically principled, and we can return to the particularities of the case in hand. If we find some of their practices abhorrent, and think we have good reason to do so, then we try to persuade them of our evaluations while advertising their benefits. They can do the same with us. In the end, we hope, a rational, well-informed equilibrium will emerge. The concern that we could never find common ground fades against a common descriptive backdrop for our conflicting evaluations; there is a point of entry for debate, at the very least in physiological facts like pleasure and pain". If the descriptive judgment of nihilism prompts concerns for ending up in "a Naziesque world," Tartaglia reminds us that "the meaning of life has hardly proved a recipe for peace throughout the ages, and continues, in the hands of religious fanatics, to generate much of the trouble we find ourselves in today".

Inez Baranay offers a personal account of how transcultural aspects of her life inform her fiction. "It is as if the transcultural were always the destination, though it remains to be seen if it proves to be another transitional space or one that is so comprehensively inclusive that it has no limits". First, there is linguistic plurality—Hungarian, French and "the world of Englishes"—which prepares a transcultural space that ultimately opens up via the experience of migration: "in here everyone belongs because of their non-belonging […]. But know this: it is not the end of difference. There's space for a melting pot, there are countless versions of hybridisation and fusion (cultural, personal) and there is endless difference." It is inner-city culture (here Sydney) that allows for a transcultural space that in turn allows for anything, except "heteronormativity." So the writer moves from being labeled experimental, then feminist, multicultural, and finally arrives at what she calls real diversity—"from the diversity of cultures to the even greater diversity of individuals." Another line of development has the name "the global foreign" and traces the road "from travel writer to global soul." Then there is the question if and how "the transcultural space: feeling foreign everywhere" can be a home: "As Helene Cixous wrote about dreams, 'foreignness is a fantastic nationality'". Finally there is the question if post-colonialism's vocabulary—"categories of dominant and subordinate, coloniser and colonised, subalterns and superiors, orientalists and occidentalists" fits the transcultural. Here the answer of fiction has it somewhat easy and can be categorical: "Look, I answer, when we enter Transcultural Space we are in a space where such phenomena cannot exist. It's a notional space, an ideal, and we can decide how it feels to live there. […] And all of this *matters* in a world that needs ideals to be articulated".

Conflicts of Interest: The author declares no conflict of interest.

Article

Genealogies and Challenges of Transcultural Studies

Bernd Fischer

Department of Germanic Languages and Literatures, The Ohio State University, Columbus, OH 43210, USA;
fischer.5@osu.edu

Academic Editor: Albrecht Classen
Received: 21 November 2016; Accepted: 15 February 2017; Published: 24 February 2017

Abstract: My introductory essay discusses some of transculturalism's enduring conceptual challenges from the perspective of the history of German cultural and political theory. I am particularly interested in the discursive space between Immanuel Kant's individualism and Johann Gottfried Herder's and Moses Mendelssohn's concepts of cultural identity. My hope is that such a discussion can enrich some of our current questions, such as: Have culture studies placed too much emphasis on difference, rather than on commonality? Can a renewed interest in the cosmopolitan individual surpass the privileged position of academic or upper-class internationalism? Can concepts of transculturality avoid the pitfalls of homogenizing politics or overstretched individualism? After mentioning a few challenges to current conceptions of transculturalism that may arise in the wake of recent developments in the natural sciences, I end my remarks with a brief example of a possible intersection of literary studies and science. The essay engages three topics: (a) the question of culture; (b) transcultural participation; and (c) transcultural empathy and the sciences.

Keywords: political philosophy; transculturalism; empathy; Foucault; Kant; Herder; Mendelssohn

---

1. The Question of Culture: Kant, Mendelssohn, and Herder

When Immanuel Kant presented in his *Answer to the Question: What is Enlightenment* (1784) the notion of a self-enlightening public, he was notably battling the specific political constrictions of late 18th-century absolutism. Although his concerns about a functioning public sphere would soon be eclipsed by the muddy realities of radically different power politics—i.e., the distinctly unenlightening media campaigns for and against the French Revolution, followed by wickedly deceptive strategies within the pro- and anti-Napoleonic propaganda wars, and, of course, the censorship decrees after the Congress of Vienna—, the idealistic passion of Kant's account has survived to this day.

Michel Foucault proposes that the ongoing appeal of Kant's brief essay can, in part, be explained by its curious status within Kant's oeuvre. In Foucault's reading, the essay is not embedded in a one-dimensional historical teleology; rather, it is concerned with finding ways out of the misery of enslaving immaturity at any stage of history and articulates the use of individual reasoning as a shift in attitude. By asking for a new arrangement of the relations between will, authority, and the use of reason, Kant is no longer content with the right to freedom of thoughts, but rather insists on the freedom of the public word. With this demand, the Enlightenment becomes a political problem for any authority. Foucault uses a Kantian term for this new attitude, "räsonnieren" (public reasoning), and contends that it holds a central position in Kant's philosophical project in that it is ultimately responsible for his decision to take on the tremendous task of writing the three *Critiques*. If public reasoning is to serve as an ongoing critical commentary on all of society's affairs, the need arises for an accurate account of its inner workings, its preconditions, and its limits. Foucault goes so far as to suggest that Kant's introduction of the new attitude of public reasoning marks a starting point of modernity, which, in turn, should also be understood as a shift in attitude: "a mode of relating to contemporary reality, a voluntary choice made by certain people; in the end, a way of thinking and feeling; a way, too, of acting and behaving that at one and the same time marks a relation of belonging and presents itself as a task" [1]. This choice amounts to a new "philosophical ethos that could be described as a permanent critique of our historical era" [1]. This ethos is in part negatively defined as the rejection of all teleological master discourses—"of another society, of another way of thinking, another culture, another vision of the world," which would only lead "to the return of the most dangerous traditions" [1].[1] Rather, modernity's attitude of public reasoning is to be historio-critical and experimental in the face of contemporary questions and problems. Foucault's conceptions of archeology and genealogy have replaced Kant's transcendentalism. This is not the place to debate how successful Foucault is in explaining his philosophical attitude from a Kantian tradition; important for my topic is, however, that he (perhaps even more so than Kant) is concerned with the primacy of critical philosophy, its methodology, potential, and limits. Foucault presents the program of historio-critical enlightenment as a guide for the individual philosopher. There is no room for culture; the one time its name appears, we find it in a list of things that we should not do, namely falling for master discourses of 'a new way of thinking, a culture, a vision of the world'; for that would imply a 'return to the most dangerous traditions'. Foucault's interpretation of Kant's use of reason stresses its most ambitious feature: its advocacy of permanent public critique without the ideological backing of an alternative vision of a new political power. (It is in this sense somewhat reminiscent of Mendelssohn's approach, as we can hopefully see below.)

How does culture fare in Kant's essay? We may begin by looking at his specific explanation of the Enlightenment's historical foil: What or who—in addition to the cowardice and laziness of individuals, who are equipped to use their powers of reason, but avoid employing it whenever it is convenient—, is responsible for mankind's proclivity for submissive immaturity? The first two items Kant mentions are books that think for us and priests that display a conscience for us. They serve as examples of all those guardians ("Vormünder") that are empowered to do the thinking and feeling for us. They coerce and exploit us with methods that Kant describes as follows: "Having first infatuated their domesticated animals, and carefully prevented the docile creatures from daring to take a single step without the leading-strings to which they are tied, they next show them the danger which threatens them if they try to walk unaided." ([2], p. 35)[2] This "Gängelwagen" (as Kant calls it) constitutes a predominant tradition for the majority of the population. It describes its habitual culture, notwithstanding the observation that, depending on their geographical and historical circumstances, people have developed various cultural formations that entail different degrees of habitual immaturity. If Kant proposes public self-enlightenment as an "attitude" that searches for a "way out", then the out-of-what question can (even in the most advanced societies) be answered with: out of habitual culture. In this sense, Kant's essay may indeed prepare the way for the kind of a radical individualism that Foucault finds in modernist art. His prime example is the extreme self-stylization that he observes in Baudelaire's figure of the dandy, i.e., the retreat of culture to the individual body.[3] Both, Kant and Baudelaire, seek, in Foucault's words, "the autonomy of the modern subject in the context of the present" and attempt "to free individuals from the normative and materialist chains of society, as well as from religion, moralism and tradition" [1,3]. What is really at stake in the modern approach to the

---

1   I will not address the problem that Foucault too cannot fully avoid presenting a latent master discourse, as the word choices in Catherine Porter's translation give away easily. Foucault seems to differentiate between new ways of thinking that are bound to (teleologically structured) philosophical, political, and/or cultural master discourses and a new mode of reasoning that gains its energy from a keen awareness of the ideological pitfalls of all master discourses. His 'Kantian' mode of critical reasoning can perhaps best be illustrated as a philosophical analogy to a scientific ethos, in as much as it operates outside of cultural, political, and ideological limitations.

2   "Nachdem sie ihr Hausvieh zuerst dumm gemacht haben und sorgfältig verhüteten, daß diese ruhigen Geschöpfe ja keinen Schritt außer dem Gängelwagen, darin sie sie einsperrten, wagen durften, so zeigen sie ihnen nachher die Gefahr, die ihnen droht, wenn sie es versuchen allein zu gehen" ([2], p. 35).

3   We will see in the second part of this essay that Foucault's radical individualism resembles in this sense conceptions of transculturality that locate cultural diversity in an individual's complex net of unique cultural influences, belongings, and enactments.

shackles of culture—"religion, moralism and tradition"—is, above all, the matter-of-course character of cultural practices, unexamined cultural institutions and performances and unquestioned habitual observances. This describes not only aspects of everyday life and philosophical attitude, but it may, if we follow Foucault, also explain a radical shift within modern culture itself—for instance, modern art's and literature's emphasis on stylized idiosyncratic eccentricity, the lone cry against the customary cruelty of society's overt or hidden norms, and so on.

In Foucault's conception, the modern attitude of "räsonnieren" comes primarily and most notably into its own in philosophy. It demands a cultural shift in philosophy itself. Kant, on the other hand, does not expose the philosopher as public intellectual, and his methodological demands seem somewhat less stringent. Although he suggests that reasoning in the public sphere should operate similar to scholarly thought, the grammatical logic of the analogical structure leaves little doubt that he aims beyond the academic discourse of philosophy and science. Kant's public sphere leads us, in my way of reading the essay, out of culture, but not necessarily into political philosophy; in other words, the essay's reach does not end with a new academic attitude, as Foucault's interpretation suggests, but rather prepares the ground for what becomes more explicit ten years later in Kant's essay "On Perpetual Peace", namely civic discourse in a constitutional republic; a critical discursive attitude that is to become part of a life-style that Kant labels unsocial sociability ("ungesellige Geselligkeit").

Kant's design of the public sphere and his political vision are closely interconnected and circle essentially around the same center: the conditions for the possibility of autonomous individuality in a thusly structured conception of civic society. It should not come as a surprise that culture raises its (still) ugly head again, when Kant proposes political principles ('definitive articles') that could put Europe (and eventually the world) onto a track towards the ultimate political hope: perpetual peace. In Kant's conception, such a peace can only be secured through the rule of constitutional law that governs both the relations of autonomous individuals in each country and the relations between autonomous countries. Both are considered autonomous or free, as long as they submit consciously and willfully to the rule of constitutional law. It is again quite difficult to locate the place of culture in this scenario, as Kant offers only one sentence to concede its presence.[4] Yet, this half-hearted concession is capable of tearing down the beautiful design that Kant had projected in previous political essays, namely, the republic of republics (or world republic).

By the time Kant writes *On Perpetual Peace* (1795), he feels the need to concede that his audience does not prioritize the benefits of the republic of republics for the following reason. People insist on their cultural differences, and striving for (national) cultural recognition is more important to them than equality, political representation, or even peace. Reluctantly, Kant replaces the logic of a world republic with the less stringent idea of an alliance or federation of states ("Völkerbund"). The second "definitive article" reads: "The Right of Nations shall be founded on a Federation of Free States" ([4], p. 42).[5] The downside of a mere federation or alliance, rather than a federal republic, lies in its inability to guarantee and enforce the law between its member states, and Kant has good reason to doubt that a mere federation can guarantee a lasting peace between nations.

> For states viewed in relation to each other, there can be only one way, according to reason, of emerging from that lawless condition which contains nothing but occasions of war. Just as in the case of individual men, reason would drive them to give up their savage lawless freedom, to accommodate themselves to public coercive laws, and thus to form an ever-growing state of nations, which would at last embrace all the nations of the earth. But as the nations, according to their ideas of international law won't have this under any circumstances and therefore reject *in hypothesi* what is right *in thesi*, the place of the positive

---

4   Tellingly, Kant's acknowledgement of culture is accompanied by a footnote that immediately challenges its reasonability.
5   I have occasionally clarified or modernized W. Hastie's translation. "Das Völkerrecht soll auf einen Föderalism freier Staaten gegründet sein" ([5], p. 354).

idea of a *world-republic*—if all is not to be lost—can only be replaced with the *negative* surrogate of an ever growing *alliance*. ([4], pp. 43–44)[6]

Nations that prefer such an alliance may believe that they can protect their autonomy, but they also remain quite dangerous. Kant uses a quote from Virgil's *Aeneid* to describe them: "Imprisoned fury roars with bloody mouth" ("Furor impius intus—fremit horridus ore cruento.") ([4], p. 20). For Kant, history has shown that the character of autonomous states is best understood as evil: "The depravity of human nature is exhibited without disguise in the unrestrained relations of the nations to each other [. . .]" ([4], p. 42).[7]

Why then do we have to accept that nations are more inclined to seek cultural recognition, rather than adhere to political reason? Notwithstanding his critique of Herder's philosophy of culture, Kant gives the battle for cultural recognition a positive spin, by providing a logical place for cultural identity that is still all too familiar to us: Although the desire for cultural recognition complicates the project of a federal republic of republics to the breaking point, it guards against homogeneity, an implicit danger of any world state. The price of international peace, so it seems, is diversity, that is, freedom. After all, even the tyrannical rule of absolutistic empires can provide for peace, albeit the peace of a graveyard. (Kant expresses the duplicity of 'universal and perpetual peace' by employing the name of a graveyard inn—"Zum ewigen Frieden"—for the title of his essay.) Nature resists enslavement through homogenization by employing "two means to prevent the peoples from intermingling, and to keep them apart: the differences of *languages* and *religions*" ([4], p. 48). The back side is that these cultural differences bring with them "a tendency for mutual hatred and furnish pretexts for war" ([4], p. 48).[8] The upshot is that Kant is fully aware that the non-constitutional federation of autonomous states, which he feels compelled to propose, suffers from a major inherent contradiction. On the one hand, peaceful states can only exist in a constitutional relationship with each other that mirrors the constitutional relationship of citizens within the state ("Surrogat des bürgerlichen Gesellschaftsbundes" ([5], p. 356)). On the other hand, this cannot

> take the form of a state made up of these nations. For that would involve a contradiction, since every state, properly so called, contains the relation of a superior as the lawgiver to an inferior as the people subject to their laws. Many nations, however, in one state, would constitute only one nation, which is contradictory to the principle assumed, as we are here

---

6 "Für Staaten im Verhältnisse unter einander kann es nach der Vernunft keine andere Art geben, aus dem gesetzlosen Zustande, der lauter Krieg enthält, herauszukommen, als daß sie eben so wie einzelne Menschen ihre wilde (gesetzlose) Freiheit aufgeben, sich zu öffentlichen Zwangsgesetzen bequemen und so einen (freilich immer wachsenden) Völkerstaat (*civitas gentium*), der zuletzt alle Völker der Erde befassen würde, bilden. Da sie dieses aber nach ihrer Idee vom Völkerrecht durchaus nicht wollen, mithin, was *in thesi* richtig ist, *in hypothesi* verwerfen, so kann an die Stelle der positiven Idee einer Weltrepublik (wenn nicht alles verloren werden soll) nur das negative Surrogat eines den Krieg abwehrenden, bestehenden und sich immer ausbreitenden Bundes den Strom der rechtscheuenden, feindseligen Neigung aufhalten, doch mit beständiger Gefahr ihres Ausbruchs (*Furor impius intus—fremit horridus ore cruento.* Virgil)" ([5], p. 357). The same rule that applies to the constitutional state must also apply to an alliance of states: its laws must be public ("öffentlich"). Kant elevates this rule to a transcendental status (*transzendente Formel*). In the second addendum, "Of the Accordance of Politics with Morals according to the Transcendental Conception of Public Right," he writes: "Abstraction being thus made from everything empirical that is contained in the conceptions of national and international right, (such as the evil disposition of human nature which makes coercion necessary) the following proposition arises, and it may be called the transcendental formula of Public Right. 'All actions relating to the rights of other men are wrong, if their maxim is not compatible with publicity'" ([4], p. 56). "Nach einer solchen Abstraction von allem Empirischen, was der Begriff des Staats- und Völkerrechts enthält (dergleichen das Bösartige der menschlichen Natur ist, welches den Zwang nothwendig macht), kann man folgenden Satz die transscendentale Formel des öffentlichen Rechts nennen: ,Alle auf das Recht anderer Menschen bezogene Handlungen, deren Maxime sich nicht mit der Publizität verträgt, sind unrecht'" ([5], p. 381).

7 "Bei der Bösartigkeit der menschlichen Natur, die sich im freien Verhältnis der Völker unverhohlen blicken läßt [. . .]" ([5], p. 355).

8 "Aber die *Natur will* es anders.—Sie bedient sich zweier Mittel, um Völker von der Vermischung abzuhalten und sie abzusondern, der Verschiedenheit der *Sprachen* und der *Religionen*, die [. . .] den Hang zum wechselseitigen Hasse und Vorwand zum Kriege bei sich führt [. . .]" ([5], p. 367). Kant's ambiguity finds an expression in the accompanying footnote on the impossibility of different religions. While he acknowledges different religious histories that rely on variations of mythological and literary traditions and may constitute different belief systems, he insists that there can ultimately only be one moral religion—just like it is unthinkable to him that there could be more than one ethics.

considering the right of nations in relation to each other, in so far as they constitute different states and are not to be fused into one. ([4], p. 42)[9]

If the aggressive nature of national cultures (with a small c) is the price to be paid for avoiding the compulsory homogeneity of a world state, Kant's hope for peace rests, in part, on a specific aspect of Culture (with a capitalized "C")—that is, in the expectation that the latently dangerous cultural differences between nations can be somewhat diffused through a common culture of reciprocal recognition, which for Kant develops primarily as a side effect of international commerce. This kind of transcultural understanding

> is effected by the commercial spirit which cannot exist along with war, and which sooner or later takes hold of every people. Among all the means of power under state rule, the power of money is the most reliable, and thus the states find themselves driven to further the noble interest of peace, although not directly from motives of morality. ([4], p. 48)[10]

Economic globalization will bring about new perspectives on a common humanity, which will eventually reach into the far corners of the world.

> However, as civilization increases, there is a gradual approach of men to greater unanimity in principles, and to a mutual understanding of the conditions of peace even in view of these differences. This pacific spirit, unlike that despotism which revels upon the grave of liberty, is developed and secured, not by the weakening of all the separate powers of the states, but by an equilibrium which is brought forth and guaranteed through their rivalry with each other. ([4], p. 48)[11]

If there is anywhere in Kant's political essays space for a constructive role of culture, it can most likely be located in the vicinity of his ideas about transcultural understanding, reciprocal recognition, and the promotion of a set of judicial and civic principles, which lie at the core of his design of a society that is to enable competitive personal growth and individual autonomy. His brand of transculturalism stands in dynamic friction with two contemporaneous conceptions of culture that are also still with us: (a) culture as an expression of a people's identity, which exists primarily as a new subject and methodology of scholarly inquiry and has in the 18th century become part of the academic public sphere; and (b) cultural politics—the construction of a people as an audience (Publikum) through language-bound definitions and delineations of a national public sphere that would latently be engaged on the opposing side of Kant's transcultural project. The two conceptions of culture are interrelated and are both most prominently presented in Herder's writings—although, I believe, the case could be made that the transcultural approach is also within the theoretical reach of Herder's notion of culture studies and cultural history.

I would like to interject a word about a possible place for Kant's critique of aesthetic judgment within the political struggle about culture. Kant's analysis of aesthetic judgments as "subjective universal verdicts"—a search for commonality that emerges from a deeply personal experience—shows structural analogies with the political weight that he puts on the autonomy or freedom of an

---

9 "Darin aber wäre ein Widerspruch: weil ein jeder Staat das Verhältniß eines Oberen (Gesetzgebenden) zu einem Unteren (Gehorchenden, nämlich dem Volk) enthält, viele Völker aber in einem Staate nur ein Volk ausmachen würden, welches (da wir hier das Recht der Völker gegen einander zu erwägen haben, so fern sie so viel verschiedene Staaten ausmachen und nicht in einem Staat zusammenschmelzen sollen) der Voraussetzung widerspricht" ([5], p. 354).

10 "Es ist der Handelsgeist, der mit dem Kriege nicht zusammen bestehen kann, und der früher oder später sich jedes Volks bemächtigt. Weil nämlich unter allen der Staatsmacht untergeordneten Mächten (Mitteln) die Geldmacht wohl die zuverlässigste sein möchte, so sehen sich Staaten (freilich wohl nicht eben durch Triebfedern der Moralität) gedrungen, den edlen Frieden zu befördern [. . .]" ([5], p. 368).

11 "[. . .] aber doch bei anwachsender Cultur und der allmähligen Annäherung der Menschen zu größerer Einstimmung in Principien zum Einverständnisse in einem Frieden leitet, der nicht wie jener Despotism (auf dem Kirchhofe der Freiheit) durch Schwächung aller Kräfte, sondern durch ihr Gleichgewicht im lebhaftesten Wetteifer derselben hervorgebracht und gesichert wird" ([5], p. 367).

individual's rational acceptance of constitutional rule. Aesthetic reconciliations that come about in the "free play" between the cognitive faculties of imagination and understanding can, from this political perspective, be seen as guide posts in the individual's quest for unknown universals (Kant's definition of a class of reflective judgments that includes aesthetic judgments). The political nature of this search for unknown territories of subjective/objective normativity is inherent in the public discourse about taste, namely, its exploratory examination of the possibility of an aesthetic *sensus communis*, a community of taste (Hannah Arendt). Aesthetic judgments must be pure and deeply personal, but carry, coinstantaneously, a strong desire for social recognition; an individual's taste stands in this sense, in no small measure, for both her expression of autonomy and her longing for community. One cannot argue about taste, and yet that is precisely what one feels compelled to do—another aspect of Kant's notion of modernity's 'unsocial sociability' and a formulary that carries his conception of public reasoning into a public discourse of aesthetic criticism. To put it into a more modest perspective (that can also serve as a transition to Mendelssohn), aesthetic judgments allow us to sense something about who we are and perhaps even more about how and with whom (in what kind of a community) we would like to live.

In his essay "On the Question: What Does It Mean to Enlighten" (1784), Moses Mendelssohn attempts to bring the three perspectives on culture that we have discussed (transcultural impetus, cultural history, and cultural politics) into a systematic structure that is anchored by a concept of "Bildung" (a term that famously connects individual education and character building with identity construction). Mendelssohn understands "Bildung" as a synthetic concept that requires both enlightenment (understood as theoretical progress) and culture (understood as practical improvement). With regard to public reasoning, Mendelssohn agrees with Kant's call for an autonomous public sphere. A state that, by censoring the public use of reason, admits that it cannot provide for the essential conditions for humanity's self-improvement (in Mendelssohn's version, the harmonization of humans as humans with their role as citizens); that is, a state that cannot allow for enlightenment to spread into all estates for fear that it will collapse, is philosophy's ultimate challenge and confronts it with its inherent limits. Living under such rule, philosophy has no choice, Mendelssohn suggests, but to cover its mouth. It should not become complicit with the politics of such a state, but it should also be aware of its own political limitations and dangers (herein lies the foreshadowing of Foucault's anti-ideological stand). In particular, it must take into account its potential for inadvertently wrecking established cultures and societies when it confronts them abruptly with a bout of enlightened thought, rather than painstakingly preparing the road for developing a higher degree of 'Bildung'. For Mendelssohn, enlightenment and culture must develop in lockstep. But even if things seem to work out perfectly, there is ultimately a limit to 'Bildung', that is, a 'Bildung' that assumes it has accomplished all that can be accomplished and is ready to leave enlightenment and culture behind. Nations that approach the pinnacle of 'Bildung', Mendelssohn cautions, are in danger of falling ill from an overdose of national intemperance and overindulgence. Healthy nations, Mendelssohn seems to imply, need the spike of an ongoing inner strife of divergent particularities, as well as a continuing struggle between theory and practice (enlightenment and culture). For Mendelssohn, particularity (culture with a small c) is there to stay and his enlightened reasoning occurs in two differentiated public spheres—most clearly demonstrated by his separate publishing venues (for instance, the Hebrew literary monthly he founded [*Ha-Me'assef*—The Collector] and the German monthly he co-edited [*Briefe die neueste Literatur betreffend*]). The particular cultural sphere of his personal belonging (language and religion) constitutes a cultural *sensus communis* that is, in no small measure, defined by its struggle for recognition and inspires him to become the premier advocate for improving his culture's 'Bildung'—linguistic and religious reform. The cosmopolitan (or transcultural) public sphere of scholarly and aesthetic reasoning allows him to establish himself as a leading philosophical player on the grand stage of 18th⁻century Europe. In Mendelssohn's conception, neither the national nor the transcultural push of 'Bildung' has an end point (no utopian notion of a universal republic or a unified culture), and the struggle for the recognition of cultural particularities remains as essential as the struggle for the recognition of an individual's place in society. A particular culture can and should become more refined, but it cannot end, as it is for Mendelssohn as much (or perhaps even more so) a part of society's engine of progress, as the competitive striving of autonomous individuals is for Kant.

2. Transcultural Participation

In contrast to Mendelssohn, Kant's political philosophy (much like his moral philosophy) envisions an immensely autonomous individual, which Charles Taylor has interpreted as a marker for the emergence of modernity. This vision of a modern self disrupted late medieval notions of strictly regimented and regulated castes, estates, and guilds and replaced them with an emphasis on individual authenticity and ethical integrity—traits that became ever more important for the meritocratic and flexible labor force that the economic and administrative policies of Europe's absolutist states demanded ([6], pp. 25–73). However, Taylor has also shown that individual authenticity proved to be a tall order and was soon supplemented with new notions of collective identities, this time primarily fashioned by an emerging discourse on cultural and regional traditions [6–8]. In his *Ideas for a Philosophy of Human History* (1784–1791), Herder elaborated a formula for this complex development that is still of significance today. In his brand of historicism, every human carries a unique measure of his own humanity within him/herself—so to speak, a peculiar attunement of all his sensuous experiences and feelings [9]. But Herder also stresses that, just like every individual self, each people (Volk) holds its own unique measure within itself and carries its own unique demands for an authentic self—in Taylor's words:

> Just like individuals, a *Volk* should be true to itself, that is, its own culture. Germans shouldn't try to be derivative and (inevitably) second-rate Frenchmen [. . .]. And European colonialism ought to be rolled back to give the peoples of what we now call the Third World their chance to be themselves unimpeded. We can recognize here the seminal idea of modern nationalism, in both benign and malignant forms ([6], p. 31).

For Herder, humans should not only be recognized as authentic individuals, but also as culturally determined beings, as members and representatives of a culture. As such, they demand respect for the authenticity claims of their culture, whereby assertions of one's culture and one's selfhood can easily stand in for each other in a kind of circular argument. It seems that by the beginning of the 19th century the modern individual was willing and interested—far more than, for instance, Kant could foresee—to delegate claims of authenticity to stories of cultural heritage and belonging, which soon morphed (not the least because of the impact of anti-Napoleonic politics) into the political claims of cultural nationalism [10].

With this historical backdrop, Taylor draws a line between the politics of equal dignity (principally theorized within a constitutional frame of equal rights) and the politics of difference.

> With the politics of equal dignity, what is established is meant to be universally the same, an identical basket of rights and immunities; with the politics of difference, what we are asked to recognize is the unique identity of this individual or group, their distinctness from everyone else. The idea is that it is precisely this distinctness that has been ignored, glossed over, assimilated to a dominant or majority identity. And this assimilation is the cardinal sin against the ideal of authenticity ([6], p. 38).

In the face of radical culturalism, it may be appropriate to point to historical indications that the dignity of difference, nevertheless, tends to fare best in democratic republics, whose concepts of national identity rest primarily on constitutional (rather than cultural) histories so that anxieties about the authenticity of a unified national culture tend to play a lesser role, while autocratically run countries tend to fear and suppress cultural difference to a higher degree. This holds also true for the homogenizing pressure that a culture fighting for the dignity of difference puts on the individual designs of its own members—its children, in particular. It is perhaps one of the least examined presumptions (a somewhat hidden culturalist bias) that pressures to adhere to homogeneous judgments, preferences, education, and life styles are somehow mitigated in communities that assert an ethnically or culturally defined particularity in order to gain a political voice (that is power). Furthermore, equating cultural (national) authenticity with freedom (a common intellectual automatism) tends to discount a core problem of Herder's brand of cultural criticism, namely the contradictory interplay of universality and particularity—i.e., Enlightenment's universal demand to recognize a culture's right to its unique particularity, even if the cultural entity at question may itself not be ready to return the favor of granting such rights to other cultures.

Wolfgang Welsch's Theory of Transculturalism

Since the 1990s, Wolfgang Welsch has attempted to confront some of these theoretical dilemmas by complementing traditional notions of cosmopolitanism with a theory of transculturalism. The hope is that a proper concept of transculturality can describe today's pervasiveness of cosmopolitan identities. For Welsch, transculturalism characterizes a growing number of real life stories in a globalized world, biographies that entail both new possibilities and new problems. For others, such as Kwame Anthony Appiah, their cosmopolitan potentials are of decisively political and ethical importance [11].

Welsch has developed his theory of transculturalism as a response to theoretical and political difficulties that he attributes to concepts of interculturalism and multiculturalism [12]. The basic problem of interculturalism lies for Welsch in its culturalist heritage, in that it continues to emphasize and celebrate cultures as separated and closed units. Although one should consider here that intercultural theories have stressed the historical variability of cultural markers and made problems of cultural lineages, borders, and overlap important topics of discussion, these refinements cannot really disqualify Welsch's observation that intercultural concepts remain fixed on the importance of the cultural authenticity of difference between peoples and nations. At the very least, transculturalism and interculturalism diverge in political temper and sensibility—to borrow a term from William Connolly ([13], p. XI). One highlights potential commonalities of richly differentiated individuals and aims for their political recognition; the other advocates the recognition of national or subnational differences that ought to be protected.

The term multiculturalism shows, from Welsch's point of view, a similar structure and attempts to navigate conflicts that arise with the confrontation of cultures or subcultures within a given society. To be sure, both interculturalism and multiculturalism have been influential in developing strategies for peaceful collaborations among cultures, for instance, by attempting to integrate the outside view into the view of oneself so that a buffer of cultural understanding can allow for a tolerant mode of living with each other.[12] However, from a transcultural perspective, they stick to the premise that identity-relevant cultural markers are principally exhausted by identifying and explaining the specificities of their ethnic and national heritage. Interculturalism and multiculturalism remain in this sense indebted to the colonial paradigm of cultural (rather than political) notions of nationhood. Whatever one may think of Welsch's attacks on intercultural hermeneutics ([15], p. 18), one can easily concede that the goal can indeed not be to institutionalize problems of cultural understanding as insurmountably fixed, and that recognizing transcultural life stories and personality designs can offer new strategies for cultural connectivity, intersection, and transition ([15], pp. 22–30).

Furthermore, Welsch's notion of transculturalism offers a unique answer to the fear of global homogenization. He argues that his understanding of transculturality does not destroy diversification, but rather modifies it in specific ways. "What changes is the type of cultural variety. Differences no longer emerge between different kinds of monolithic identities, but between identity configurations that have some elements in common while differing in other elements, in their arrangement as a whole, and often in their complexity" ([16], p. 6). In addition, Welsch contends that the term national culture

---

[12] This strategy has, for instance, been elaborated in Intercultural Literary Studies [14].

as used by today's adherents of interculturalism has become misleading: "what we really have in mind when speaking this way are *political* or *linguistic* communities, not truly *cultural* formations" ([16], p. 4). While differences between culturally defined societies may indeed be deemphasized in transcultural studies, new diversification arises in the individual self, in its network of particular and peculiar modes of life, heritage, education, tastes, and participations that latently portray a much greater abundance of cultural variability than closed-off cultures. "So difference is not vanishing, but its *mode* is changing. Difference, as traditionally provided by single cultures, certainly is diminishing. Instead differences between transcultural networks arise. These networks, however, also have some elements in common while differing in others. So there is always some overlap between them—'family resemblances', as Wittgenstein put it" ([16], p. 8).

At least at an abstract level, Welsch's notion of transcultural individuality offers an innovative approach to the antinomy of a political enlightenment that is simultaneously directed at universality and particularity, which we encounter in Kant's unease with his retreat from the republic of republics, as well as in the paradoxical structure of the Enlightenment's particular demand for the universal recognition of particular cultures (Herder)—a position that also falls short of circumventing the political drive to extend the reach of its own particularity (the universalism of human rights). In a way, individuality and diversity collapse in Welsch's concept of transculturality—to the degree that the individual's unique authenticity lies in evolving networks of cultural participation and not in static belongings. It is, once again, the individual self that can, in this model, insist on claims for individual integrity and authenticity and no longer her assigned cultural heritage for which she can no more stand in as it can stand in for her. Perhaps most importantly, transculturality offers room for individual cultural specifications without having to limit the demands of universal values in improper ways. A transcultural conception of society assumes accordingly that humans reach their specific individuality through a lifetime of dynamic participations in ancestral and educational, particular and universal, local and cosmopolitan, and immediate and mediated formations of belonging.

The consequences that the reintroduction of the individual as cultural agent could have for intercultural hermeneutics can hardly be overestimated. Horst Steinmetz, for instance, warns against the pervasive de-aestheticization in current intercultural literary studies and laments that, in spite of its inflated theoretical superstructure, truly intercultural text explication happens, if at all, intuitively and sporadically, and by no means methodically and systematically ([17], p. 467). Implicitly, he closes the circle back to Herder's concept of knowledgeable intuition and interpretative sensibility. It stands to reason that this is no accident, as it is indeed important to acknowledge that a transcultural orientation can be traced back to the very beginning of culture studies in the late 18th century, as I have tried to demonstrate elsewhere in regard to Herder [18].

Transcultural studies—and this is not to be taken lightly—have always been a quite elitist scholarly undertaking. Herder's scholar, for instance, reaches a "transcultural" understanding because of raw talent and, equally important, exhaustive studies and endless reading, which allow him (as Herder puts it) to feel himself into another culture, without having to live or even witness it. Even though more and more men and women may today live transcultural lives, there is reason to suspect that transcultural studies remain, nevertheless, dominated by modes of highly educated, aesthetic participation.[13] On the other hand, it seems quite preposterous, as Welsch puts it, when contemporary cultural studies surround themselves with a nimbus of liberation, while their micro-analytical studies have, in Welsch's view, nothing to offer than the choice between "different cells of a prison and by no means freedom" ([19], p. 7). For Welsch, intercultural hermeneutics is in this sense the latest garb of radical historicism ([19], p. 3).

---

[13] While the term "participation" offers, in my view, a realistic and politically desirable description of transculturality, its elitist genealogy may pose a level of concern.

With all this, transculturalism—understood as a description of individually diversified modes of life beyond the limitations of particular cultural frameworks—cannot forego reaching for a level of understanding that extends beyond individual cultures and latently touches all known cultures. For me, one of the more interesting questions is, if Herder's strategy to fill this space with his (already tautologically structured) concept of humanity ("Humanität") can perhaps turn into a new direction in culture studies that take the open-ended quality of "trans" at heart. For the impetus of transcultural scholarship is bound to envision a public sphere of universal and inclusive participation, that is, a scholarly culture of fair communication and interaction. Such participatory cosmopolitan cultures have historically been available primarily for two groups: economic and political elites (high aristocracy, high finance, and international business and trade) and, secondly, scholars and artists. There are no principal reasons that would preclude this level of transcultural (cosmopolitan) participation from becoming available to the populations at large—of all communities and in all corners of the world. There are, however, some preconditions for such a level of universally extended transcultural participation in a kind of world culture that can hold its own in the midst of (and while recognizing) all the particular cultures and subcultures. One has already been pointed out as Herder's paradox of universal particularity. Taken as a condition for a (world) culture of transculturality (if the paradoxical structure makes sense at this point), it demands that no culture can claim exclusivity and insist on incompatibility. In other words, it stands to reason that, in addition, to our individual cultural and subcultural participations and inclinations, we need to develop and defend an inclusive culture of universality, cosmopolitanism, and internationalism (to name some of the traditional theories that aim at such a world-cultural level). I trust that the possibility of such an inclusive transcultural culture is a worthwhile guide post for scholarship in the humanities—if we are inclined to battle current forces of xenophobic and nationalistic demagoguery and power politics that threaten to carry the day.

In recent years, Welsch has complemented his theory of transculturalism by incorporating popular developments in evolutionary anthropology and other 'hard' human sciences (cf. also [20]).

> For there *is* another type of commonalities, one *preceding* cultural difference. We tend to overlook the amount of commonalities humans already share before cultural differences get off the ground. What I have in mind here, is roughly what was formerly referred to as universals: determinants common to all cultures. [...] My current picture is that transculturality—the existence of cross-cultural commonalities—is fostered by two quite different factors operating at very different levels (though there is, as I will show, also some connection). One is the current process of the permeation of cultures—a process creating commonalities by *overcoming* differences. The other is much older and related to the human condition as such. It *underlies* all formations of difference.—If we take *both* aspects into account, then we might, I suspect, arrive at a more complete picture of transculturality altogether. ([16], p. 2)

Welsch knows, of course, that deep structures of transcultural commonalities that can be expounded in the terminology of evolutionary theory have been met with suspicion and unease. "Reference to cultural universals must reckon with resistance. In the realm of cultural studies an extreme form of difference thinking is today dominant. Under its auspices cultural studies flourish. To refer to universals there seems almost to be a sacrilege" ([16], p. 9). For him, culture studies that refuse to engage in a critical debate with other sciences operate in untenable isolation. "The dogma of radical cultural relativism broke down in anthropology (it has survived only in cultural studies in America and Europe)" ([16], p. 14).

Better known examples of the kind of proto-cultural commonalities that Welsch has in mind include, for instance, facial expressions, gestures, aesthetic preferences of certain designs and images (as well as face and body shapes), logical structures, and linguistic deep structures [21]. To the degree that such proto-cultural commonalities can be explained as results of biological feedback effects (cf. [16], p. 16), Welsh implores the humanities "to take the entire origin of humanity into account—not only the historical development of humans, but also their proto-historical and evolutionary origin. For human cognition and sensation is not a free (merely historically formed) construction of objectivity, but, at a fundamental level, also a reflex of the world in and through which we became what we are" ([19], pp. 108–9). In the last five years, Welsch has even attempted to offer a comprehensive grounding of philosophy that questions the anthropomorphic basis of our thought in radical ways [22,23].

This is, of course, not the place to engage Welsch's anti-anthropomorphism; rather, I would like to point to a few scientific contexts that might eventually challenge some of our assumptions. The most obvious concern stems from the possible impact of advances in reproductive selection, high-cost medicine, and genetic engineering for privileged populations. Some go as far as to speculate that the top one percent of the world's population will put part of its vast resources into transforming itself into a new (arguably superior) human species [24]. Other concerns involve, for instance, studies of stress hormones in the presence of strangers or microbial research that suggests evolutionary explanations for both the primary importance of human individuality and communal tastes and mentalities [25]. Further discussions of proto-cultural universals that can potentially invite a range of unpredictable political interpretations could eventually arise from genetic discoveries of cross-species breeding. As it turns out, genetically pure samples of the species *Homo sapiens* can primarily be found on the African continent. On the other continents, the genome was supplemented with genetic material from *Homo neanderthalensis* and (at least in East Asia) from *Homo denisova* (perhaps *Homo floresiensis*)—and it remains to be seen what additional genetic traces of the apparently quite variegated human genus might still be found. Traces of genetic material from other species do not necessarily imply a higher degree of genetic diversity. Quite to the contrary, the human genome is on the African continent more varied than on the European or Asian continents.

Of more immediate consequences for our understanding of human diversity could be the not impossible inference that, just like bodily traits, emotional potentials can be epigenetically actuated so that they can, in part, be understood as response patterns that were initially stimulated by specific environmental and societal circumstances that may no longer be relevant. If such epigenetic information can be inherited by up to four generations (as has been observed in medical studies), then epigenetics may perhaps contribute to a scientific explanation of phenomena that we tend to bundle under an undefined notion of ethnic traits and differences [26,27].

3. Transcultural Empathy and Literary Imagination

Cultural studies have a long history of engaging social and psychological approaches to questions of phylogenetic developments of emotional potentials (from family settings and educational institutions to psychoanalysis). However, these too can appear in a different light when seen from current scientific perspectives. Consider, for instance, the role of fiction.

(1) Fiction in brain science: Neuronal connections that accompany and enable the development of a child's basic cognitive abilities (such as hearing, seeing, feeling) develop during distinct windows of time. During these developmental stages, the brain makes a very large number of neurons available for the structural formation of a specific network. Only those neurons and neuronal structures that the child uses over and over again in active interactions with its environment have a chance for survival. Neurons that are not being used for specific skill related connections (30 to 40 percent) remain forever unused. Only those that fire together wire together [28]. Play (and this means, to a large extent, fictional play) is of central importance during these developmental stages. This holds, of course, true for the essential ability to comprehend other humans as beings with sovereign emotions and, through a mirror of reciprocity, for the acquisition of a sense of self. The child imagines the inner condition of another person and is guided by (often exaggerated and in this sense fictional) facial expressions, body movements, voice intonations, etc. This triggers processes of learning that lead (if everything goes right) to ever more accurate and intimate processes of empathetic emotions, sympathetic thoughts,

and the emergence of a social self.[14] It is not unreasonable to assume that abilities for emotional and intellectual empathy can already at this stage develop in different ways or to different degrees. Irrespective of the question if the assumption of specific "mirror" neurons is needed for the reflection of the other in the self (and vice versa), it seems to hold true that the same regions of the brain are active when we experience a specific emotional situation, observe someone who experiences this situation, or hear (or read) a story of someone who experiences it [31]. In this context, it is important to consider the brain's astonishing potential for autopoietic input/response patterns.[15] We cannot remember the endless training sessions that contributed to the hardwiring of our fundamental neuronal structures, because they happen primarily in the first two years of our lives, before the structures for a declarative memory have been completed.

Consequently, adults are, so to speak, confronted with two levels of unquestionable factuality (a priori); one emerged over millions of years as the result of evolution and has found an expression in the architectonic structure of the brain; the other emerges as individual neuronal structures in the first years of childhood. This second level of a priori facticity is bound to the child's high level of neuronal plasticity, in order to allow for adaptations to specific cultural (historically and socially variable) environments. It is influenced by sensory stimulations that may be differently weighted in different cultural and social settings. In this sense, the brain contains already within its developed neuronal structures a level of socio-cultural information, which the individual, however, experiences to a large extent as natural (a priori) facts of her world. It is not unreasonable to assume that this neurologically anchored level of socio-cultural difference does extend to variations of empathic inclinations.[16]

(2) Fiction in literature: The drastically reduced plasticity of an adult brain does not mean that adults cannot acquire, exercise, and improve behaviors, preferences, mentalities, emotions, skills, and logical structures; it may mean, however, that these later acquisitions lack the same level of unquestionable facticity, which characterizes neuronal structures that formed, so to speak, pre-consciously during earlier years. The function of empathetic imagination is also not limited to the child's formative processes of self and other. To the contrary, empathy, imagination, and autopoietic fiction describe fundamental ways of being, which accompany us for the rest of our lives. Fictional literature, in particular, has the advantage that it can actuate, mediate, and relate (communicate) basal, cultural, psychological, societal, political, and many more markers and aspects of empathetic potentials in complex, comprehensive, and yet very immediate ways (on cognitive, emotional, and aesthetic levels)—which can easily exceed the limitations of other experimental settings (in particular, those that have to adhere to scientific norms). What kind of relations can we assume between the early neurological formation of empathetic potentials and the potentials and functions of imaginary or fictional experiences of empathy that adults seek in plays, movies, and novels? Of particular interest is, from my point of view, the question if adult strategies for improving, refining, or testing their empathetic potentials can only be achieved second hand by way of intellectual understanding—i.e., through rational processes, which quickly drift into the domains of duty and ethical self-awareness—, or if aesthetic sensations (that is their potentially trans-intellectual dimension of social experience) can still offer an immediate approach to empathic emotions and considerations at any age.[17] If so, what kind of role could aesthetic experiences continue to play for processes of identity construction? I can

---

[14] The model jibes in some ways the model of intersubjective identity construction that was proposed as early as 1797 in J. G. Fichte's *Foundation of Natural Law* and has, via its Hegelian adaptation, been developed into a modern social theory by Axel Honneth and others [29,30].

[15] Most of our experiences feed to a large extent on autopoietic information. The more complex the neuronal architecture is in the animal kingdom, the more importance is put on internal computations, i.e., more areas of the brain process information that is initiated within the brain itself, while relatively little energy is expended on processing sensory data.

[16] There is, of course, also the possibility that sensoric deprivation, due to biological or social irregularities or catastrophes, can lead to insufficient formations of empathetic capacities (such as Autism, Asperger Syndrome, or sociopathic behavior).

[17] Theodor Lipps' strategies to link aesthetics and empathy in a comprehensive (phenomenological and psychological) model are, in this context, still of interest today [32–34]. For narrative settings of cultures of empathy cf. [35].

only propose a rather simple idea borrowed from the historical fundus of literary culture that brings us back to the first part of this essay.

It seems to be no coincidence that popular genres that developed around aesthetics of empathy, such as sentimental comedies and bourgeois tragedies (prevalent in today's mass media), tend to accompany the economic, ethical, and political aspirations of an emerging bourgeoisie. It is certainly no historical accident that at the height of enlightened cosmopolitanism (within the confines of colonialism and anti-colonial counter thought) an elaborated cultural theory took center stage that was directed at recognizing and empathizing with the human in foreign cultural settings via aesthetic immersion.[18] I believe that this aspect of the Enlightenment project—a kind of sympathetic sense for recognizing cultural difference that relies, in the end, on the assumption of and trust in a common humanity—must itself be understood as a cultural achievement, from which we feed to this day. In that sense, it remains indispensable that we keep in mind that the priority of aesthetic empathy within the Enlightenment project and the discovery of the humanity of difference are not understood, when we ignore their political foundations and conditions. Kant's first 'definitive article' in his essay *On Perpetual Peace* is also in this sense as true as it ever was.

Conflicts of Interest: The author declares no conflict of interest.

References

1. Michel Foucault. "What Is Enlightenment? (Was ist Aufklärung?)." Translated by Catherine Porter. Available online: https://drive.google.com/file/d/0B5t_gfMVp1JIbHN6M3hSSmM1b3M/view?pli= (accessed on 4 November 2015).
2. Immanuel Kant. "Was ist Aufklärung? " In *Gesammelte Schriften (Akademie Ausgabe)*. Berlin: de Gruyter, 1923, vol. 8, pp. 35–42. (Electronic Edition).
3. Anita Seppä. "Foucault, Enlightenment and the Aesthetics of the Self." Available online: http://www.contempaesthetics.org/newvolume/pages/article.php?articleID=244 (accessed on 4 November 2015).
4. Immanuel Kant. *Kant's Principles of Politics, Including His Essay on Perpetual Peace. A Contribution to Political Science*. Translated by William Hastie. Edinburgh: Clark, 1891. Available online: http://oll.libertyfund.org/titles/358 (accessed on 12 October 2016).
5. Immanuel Kant. "Zum ewigen Frieden." In *Gesammelte Schriften (Akademie Ausgabe)*. Berlin: de Gruyter, 1923, vol. 8, pp. 342–86. (Electronic Edition).
6. Charles Taylor. "The Politics of Recognition." In *Examining the Politics of Recognition*. Edited by Charles Taylor. Princeton: Princeton University Press, 1994.
7. Odo Marquard. *Zukunft braucht Herkunft. Philosophische Essays*. Stuttgart: Reclam, 2003.
8. Odo Marquard. *Schwierigkeiten mit der Geschichtsphilosophie*. Frankfurt: Suhrkamp, 1982.
9. Bernhard Suphan. *Herders Sämtliche Werke*. Edited by Bernhard Suphan. Berlin: Weidmann, 1887, vol. 13.
10. Bernd Fischer. *Das Eigene und das Eigentliche: Klopstock, Herder, Fichte, Kleist. Episoden aus der Konstruktionsgeschichte nationaler Intentionalitäten*. Berlin: Schmidt, 1995.
11. Anthony Kwame Appiah. *Cosmopolitanism: Ethics in a World of Strangers*. New York: W.W. Norton & Co., 2006.
12. Wolfgang Welsch. "Transculturality—The Puzzling Form of Cultures Today." In *Spaces of Culture: City, Nation, World*. Edited by Mike Featherstone and Scott Lash. London: SAGE, 1999, pp. 194–213.
13. William E. Connolly. "The Left and Ontopolitics." In *A Leftist Ontology. Beyond Relativism and Identity Politics*. Edited by Carsten Strathausen. Minneapolis: University of Minnesota Press, 2009, pp. IX–XVII.
14. Alois Wierlacher, and Andrea Bogner, eds. *Handbuch interkulturelle Germanistik*. Stuttgart: Metzler, 2003.

---

[18] The hypothesis cannot entirely be dismissed that the cultural evolution of empathetic formations was, in various historical periods, bound to transcultural (cosmopolitical) ideas of humanity; in which case the formation of empathy and transculturality can be understood as a reciprocal relation.

15. Wolfgang Welsch. "Rolle und Veränderung der Religion im gegenwärtigen Übergang zu transkulturellen Gesellschaften." In *Religionen in der Pluralität. Ihre Rolle in Postmodernen Transkulturellen Gesellschaften. Wolfgang Welschs Ansatz in Christlicher und Islamischer Perspektive.* Edited by Dirk Chr. Siedler. Berlin: Alektor, 2003, pp. 13–47.

16. Wolfgang Welsch. "On Acquisition and Possesion of Commonalities." Paper presented at the ASNEL Conference "Transcultural English Studies", Frankfurt, Germany, 19–23 May 2004. Available online: http://www2.uni-jena.de/welsch/papers/W_Wesch_On_Acquisition_and_Possession.pdf (accessed on 4 November 2015).

17. Horst Steinmetz. "Interkulturelle Rezeption und Interpretation." In *Handbuch interkulturelle Germanistik.* Edited by Alois Wierlacher and Andrea Bogner. Stuttgart: Metzler, 2003, pp. 461–67.

18. Bernd Fischer. "Herder Heute? Überlegungen zur Konzeption eines transkulturellen Humanitätsbegriffs." *Herder Jahrbuch* VIII (2006): 175–93.

19. Wolfgang Welsch. "Der Mensch—Und immer nur der der Mensch (The Human—Over and Over Again)." In *Weakening Philosophy. Essays in Honour of Gianni Vattimo.* Edited by Santiago Zabala. Montreal: McGill-Queen's University Press, 2007, pp. 87–109.

20. Winfried Menninghaus. *Das Versprechen der Schönheit.* Frankfurt: Suhrkamp, 2003.

21. Wolfgang Welsch. *Ästhetische Welterfahrung—Zeitgenössische Kunst zwischen Natur und Kultur.* Munich: Fink, 2016.

22. Wolfgang Welsch. *Mensch und Welt. Eine evolutionäre Perspektive der Philosophie.* Munich: Beck, 2012.

23. Wolfgang Welsch. *Homo mundanus—Jenseits der anthropischen Denkform der Moderne.* Weilerswist: Velbrück Wissenschaft, 2015.

24. Juan Enriquez, and Steve Gullans. *Evolving Ourselves. How Unnatural Selection and Nonrandom Mutation Are Changing Life on Earth.* New York: Portfolio/Pinguin, 2015.

25. Stephen M. Collins, Zain Kassam, and Premysl Bercik. "The Adoptive Transfer of Behavioral Phenotype via the Intestinal Microbiota: Experimental Evidence and Clinical Implications." *Current Opinion in Microbiology* 16 (2013): 240–45. [CrossRef] [PubMed]

26. Eva Jablonka, and Marion J. Lamb. *Evolution in Four Dimensions: Genetic, Epigenetic, Behavioral, and Symbolic Variation in the History of Life.* Cambridge: MIT Press, 2005.

27. Milton Brener. *Evolution and Empathy. The Genetic Factor in the Rise of Humanism.* Jefferson: McFarland & Company, 2008.

28. Wolfgang Singer. "Was kann ein Mensch wann lernen?" In *Die Zukunft der Bildung.* Edited by Linda Reisch, Jürgen Kluge and Nelson Killius. Frankfurt: Suhrkamp, 2002, pp. 78–99.

29. Axel Honneth. *Kampf um Anerkennung. Zur moralischen Grammatik sozialer Konflike.* Frankfurt: Suhrkamp, 1992.

30. Axel Honneth. *Das Ich im Wir. Studien zur Anerkennungstheorie.* Frankfurt: Suhrkamp, 2010.

31. Claus Lamm, and Jasminka Majdandžić. "The Role of Shared Neural Activations, Mirror Neurons, and Morality in Empathy—A Critical Comment." *Neuroscience Research* 90 (2015): 15–24. [CrossRef] [PubMed]

32. Theodor Lipps. *Ästhetik—Psychologie des Schönen und der Kunst.* Leipzig: Voss, 1903, vol. 1.

33. Theodor Lipps. *Vom Fühlen, Wollen und Denken.* Neudruck. Norderstedt: Vero, 2015.

34. Theodor Lipps. *Ästhetik—Psychologie des Schönen und der Kunst.* Leipzig: Voss, 1920, vol. 2.

35. Fritz Breithaupt. *Kulturen der Empathie.* Frankfurt: Suhrkamp, 2009.

Article

Transcultural Experiences in the Late Middle Ages: The German Literary Discourse on the Mediterranean World—Mirrors, Reflections, and Responses

Albrecht Classen

Department of German Studies, The University of Arizona, Learning Services Building 301, Tucson, AZ 85721, USA; aclassen@email.arizona.edu; Tel.: +1-520-621-1395; Fax: +1-520-626-8268

Academic Editor: Bernd Fischer
Received: 11 September 2015; Accepted: 10 October 2015; Published: 20 October 2015

Abstract: As recent scholarship has demonstrated, the world of the Mediterranean exerted a tremendous influence not only on the societies and cultures bordering the Mediterranean Sea during the late Middle Ages, but had a huge influence on the mentality and culture of the world north of the Alps as well because it was here where East and West met, exchanged ideas and products, and struggled to find, despite many military conflicts, some kind of transcultural. The highly complex conditions in the Mediterranean realm represented significant challenges and promises at the same time, and no traveler from Germany or England, for instance, whether a merchant or a pilgrim, a diplomat or an artist, could resist responding to the allure of the Mediterranean cultures. The corpus of travelogues and pilgrimage accounts is legion, as scholars have noted already for quite some time. But we can also observe literary reflections on the Mediterranean especially during the fifteenth century. The emergence of the late medieval and early modern prose novel is often predicated on transcultural experiences, whether they entailed military conflicts or peaceful encounters between Christians and Muslims. These literary texts did not necessarily respond to the historical events, such as the fall of Constantinople in 1453, but they document an intriguing opening up of German, English, French, and Flemish, *etc.*, society to the Mediterranean world. The prose novels discussed in this paper demonstrate that Germany, in particular, was a significant *hinterland* of the Mediterranean; somewhat farther apart, but still closely connected. The literary evidence will allow us to identify how those transcultural encounters were recognized and then dealt with.[1]

Keywords: the Mediterranean; transcultural experiences; late medieval German prose novels; *Königin Sibille*; *Melusine*; *Pontus und Sidonia*; *Fortunatus*; Ottomans; crusades; travel experience; Elisabeth von Nassau-Saarbrücken; Thüring von Ringoltingen; Eleonore of Austria

---

1. Mediterranean Culture and Transculturality in the Late Middle Ages

Mediterranean Studies have made big headway in the last few decades, beginning with Fernand Braudel's famous study on the *Méditerranée et le monde méditerranéen à l'époquede Philippe II* (1949), so it is pretty clear by now that we can only approach this entire world extending from the Straits of Gibraltar to Eastern Anatolia, from the southern slopes of the Alps to the northern Sahara if we recognize this as one, though highly complex geopolitical and culturally interacting entity [1].

---

[1] This article resulted from research that I could carry out within the framework of and subsequent to the National Endowment of the Humanities Summer Institute, "Negotiating Identities: Expression and Representation in the Christian-Jewish-Muslim Mediterranean," Barcelona, Spain, July 2015, organized by Brian Catlos and Sharon Kinoshita. I am very grateful for this wonderful opportunity, which made it possible for me to combine my own investigations on late medieval German literature with the project presented and explored from many different perspectives, the medieval Mediterranean world.

Humanities **2015**, *4*, 676–696

Moreover, the Mediterranean world was not limited to the shore lines, but there were also countless hinterlands, so the connections to England, Germany, or even Poland and the Baltic Sea, and then to Niger, Mali, and the countries we call today Syria or Iraq are to be reckoned with all the time, and this in economic, religious, political, artistic, and literary terms [2]. Both the trade across the Mediterranean via shipping and transportation over land and the multilingual conditions prevalent in virtually all coastal areas facilitated the creation of a cultural unit throughout the ages irrespective of often changing political, religious, and military constellations, as Peregrine Horden and Nicholas Purcel have famously concluded their encyclopedic study:

> The region is only loosely unified, distinguishable from its neighbours to degrees that vary with time, geographical direction and topic. Its boundaries are not of the sort to be drawn easily on a map. Its continuities are best thought of as continuities of form or pattern, within which all is mutability. ([3], p. 523)

While the contributors to *Das Mittelmeer—die Wiege der europäischen Kultur* emphasize, above all, the significant impact of the Roman Empire on the Mediterranean, some of them also extend their investigations to the Middle Ages and highlight the surprisingly close relationships between Muslims, Jews, and Christians, at least in economic terms [4]. Many other scholars have followed their paths, probably because the topic of the Mediterranean world itself proves to be just too fascinating and irresistible since the countless connections between the various areas, cultures, political entities, religious groups, and economic markets open up many heretofore unexplored perspectives. We can certainly identify the Mediterranean as one of the most transcultural areas in the world, both in antiquity and ever since [5]. Travelers criss-crossed the sea and brought with them products and stories, experiences and impressions, and hence increased their knowledge and awareness of other cultures tremendously, which invited their audiences to respond in kind [6,7]. Once they left to return home, they carried much more with them in the vessels than material goods, so ultimately a Mediterranean culture emerged that continues to exist in many different ways until today held together in a productive equilibrium [8].

The intellectual transfer from the Arabic world to the north via Italy and Spain finds a curious but most striking example in the many cookbooks from the late Middle Ages which also pursued dietetic and medical purposes [9]. Arabic recipes and medical treatises, often in conjunction with each other, enjoyed a growing popularity first in Italy and then north of the Alps. Art-historical evidence has amply confirmed the extensive exchange among the Mediterranean cultures and between the Mediterranean world and its *hinterland* [10]. And we know already for a long time how much Arabic sciences, mathematics, astronomy, and philosophy, inherited from the Greeks, contributed to the rise of the so-called Renaissance of the Twelfth Century [11–13].

2. The Mediterranean World

There is hardly any other region in Europe that was as much determined by ancient and medieval influences as the Mediterranean world, as scholarship has consistently emphasized, pursuing ever new perspectives in this regard [14]. Some researchers have grounded their investigations in one country or region, such as medieval Iberia, and have examined how the Mediterranean at large impacted the culture and political conditions there [15]. But this does not change anything with regard the global interconnectedness predicated on the Mediterranean and its neighboring countries and cultures. Michel Mollat du Jourdin goes so far as to define Europe primarily by way of reference to the Mediterranean [16].

However, all this would only make sense if we do not draw too narrow limits and hence do not cut off the *hinterlands*. A vast number of travelers reaching the Mediterranean—pilgrims, merchants, diplomats, scholars, artists, rulers, preachers, medical doctors, *etc.*—came from the north or the east, and probably also from the south, that is, for instance, the Kingdom of Mali [17,18], and while the Mediterranean Sea was certainly the central meeting place, the mix of people in that region can only be identified as massive and highly complex. The number of travelogues and pilgrimage accounts, above all, is truly legion [19]. We would not go wrong, in other words, to speak of a Mediterranean cosmopolitanism, since the Mediterranean attracted individuals from every direction and proved to be the central hub of a global compass, as the contributors to *Cosmopolitanism and the Middle Ages* (2013) elucidate nicely by focusing on such well-known cases as Marco Polo, Ibn Battuta, then on the situation in the Iberian Peninsula, Mediterranean trade, but then also Langland's *Piers Plowman* and Chaucer's "Man of Law's Tale." Following Janet Abu-Lughod's observation or claim that the Middle Ages were a world still not yet dominated by a global hegemonic thinking [20], the editors suggest an approach to that past culture in which "international commerce and cross-cultural contacts can happen frequently and across great distances in the absence of a universally imposed system of exchange" ([7]; [21], p. 3).

Of course, with the "discovery" of the New World through Christopher Columbus in 1492 a paradigm shift occurred, since the perspectives then moved toward the Atlantic and also, in the wake of further discoveries (Vasco da Gama, 1498) toward Asia [22]. Nevertheless, in many respects the Mediterranean maintained its central magnetisms, which is reflected in political, economic, literary, and artistic history from the Middle Ages and far beyond.

For the subsequent investigations it is centrally critical to build on this broad base, since we can thus gain full support from social, religious, art-historical scholars when we investigate what we know about the literary documents from the late Middle Ages that reflect in one way or the other on the Mediterranean which Sharon Kinoshita calls, herself drawing from Peregrine Horden's and Nicholas Purcel's *The Corrupting Sea* [3] and from the research by Brian Catlos, a "zone of intelligibility" [23]. Although the tensions were often very high between the representatives of the three Abrahamic faiths, it would be only correct to assume an impressive degree of contact, exchange, and cohabitation [24]. This finds an intriguing expression particularly in late medieval literature, especially when composed in the Mediterranean *hinterland*, which is the topic of this paper.

The purpose does not consist of identifying direct influences or of situating literary texts from the north at the intersection of cultural contacts; instead the topic will focus on the question how northern European writers, here especially from German-speaking lands, responded to and interacted with the Mediterranean horizon and thus reflected, to some extent, transcultural experiences, such as we know from the South-Tyrolean poet Oswald von Wolkenstein (1376/77–1445) [25,26].

Sharon Kinoshita has already discussed this phenomenon in light of high and late medieval French and Italian literature, encouraging us to regard the Mediterranean not as a place of nations and religions, hence of origins, development, and expansion, but as a place of "contact, interaction, and circulation" ([27], p. 39). As she confirms, "Beneath the grand history of the crusades, specialists routinely document the multiple kinds of exchange that constituted business as usual in the medieval Mediterranean" ([26]; [27], p. 40). Neither religions nor languages were defining barriers because more often than not there was a shared sense of local identity, although we would now be best advised to recognize more a form of "conveniencia" than a form of "conviviencia" [28–31].

Consequently, it comes as no surprise to realize that the various social groups all over the Mediterranean entertained considerable contacts with each other and pursued extensive exchange since there were many areas of shared interests. The crucial question that I want to pursue, here, however, pertains to the issue how much northern Europeans participated in this Mediterranean world by way of the literary discourse. Concerning the high Middle Ages, Sharon Kinoshita has noted, for instance, the extent to which Chrétien de Troyes operated with numerous significant references to Mediterranean cities, which thus allowed him to create a kind of *translatio imperii* and hence a *translatio studii*, that is, transferring the glorious cultural past of Greece and Rome to medieval France, establishing a remarkable bridge between the south and the northwest of Europe [32]. For Chrétien this was the ideal opportunity to compete with the German claims on this famous tradition, but we can deduce much more from these few allusions, apart from the political implications since this phenomenon, both *translatio imperii* and *translatio studii*, was a universal concept intensively pursued by intellectuals and poets throughout the Middle Ages ([33], pp. 29–30; [34]). The Mediterranean world

Humanities **2015**, *4*, 676–696

mattered significantly for this and many other authors of courtly romances, even if their world view was still pretty limited, at least compared to the early modern world. A significant German example would be the anonymous verse narrative *Mauritius von Craûn* from *ca.* 1220/1230 ([35], pp. 15–51), where the ideals of knighthood are described as residing in France, finally, after they could not be sustained any longer in Greece and Rome. Another good case in point, even more impressive with respect to the Mediterranean world, would be Rudolf von Ems's *Der guote Gerhard* (*ca.* 1230/1250), where the Cologne merchant experiences a warm welcome by the Count Stranmur, the leader of the Moroccan harbor of Castelgunt, after Gerhard had traversed many countries to the east for the purpose of trade and after he had almost been shipwrecked in the Mediterranean [36,37]. The mutual respect shown between Gerhard and Stranmur signals what transculturality could mean in the literary context, that is, the acknowledgement of representatives of other cultures in their own terms, without imposing the own value on the foreign culture. I will discuss this issue further below.

The many allusions to the Mediterranean both here and in many other texts from the entire Middle Ages indicate a constant interest in transcultural experiences. A number of pan-European narratives, such as *Apollonius of Tyre, Flore and Blanscheflur,* and *Manekine* (also known in Middle High German as *Mai und Beaflor*), signal how much the literary discourse tended to veer off to the eastern Mediterranean as the most fascinating area for many poets because there the conflicts between Christians and Muslims could be functionalized for the exploration of unexpected transcultural love affairs, such as in the verse narrative *Diu Heidinne* (late thirteenth century) [38].

Boccaccio's *Decameron* from *ca.* 1351 contains numerous examples for this phenomenon, especially the story about the Muslim princess Alatiel (story seven of day two) ([39,40]). Another interesting example would be Konrad von Würzburg's *Partonopier und Meliur* (*ca.* 1280) where the major plot development happens in the Byzantine Empire and where the Christian protagonist Partonopier faces, as his most serious contender for the hand of the Byzantine Princess Meliur, the Persian prince. Despite the religious difference, there is little in the way for Meliur to marry this shining knight from the east, until Partonopier appears again and defeats him. Similarly, in the more or less contemporary anonymous crusading romance *Reinfried von Braunschweig* the Christian protagonist strikes friendship with the Persian prince and tours his vast empire in a most peaceful and touristic fashion, quickly forgetting all of his crusading ideals [41].

Even though we cannot determine fully to what extent the various poets pursued truly transcultural interests, our critical analysis clearly indicates that their choice of narrative material was undoubtedly predicated on the awareness that such transcultural experiences seem to have happened at a large scale and that the description of such events would hence appeal to their contemporary audiences [42,43]. Specifically, here I would like to examine how much the Mediterranean world mattered for the authors of fifteenth-century German prose novels and how this might have contributed to a transcultural experience, both in positive and in negative terms. After all, transculturality does not naively imply that the representatives of two different cultures simply embrace each other; very often the opposite is really the case. The choice of the genre of these prose novels ("Volksbücher") finds its justification in the facts that they were all composed at a critical juncture in the history of the late Middle Ages moving toward a major paradigm shift; that many of them were German translations of French sources; that they were written in prose, reflecting the rise of a new form of mercantile, urban readership; and that they reached out both to the urban elite and the aristocratic circles, and this at a time when the interest in pilgrimage and travel to the Holy Land increased tremendously.

3. Fifteenth-Century Prose Novels ("Volksbücher") and Transculturality

Even before the invention of the printing press by Johannes Gutenberg in *ca.* 1450, numerous German authors appeared producing prose novels that were either based on Italian, French, Latin literature, or they drew their material from Middle High German heroic poems and courtly romances. Some of those new novels present innovative creative material, such as *Alexander von Metz, Barbarossa, Brissonetus, Faustbuch, Fortunatus, Wagnerbuch, Ritter Galmy,* and *Gabriotto und Reinhart.* Others were

Humanities **2015**, *4*, 676–696

didactic narratives, drawing from everyday experiences and from the learned tradition, such as *Claus Narr, Till Eulenspiegel, Der Finkenritter, Die Gartengesellschaft, Wendunmuth, Rastbüchlein, Katzipori,* or *Schimpf und Ernst* [44]. Recent scholarship has slowly discovered the significance of this large corpus of prose works, which is oddly situated between the Middle Ages and the Renaissance, especially because most of the literary material derives from the twelfth and thirteenth centuries, and yet it suddenly appealed again to the new audiences in the fifteenth and sixteenth centuries, probably also because it was rendered into prose and adapted in style and outlook to the new tastes [45].

Even though the focus never really rests on the Mediterranean exclusively, we constantly come across significant references to that world, and these allow us to probe more deeply the transcultural experiences which are reflected in a variety of those prose novels insofar as many of the protagonists have to leave home, traverse the world, cope with foreign cultures, and then also must realize that that foreignness is actually hidden in their own cultural core, their identity. Previously, in her broad survey, Xenia von Ertzdorff had isolated only a few major themes, such as (marital) love and heroic accomplishments ([46]; *cf.* also [47]), and then she also examined the specific nature of the novella type narrative within the European context, which was also the focus of Klaus Grubmüller's study [48]. By contrast, the employment of the Mediterranean chronotope in those novels, a concept developed by Bakthin, has not been fully recognized until today.[2]

The purpose of this paper cannot be to revisit the entire genre and to introduce and discuss the individual novels, which would amount to a whole monograph by itself [45]. Instead, following the precepts as outlined by recent Mediterranean Studies and buttressed by the theoretical insights of Transcultural Studies, I will examine only specific elements that appear sprinkled throughout the various texts explicitly signaling a concrete interest in the exotic and foreign, normally situated in the Mediterranean, which thus promises us to explain the astounding success of those novels on the early modern book markets [51]. Scholars such as Jan-Dirk Müller have rightly underscored the importance of the adventurous elements in these texts, since the male protagonists tend to travel far and wide and thus set the narrative markers characteristic of these popular novels ([52], pp. 997–99).

Transculturality in the Late Middle Ages?

Altogether, as we will observe, both crusading topics and mercantile interests matter the most, emphasizing the extent to which the authors were keen on connecting their own world and culture with the globally conceived Mediterranean. This automatically implied transcultural experiences, though not quite in the way as Johann Gottfried Herder was to define it in his famous *Auch eine Philosophie der Geschichte zur Bildung der Menschheit* (1774) and in his equally significant *Philosophie der Menschheit* (1784–1791) [53]. In a rather curious opposition to Herder, Wolfgang Welsch has recently suggested that culture is a phenomenon that "passes through classical cultural boundaries" ([54], p. 197), which constructively problematizes the issue. Hence, Bernd Fischer has rightly raised some doubt about the idealizing concept of transculturality since it normally requires a "Verstehensorientierung" (an orientation based on mutual understanding) ([55], p. 88; see also his previous reflections on this topic, note [56]). But culture constantly undergoes change and experiences transformations. Xenophobia, for instance, tends to arise out of the encounters between two or more cultures, which suggests that the earlier stage was certainly less dominated by this kind of hostility, perhaps out of ignorance, or as the result of the absence of direct contact points.

Transculturality begins when representatives of one culture react to elements of another culture, even when this happens in negative terms at first. The concept of Mediterranean Studies will facilitate our investigation of pre-modern phenotypes of transcultural contacts and exchanges. Most

---

[2] There is much research on how to understand and apply Bakthin's concept of the chronotope, such as the study by Vice [49]; but I found the online article at https://en.wikipedia.org/wiki/Chronotope to be the most concise and pragmatic; see also note [50].

helpfully, hence, Rolf-Peter Janz now emphasizes, "Im Fremden war immer schon die Projektion eigener Wünsche oder Befürchtungen zu erkennen...statt von dem Fremden zu reden, ist es geboten, von der komplexen Vielfalt fremder Kulturen auszugehen; was als fremd wahrgenommen und bezeichnet wird, wird in der jeweiligen Epoche innerhalb verschiedener Gesellschaften 'ausgehandelt', es wird 'erfunden' oder 'konstruiert'" (The projection of one's own wishes or fears have always been recognizable in the foreign itself...instead of talking about the foreign, it would be appropriate to accept first of all the complexity of foreign cultures; what we recognize as foreign and call as such, is being "negotiated", "invented", or "constructed") ([57], p. 19). Transculturality consists, as Steven Martinson avers, in the "wechselwirkenden Interaktion verschiedener kultureller Elemente *und*, zweitens, in der Transformation von zwei oder mehr Kulturen in ausgeweiteten Identitäten, während diese Kulturen ihre authentischen Grundformen behalten" ([58], p. 75; the mutually influential interaction of diverse cultural elements *and*, secondly, in the transformation of one or more cultures in expanded identities, while these cultures hold on to their authentic basic forms). In order to explore this issue further, and particularly in order to recognize its historical dimension and problematic nature, next I will turn to fifteenth-century prose novels where we discover intriguing, though only nascent elements both of transculturality and Mediterraneanism.

Understandably, most scholars working on transculturality are primarily concerned with the traditional concept of nationhood, political identity, and the breaking up of those boundaries in the present world of the late twentieth and early twenty-first centuries where transcultural phenomena begin to emerge globally [59]. But transculturality developed much earlier, particularly in the late Middle Ages, when writers and poets already explored the encounters of representatives of different cultures, religions, and languages by presenting their protagonists as traversing many lands and large bodies of water, meeting foreigners, engaging with them constructively, and reflecting on the commonalities connecting all people with each other irrespective of political or ideological oppositions.

We have always to keep in mind the strong workings of the Christian paradigm throughout the pre-modern world, and beyond, which, however, is quite often almost undermined by the writers of those prose novels and of their predecessors, who often composed verse narratives where Christians and Muslims successfully operated together in disregard of their religious differences. Transculturality hence here implies, in the medieval context, an opening up of the protagonist's mind-set through travel experiences and meetings with foreigners, who soon enough lose their foreignness and demonstrate that all tensions and conflicts in life are really human-made and could be taken care of by way of communications across cultural barriers. A surprisingly large number of literary examples, especially from the late Middle Ages, here the German prose novels, indicate already what transculturality could have meant in the pre-modern world.

4. Elisabeth von Nassau-Saarbrücken's *Königin Sibille*—The Suffering Female Protagonist in a Transcultural Context

I will first study the novel *Königin Sibille*, which Elisabeth von Nassau-Saarbrücken had translated from French into German in 1437 [60,61], where representatives of the East (Byzantium) and the West (the Frankish kingdom) find ways of close cooperation and cohabitation (marriage). *Mutatis mutandi* we could also claim that early forms of transculturality occurred in the source text (as is also the case with most other examples in this article), but this would only add more confirmation to the fundamental epistemological process that I want to describe in this and other German novels. At the beginning we learn that King Charles has married Sibille, the daughter of the Emperor of Constantinople, Richart ([60], p. 149), but their marriage breaks up even before she can deliver their first child (Ludwig) because sinister accusations against her make him believe, quite absurdly, that she had an affair with an ugly dwarf who had suddenly arrived at the court and had pushed his way into the inner circle around the king.

At first Charles, also known as Charlemagne, intends to have her burned at the stake as a punishment for her allegedly egregious adultery, but he later agrees to exile her instead. This then triggers a long series of events that take Sibille back to her father in Constantinople, from there to the pope in Rome, and then, ultimately, to France again. By then her son, Louis, has grown up and leads the army against his own father, who finally has to accept the truth that he had been misled by evil members of his court. The union of husband and wife concludes this novel, but her enormous suffering as an innocent victim, and this for many years, highlights the author's major narrative thrust.

The cultural background, however, harkens back to ancient political contacts between the Byzantine Empire and the Holy Roman Empire. Of course, by the mid-1400s Constantinople was already dramatically decimated through the constant onslaught by the Ottoman, who eventually captured that city in 1453, bringing about a traumatic paradigm shift for all of Europe since this meant the complete and final disappearance of the Roman Empire [62]. But poets did not compose their works in direct correlation with the historical conditions, and it would take a long time until the total loss of Constantinople fully sank into the European consciousness, as reflected, for instance, by the anonymous *Fortunatus*, first printed in 1509 (see below). Elisabeth von Nassau-Saarbrücken was likewise not concerned with specific historical details; instead in her novel she highlights the suffering of the female protagonist who has to travel for a very long time until she can finally reach her father's court again, from where she then endeavors slowly but surely to regain her husband's support and love.

Basically, the king has to be forced to let go of his foolish grudge against his wife and his deep misogynist distrust, but the outcome is a happy one. All this entails collective efforts on the part of many individuals and powers, which situates this novel, also extent in a French and a Spanish version, in a global context. At Charlemagne's court, which is located in Paris, the major princes come from Bavaria (Nymo), Denmark (Otger), Narbonne (Emmerich), and Brabant (Bernhart). The king sends his wife away, ordering the knight Abrye von Mondidyre to accompany her through the forest and to set her on the way to Rome where she is supposed to repent her alleged sins ([60], p. 127). Yet, she turns to Constantinople, accompanied, or rather guided, by the good and loyal peasant Warakir, since she knows that her father would help her to gain justice ([60], p. 130). On the way they make a stop in Hungary where the king has her child baptized and agrees to be the godfather ([60], p. 144).

From there the small company, which has by then grown into a group of several people, they reach Rome and inform the pope about the tragic development in France at King Charles's court ([60], p. 154). The pope is immediately ready to accompany them on their way to Constantinople, where the emperor welcomes his daughter, though with great surprise, and is soon informed about all the terrible details. In a curious, almost hilarious turn of events, upon the begard's recommendation—a holy hermit whom they had met during their journey—the emperor assembles his army and marches toward France ([60], p. 155), thus reversing the traditional military campaigns of the Crusades that had come to a complete stop in 1291 with the fall of Acre to the Muslims. Elisabeth apparently did not care particularly about geographic details and abandoned historical veracity in favor of dramatizing the tragic development in Queen Sibille's life. The narrative focuses rests on France, however, since that is the location where the subsequent battles take place and where, in the end, the royal couple finds together after all.

Irrespective of historical conditions, the author has the Byzantine emperor and the French nobles cooperate closely, besieging King Charles in Troyes ([60], p. 156). King Louis, Charles's own son and his successor (Louis the Pious) strategizes with his uncle, the emperor how best to overcome the hostile forces, and both are supported by the pope, which creates a highly unusual mix of political entities far removed from historical reality. But the author projects this conjunction of the most important individuals with the intention of casting Charles as a highly irrational and confused ruler who must be brought to reason by means of a close alliance of the Eastern and the Western Church, as if the Great Schism of 1054 never had happened [63].

However, while the geographical and historical accuracy might be lacking considerably, the novel itself signals how much the events described here take place within the larger Mediterranean world and that the history of western Europe really has to be located within the Mediterranean framework,

Humanities **2015**, *4*, 676–696

irrespective of how much the author and her audience really understood about it. The origins of the Carolingian empire are thus closely tied in with the Byzantine Empire and the papacy, and thus the Frankish *hinterland* suddenly emerges as a critical component of transcultural Mediterranean reflections. According to the narrator, once Charles and Sibille have renewed their marriage, they conceive of another son, Lohir, who was later to become the emperor of Rome ([60], p. 173), which again does not agree with the historical conditions as reflected by the relevant chronicles. However, Elisabeth thereby managed to create a transcultural map of Europe according to which all the relevant power players at that time could get together and join hands in order to overcome the traitors, liars, and deceivers who endangered the well-being of the royal court and especially of the queen.

Why does the author conceive of such a huge geographical framework, combining Paris with Constantinople and Rome? The narrative focus clearly rests on the innocent queen's suffering and the astounding support which she receives from a wide range of forces both east and west. There is no reference to the Muslim world or the Jewish culture here, but the old conflict between the Greek Orthodox and the Catholic Church has also disappeared from view because the only concern addressed in this novel pertains to ethical values within the political context.

Transculturality is, what is noteworthy in our context, simply assumed as the basis of all actions, such as the marriage between the Byzantine princess and the Frankish king, and later the close cooperation of various people from different countries and societies with the same goal of restoring Sibille's honor and status as Charles's wife, while the true evil forces rest within the western Carolingian court. Once those traitors are eliminated, King Charles finally realizes how much he had been misled by those evil courtiers and how terribly he had treated his own wife. All this is possible, however, only because the Byzantine emperor and the pope join hands and form a military and political alliance together with Charles's own son Louis and a whole array of simple people such as Warakir, the true hero behind Sibille's rescue. The novel aggressively targets the failures of courtly society and heavily relies on a transcultural background without which those traitors could not be defeated [64].

Even though the geographical map outlined here is nothing but highly spotty, and the very absence of more specific details confirms how much the author and her audience simply assumed a generic understanding of the Mediterranean world and how little they cared about actual cultural or religious differences. While the marriage of Theophano with Emperor Otto II in 972 was apparently a major deviation from the political norm even at that time [65], within fifteenth-century literary discourse this was suddenly regarded and treated as a regular and very positive development [66]. For Elisabeth, to be sure, it seemed to be a very ordinary move by King Charles to find his bride in the Byzantian empire, probably because by the fifteenth century the connections between East and West had become intensive enough both in economic and political terms to allow such a marriage to be treated as quite ordinary within the literary context ([8], pp. 137–53).

5. Thüring von Ringoltingen's *Melusine*: The Uncanny in a Transcultural Context

While Elisabeth's *Königin Sibille* has survived in only one manuscript and was never printed, the situation with Thüring von Ringoltingen's *Melusine* (1456) was a very different one, since this quickly turned into a true bestseller far beyond the Middle Ages ([44], pp. 141–62; [52], pp. 1012–87). There are many reasons for this enormous success story, but one of them does not seem to have been discussed much so far at least within the German literary context, that is, the transcultural experience within the Mediterranean context (for previous approaches to this issue in the French version, see Burns [67]). The female protagonist Melusine proves to be a hybrid creature, half human and half snake, which her husband Reymund only finds out many years after their marriage and after most of their children have already grown up. But behind this poeto-mythical dimension we can also discover numerous comments on cultural aspects of great importance for our argument here.

His own brother instigates him to investigate his wife's whereabouts on Saturdays when she regularly hides in a bath, preventing anyone from seeing her, which arouses Reymund's suspicion that she might have an extramarital affair. To his horror he has to realize her true nature, which he at first keeps a secret, but which he later makes known to the public in an emotional outburst after he has learned that his son Geoffroy had killed his brother Freymund because the latter had joined a monastery. Violence hence rests within the family, and this leads to Reymund's public accusation, and hence to Melusine being forced to depart home and hearth and to leave mankind behind for good until the Day of Judgment has come. Mythical elements combine here with narrative features drawn from a variety of literary sources, and the success which this novel experienced has certainly to do with the many different themes brought together by the original French author Couldrette (*ca.* 1400, verse romance) and his predecessor, Jean d'Arras (1393).

On the one hand the intriguing aspect of a man marrying a hybrid creature has mattered greatly in the novels' extraordinary popularity far into the eighteenth and even nineteenth century. On the other, *Melusine* is action-packed, with war, murder, and other conflicts dominating many sections, especially after Melusine's disappearance. But already in the first half of the text, where we learn much about her sons' adventures in the distant world, major conflicts emerge that must have fascinated the contemporary audience. Those accounts apparently draw from a variety of sources and are partly historically accurate, partly imaginary. All of them, specifically underscore the great interest in projecting foreign worlds and cultures with which the protagonists have to interact.

After Melusine's son Anthoni has married the Princess Cristina of Lützelburg, war breaks out in Bohemia because, as the King of Alsace is informed by his brother, the king of Bohemia, the Turkish emperor has attacked his land and is besieging the city of Prague ([52], p. 74). Of course, Anthoni and his brother Reynhart get immediately involved and rush east, where they succeed, after an intensive battle to overcome the enemies and destroy them altogether. While the Turks had first burned the king of Bohemia to death ([52], p. 79), now the king of Alsace does the same to the Turkish emperor and all of his troops whom they had captured in the fight ([52], pp. 82–83).

There is no good explanation why the author would have reconfigured historical factors, distorting them so egregiously, unless we assume, as is often the case in this genre, that references to foreign locations, cultures, and people are freely combined in order to set the stage for the protagonists who thus can demonstrate their prowess and military accomplishments on behalf of the entire European knighthood and Christianity. Relocating these religious wars at the edge of northern European kingdoms brings the traditional Mediterranean military conflicts closer to home and make them thus more dramatic and scary for the contemporary audiences.

Moreover, Thüring makes it thus possible for the Alsatian and Rhenish knights and their friends and families to imagine that they as well could accomplish triumphs on the battlefield against the Ottomans, who by that time were still far away and "only" moving north through the Balkans [68]. These military endeavors are regularly associated with experiences of love and marriage, since Anthoni has already married the Princess of Alsace—certainly another historical fiction, which serves the author well, however, because his account thus does not conflict with historical facts.

At the same time, the military operations outside of the city of Prague are described in very similar terms as those in countless courtly romances, except that here the Ottomans have replaced the Saracens, and the battle does not take place in some mysterious location in the east, but on familiar grounds, Bohemia, which yet still seems somewhat far away from western Europe, that is, Switzerland. For Thüring the battle itself proves to be an ideal occasion to reflect upon the rise and fall of fortune in such military operations because at first the Ottomans seem to be very successful, especially because the king of Bohemia, Friedrich, is killed by the arrow shot from a cross-bow ([52], p. 78), which strongly encourages them to pursue their enemies more energetically, thus almost gaining the upper hand and so the victory. But then Anthoni and Reymund arrive with their large army and can turn everything around, killing the Ottoman emperor and many of his soldiers, thus triumphing altogether and crushing the Muslim attack thoroughly.

Naturally, the foreign culture could only be perceived in military terms, since the audience expected to hear about the Christian victory, especially brought about by Melusine's sons. But this is not the only encounter with the Mediterranean world, since the other sons also gain significant victories far away, setting up their own kingdoms much further east. Uriens and his brother Gyot fight successfully in Cyprus and rise to highest honors there ([52], pp. 51ff.), which does not come as real surprises because Cyprus represented, especially in late medieval literature, a geographical trope commonly referred to as a marker of the eastern Mediterranean, a half-way stepping stone, so to speak, to the exotic Orient, a place of wealth, power, and also peace ([23,24,69]).

While the entire story of Melusine is located in the vicinity of Poitiers ([52], p. 13), the monstrous and fair-like nature of this female figure evokes distant lands and strange realms where only few humans ever set foot [70]. Hence the narrative takes a natural turn toward those far-away countries in central Europe and then particularly in the eastern Mediterranean where Melusine's sons hope to gain fame and power through military victories.

As is very common in fifteenth-century, in Famagusta (here: Famagrossa) they come to the local king's rescue who is attacked by the Muslim Sultan who is besieging the city "mit hundert tausent heyden" ([52], p. 51; with hundred thousand heathens). The king is already deeply worried that they would not be able to resist the siege much longer and might have to capitulate, which would force them to abandon their Christian faith and to be converted to Islam ([52], p. 52). When the king notices the arrival of the foreigners, which makes the Muslims turn away from the city toward the new enemies, he believes that they are in flight, so he opens the city gate and launches a sortie, but they are badly beaten back and the king himself is mortally wounded through a poisoned projectile ([52], p. 52). In the meantime the two brothers engage with the Sultan's troops and can quickly overcome them despite the huge difference in numbers. Uriens even succeeds in overcoming the Sultan and killing him, which soon brings about their victory over the enemies. We learn only then that this Sultan is the ruler of Babylon ([52], p. 54), who thus emerges as an icon of everything foreign to late medieval Europeans.

Ironically, however, while the Sultan and his soldiers represent religious otherness, Uriens himself, being Melusine's son and hence marked in his face as a descendent of a monstrous race, represents an internal, or genetic otherness, as we would say today:

> Doch was sein angesicht nit schoen/sunder einer selczamer form vnd gestalt/wann er was gar kurcz vnd vast breyt vnd flach vnder seinen augen Vnd was jm das ein aug rott vnd das ander gruen Er haett auch einen grossen weyten mund/vnd lange vnd grosse oren. ([52], p. 47)

> [But his face was not beautiful but of strange form and shape since he was very short and very wide and flat underneath his eyes. One of his eyes was red and the other was green. He had a large wide mouth and long and large ears.].

The Cypriots marvel at his appearance, but they can only express puzzlement since he has rescued them through his manly and powerful fighting against their existential threat. They make the sign of the cross when they catch sight of him out of precaution and yet admire him because he appears to them as an individual who would be able to conquer many countries ([52], p. 55). The mortally wounded king enquires about his name and then expresses his great respect for the dynasty of Lusignan, which is mentioned really only here for the first time, whereas before Melusine had not divulged anything about her own background and origin. The narrator had only signaled before that the name of "Lusinia" for one of the castles which Melusine had ordered to be built on her behalf ([52], p. 1053) would later gain in global esteem.

Jean d'Arras in his earlier version (1393) had given slightly more information about Lusignan [71], embedding the entire account in the mythical past of the noble lineage of Lusignan in Poitou ([52], p. 21). Thüring associates the entire story to that dynasty only in his epilogue in which he confirms that the fairy figure Melusine had the original castles and towers built.

Whereas Uriens is thus characterized by his inheritance and descendance from an archaic, autochtone, that is, monstrous race and thus represents the internal foreignness, the Muslims appear on the stage as external foreigners who are quickly defeated and eliminated. Even though this proves to be a traditional trope in medieval literature, which is here carried over to the fifteenth century in slightly changed configurations because of the Mediterranean setting (Cyprus), Thüring successfully translated the exotic dimension into a narrative context which here becomes digestible and understandable also for a northern European audience. There could hardly be a better example of what the *hinterland* of the Mediterranean world implied, as Melusine and Reymund establish their dynasty in France, but their sons conquer or gain kingdoms in Cyprus and neighboring countries. As concrete as those areas might be, for the poet and his audience they represented probably something what Henrie Lefebvre had called "abstract space", the product of imagination based on some elements of concrete knowledge through personal experience on travels [72].

At any rate, Uriens assumes the throne after the mortally wounded king has asked him to marry his daughter and to replace him because he can no longer defend his country and his people ([52], p. 57). After the marriage has been completed, the king addresses Uriens and identifies him as "Vriens von Lusinyen" ([52], p. 57) who is now supposed to assume the crown and continue with his successful fighting against the Muslims after he had already killed the Sultan. Immediately after the marriage the king succumbs to his wound and passes away. We only learn that Uriens and Hermyne live a happy life and have a son called Greyffe, who later accomplished many heroic deeds and conquered his own kingdom somewhere in the Asian east, called Premye ([52], p. 60). This surprisingly extends the Mediterranean far into a mythical Middle East, characterized by fictional names of those places which then belong to Premye—a narrative strategy which already Wolfram von Eschenbach had pursued at the end of his *Parzival* (*ca.* 1205) by relating the history, even if only in fragmentary form, of Parzival's half-brother Feirefiz and his wife, Repansche de Schoye, one of the maids serving the Grail, whose son was to turn into the fabled Prester John.

In *Melusine*, however, the narrative interest lingers on the Mediterranean, as imaginative as it might be presented here. We learn at the end of the chapter that shortly thereafter the King of Armenia also passes away, which makes the inheritance decision to a critical issue for the entire country. But since the king had been Hermyne's uncle and since the fame of the two Lusignan brothers has spread far and wide, the nobles of that country request that Uriens's brother Gyot be designated as the new king by marrying the Princess Florye ([52], p. 61). This happens, and the next chapter quickly informs us about the subsequent events, since the two brothers rule mightily over their lands in the eastern Mediterranean, fight with great success against the Muslims, and support the Knights of St. John, or Knights Hospitallers, on the island of Rhodes ([52], p. 62).[3] We are then only informed about the next generations who all continue successfully with the war against the Muslims and can thus maintain their own honor and reputation. Back home, Reymund resigns from the throne and travels to Rome to ask the pope for his redemption and absolution of his sins. From there he retires to the monastery of Montserrat in Aragon, which finally integrates also the Iberian Peninsula into this family history, extending another, though rather thin line of transcultural experience, but now in the western Mediterranean. This does not mean, however, that Melusine would hence be completely out of the picture because of her husband's religious conversion. Instead, briefly before his death in the monastery, she appears for three days in the air around the castle Lusignan, thus prophesying his passing away as she had foretold before her own departure from mankind ([52], p. 154).

The remainder of the novel deals with attempts by various of the sons to meet the challenge posed by their ghost-like aunts, in which they fail, and then with Geoffrey's death. The narrator only emphasizes at the end how much the dynasty of the Lusignans is connected with virtually all countries in then known Europe through marriage and military conquest: "vnd ist diser stamme also weytt vnd verr zerbreyttet jn waelsch vnd teütsche lannd" ([52], p. 174; and this dynasty is widely disseminated in French/Italian and German lands).

---

3   For fastest and concise information. Available online: https://en.wikipedia.org/wiki/Knights_Hospitaller (accessed on 18 August 2015).

Humanities **2015**, *4*, 676–696

All this does not necessarily constitute transculturality, insofar as both Reymund and his sons operate only in Christian lands and tend to fight against Muslim opponents. But the narrative is definitely anchored not only in France, but also in Bohemia, Cyprus, Armenia, and Spain, apart from the imaginary territories where Melusine and her sisters operate. This geographic network does not evoke much confidence about the author's concrete knowledge of the various countries on the European map, but the deliberate strategy to have her protagonists commonly operate in those distant lands clearly reflect an interest in foreignness by itself and especially in the Mediterranean world where Melusine's sons can gain might and political status.

6. The Scottish Princess at the Austrian Court Reflects on the Transcultural in Her *Pontus und Sidonia*

The situation concerning the transcultural experience is somewhat different and yet quite similar in the novel *Pontus und Sidonia* by Elisabeth's contemporary, the Scottish Princess Eleonor, which she completed sometime between 1440 and 1460. Eleonor had been the daughter of the Scottish King James I (murdered in 1437) and had briefly stayed at the royal court of in France between 1445 and 1448, when she was married to the Tyrolean Duke Sigmund [73]. Sometime thereafter she translated the French novel *Ponthus et la belle Sidoyne*, probably originally composed by Geoffrey de la Tour Landry (before 1330–1402/1406), into German, parallel to two other German intellectuals, but her novel was the only one that made it into early modern print (first printed in 1483) ([44], pp. 144–54, 44–47), from when on it turned into a true bestseller far into the seventeenth and eighteenth centuries.

In essence, Pontus is the son of the King of Galicia who is killed by his Muslim enemies, but he is secretly helped and can escape to the Kingdom of Brittany, where he soon emerges as a superior knight. He and the king's daughter Sidonia secretly fall in love, but they maintain strictest modesty and chastity, fighting any effort by a jealous courtier to malign them and accuse Pontus, above all, of pursuing the princess with prurient interests. To avoid any scandal, Pontus goes into a voluntary exile and travels to England where he stays for seven years. Already back in Brittany he had decisively defeated one of the Sultan's three sons, killing his opponent and scores of his fighters. In England he faces the same threat, this time by the third of the Sultan's sons, and also overcomes and kills him. At the very end Pontus returns to Galicia and accomplishes the same heroic deed there, thus eliminating all threats to western Christianity by any Muslim forces [74].

The theme of this novel focuses on the love relationship between Pontus and Sidonia, although both have to struggle long and hard to fend for their honor and freedom to choose their own marriage partner. Even though they quickly fall in love with each other, the barriers barring them from experiencing their happiness and joy are steep and require resolute and arduous actions. Pontus has to defend himself repeatedly in public against the charge of lusting after Sidonia, so he withdraws several times from the court. He returns from England only after a messenger has alerted him to the danger that Sidonia might be forced to marry the old and ugly duke of Burgundy. As soon as Pontus has arrived at the court, he joins a tournament and kills the opponent more or less by accident, thus removing this danger for their private happiness. Next, nothing seems to be in the way between the two lovers to join hands in marriage, but Pontus first has to liberate his own country, Galicia, and to regain the title of king by defeating the Muslims there.

During his absence, the jealous courtier Gendelet, has fake letters written in which Pontus alleges makes known that he would prefer if Sidonia married Gendelet, and her father strongly pushes for that marriage. However, Sidonia withdraws into a strong and well-provisioned tower and can resist the siege for a long time. At the end her father joins their company and thus has to endure famine as well. Only because he is then about to die from hunger, does Sidonia finally agree to marry the hated man, but Pontus returns just in time from Galicia and kills his opponent.

The novel has the protagonist operate in many different countries, which reflects the aristocratic culture in the fifteenth century internationally connected through marriages and military alliances. Pontus originates from Galicia in the northwestern part of the Iberian Peninsula. He finds refuge in

Brittany, and later he goes into "exile" in England. There he helps solve a military conflict with the king of Ireland and sets up peace between both sides through a marriage contract. The King of England and the King of Scotland are also connected through marital bonds. Once Pontus has returned from England, he confronts the Duke of Burgundy and kills him. During his first absence from the royal court in Brittany people assume that he might have gone to Poland, Hungary, or Germany.

After Pontus has liberated Sidonia from the persecutions by the courtier Gendelet, he returns to Galicia and defeats the Muslims there. The Mediterranean world does not exactly arise at the narrative horizon, but the connection with Spain is clearly visible. Moreover, the Sultan's three sons arrive from the eastern Mediterranean and attack first Galicia (victory), then Brittany (defeat), and finally England (defeat). Even though it remains unclear whether Eleonore of Austria was aware of the catastrophic fall of Constantinople to the Turks in 1453, her novel specifically outlines how Christianity can rally enough strength to resist and overcome this Muslim danger. Actually, all of Europe was abuzz with the terrible news about this catastrophic development in the Eastern Mediterranean, which rang in a new age of Ottoman threats to the Balkans and then to the Habsburg Empire [75–77]. However, neither Eleonore nor Elisabeth, not to mention Thüring, bothered to engage with those events specifically, and instead only project general military conflicts, conquests, and battles pitting Christians against Muslims. Each time we observe the same narrative pattern because at first the latter are very successful and take over the targeted country completely. They then rely on the traditional administrative structure, as long as the officers convert to Islam, as is the case in Galicia, and nothing seems to be in their way until the hero emerges and defeats them entirely.

In *Pontus und Sidonia* we learn, for instance, of a formerly Christian knight who now serves Sultan Produs and can do so because he has assumed the appearance of a Muslim, although in his heart he has remained a Christian ([74], p. 46). Throughout the entire Mediterranean world we hear of similar problems because many times representatives of other religions served their lords, which caused deep frictions at time and could result in direct persecutions [78,79]. In Eleonore's novel this counselor is never exposed, but he certainly operates secretly supporting the Christian cause. Every time the Sultan has a nightmare which foretells him his own tragic ending at the hand of young Pontus, this knight calms his fears and dismisses this dream vision as irrelevant and deceptive ([74], pp. 49, 138), although the very opposite will take place.

What does have to do with transculturality? At first, superficial, sight the very opposite seems to be the case insofar as the representatives of these two cultures and religions fight each other most bitterly; and the Christians do not rest until they have achieved the ultimate triumph. But the author integrated these motifs not simply for religious reasons, especially since there is no clear sense of a crusading mentality. But this and other novels clearly reflect on deep-seated fear of a Muslim take-over when the own military defense might not stand up to the danger by the Arabic or rather by then Turkish forces.

The Sultan, who resides in famous, almost mythic Babylon ([74], p. 60), has four sons, and only one, the oldest, is designated to inherit his father's empire in the east. The three others must fend for themselves and thus they extend their power to western European countries, each trying to achieve the greatest glory in winning the most lands and in converting a maximum of Christians to Islam—a standard narrative theme which we commonly find, with only slight variations, in numerous courtly romances. The Sultan's sons operate, in other words, just like any other Arthurian knight, except that they adhere to another faith. Both Eleonore and Elisabeth, among others, imagine a world where Christians and Muslims might ultimately share an interest in and with each other, competing for the control over various lands and kingdoms without much concern regarding the religious orientation, although at the present, in the time of the literary texts, the relationships are determined by military conflicts. This non-religious, and in a way also much more transcultural perspective will be increasingly noticeable soon in such texts as the anonymous *Fortunatus*.

Humanities **2015**, *4*, 676–696

7. The Ultimate Departure toward the Transcultural in the Mediterranan Context: *Fortunatus*

We notice a very different constellation in a later prose novel, the anonymous *Fortunatus* (1509) (here quoted from Müller, note [52], which also enjoyed tremendous popularity and was even translated or adapted into English by Thomas Dekker as *The Pleasant Comedie of Old Fortunatus* (1599) [80]. Fortunatus at first travels throughout western Europe and concludes his life after he has also toured the eastern Mediterranean, including Egypt and the Middle East. But he embarks on his adventurous life not at all as a wealthy person because his father, a wealthy citizen of Cyprus, has proven to be a spend-thrift who wastes all of his extensive inheritance and later also his wife's dowry. Facing poverty and misery, Fortunatus leaves home, and is lucky enough to be hired by the Count of Flanders who at that point is just about to depart from Cyprus and to return home ([52], p. 192).

Cyprus quickly disappears from our view since Fortunatus undergoes many difficult and challenging life-experiences, but once he has acquired many riches and has become an independently wealthy individual, he returns home and settles there, rising to the highest possible position within that society based on his money, which emerges as a critical new theme in early modern German literature [81]. The novel is based on the fundamental experience of the wheel of fortune, that is, very much in the sense of Boethius's teachings in his *De consolatione philosophiae* from 525 C.E., insofar as Fortunatus has to struggle hard to survive most dangerous situations. At first he loses all his money he had earned in the service of the Count of Flanders, then he works for a merchant of Florence in London ([74], p. 408), who is, however, later accused of having stolen the king's jewels, which only turns out to be wrong, but by then too late for the innocent victims. Both the merchant and his men are executed, only Fortunatus is spared by luck. Before that process is set in motion, the mob is threatening all Florentine and Lombard merchants, suspecting them of nefarious actions, which confirms the extent to which by the early sixteenth century cosmopolitan conditions dominated in such large cities as London, which are directly connected with their trading partners in the Mediterranean ([74], pp. 419–20).

The jewels are discovered later, but by that time Fortunatus has been escorted out of the country and ends up in a large forest where he finally encounters, after a life-threatening fight against a bear, a mysterious lady who offers him, as in a fairy tale, the choice among wisdom, wealth, physical strength, health, beauty, and a long life ([74], p. 430). Without much consideration, Fortunatus chooses wealth and receives a money purse that will never be empty wherever he might be. Of course, as to be expected, this new wealth makes Fortunatus rather suspicious to others, and his life from then on proves to be rather precarious, although he handles the endless amount of money quite carefully, which ultimately allows him to go on extensive travels throughout Europe and later also to Egypt and the Near East. The first part of the novel concludes with him marrying the daughter of an impoverished count in Cyprus and thus setting up his own dynasty, and this with the help of his infinite money supply. He can even win a magical cap from the Egyptian Sultan by deceiving him. This cap allows him to fly to any location in the world within seconds according to his own wishes.

Subsequently Fortunatus dies and passes his wealth and these two magical objects on to his sons, Ampedo and Andolosia. The latter quickly abuses them in order to rise in social rank, and is thus finally murdered because others begrudge his wealth and presumptuousness, while the former dies out of grief because of the disappearance of his brother. With their death the money purse and the travel cap lose their properties as well, which concludes the novel. In the epilogue the narrator offers his reflections, warning against the temptation of money and urging his readers to choose wisdom instead, especially because the biblical King Solomon had done the same ([74], p. 580; [82]).

Let us return to the first half dealing with Fortunatus's life. After all those preliminary events leading up to the scene with the magical maid in the forest, the narrative is determined for a long time by Fortunatus's travels that take him all over Europe ([74], pp. 441ff.). The narrator is fairly specific about the individual stations, but limits himself to name dropping and giving distances. Fortunatus, together with his servant Lüpoldus, embark on their trip in Nuremberg, although they had met in Nantis, or Nantes, the capital of Brittany ([74], p. 436). The German author, however, closely followed the usual outline of many contemporary travelogues, which commonly began in Nuremberg, and has the two travelers reach, in sequence, Augsburg, Nörtlingen, Ulm, Constance, Basel, Strasbourg, Mainz, Cologne, Bruges, then London, from where they turn to Scotland and then Ireland ([74], pp. 441–42; [83,84]). Subsequently they visit the so-called "St. Patrick's Purgatory" ([74], p. 443), where it would be possible to enter a cave and to get a view into the actual purgatory. In reality, there is only darkness, and the two men would almost have died in the labyrinth of the cave system, if not at the end an old monk would have rescued them ([74], pp. 445–47).

Their travel then takes them to Calais, Paris, then Bayonne, Pamplona, Burgos, Santiago de Compostela, Lisbon, Sevilla, Granada, Cordoba, and Barcelona, from where they visit the Monastery of Montserrat. The following stations simply follow the usual pilgrimage routes to Jerusalem, Alexandria, and the St. Catherine monastery in Sinai ([74], p. 449). They also reach Constantinople, which is not yet conquered by the Ottomans ([74], p. 450), which could indicate that the original text was composed before 1453 ([52], pp. 1163–64).

From here I would like to jump to a later section in the novel in order to move beyond the global Mediterranean scope, without leaving that perspective out of sight, and reflect on the aspect of transculturality once again. First, once they all have arrived at the court of the Turkish emperor, they feel safe again because in Constantinople they were attacked by their inn-keeper who tried to steal their goods, whereupon Lüpoldus killed him and then deposed off the body in the latrine. However, Fortunatus expressed his great disappointment over the many Christians who had converted to Islam in order to serve at the Ottoman court ("verlogneten christen" [74], p. 463; deceptive Christians). This finds a good parallel in Eleonore's *Pontus und Sidonia*, but there the narrator's explanation underscores the existential fear those individuals felt once the Muslims had taken over their country. Next we learn of Fortunatus's visits of the Scandinavian countries, then of Bohemia, from where he returns to Venice, and then to Cyprus. Once having established a residence on this island, and once his wife has delivered two boys, Fortunatus embarks on his next journey, which takes him, however, this time to Egypt, and from there further east.

Operating like an ordinary merchant, the protagonist arrives in Alexandria and receives a friendly welcome, as any other merchant originating from Venice or other parts of the western Mediterranean would be given. He is even allowed to see the Sultan, whom he offers a huge gift of jewels, which stuns the Sultan and makes the Italian merchants very jealous ([74], pp. 486–87), particularly because Fortunatus had never set foot in that part of the world before and does not really operate like a traditional merchant, and yet immediately outdoes them in every respect. The Sultan returns the gift with an equally valuable amount of pepper, and the two develop, irrespective of the anger by the other merchants, a good working relationship. The same happens with the Sultan's Admiral, whom the Italian and other merchants—now also including those from Catalunya or Catalonia—try to bribe hoping that he would treat Fortunatus badly, but they are simply outdone by the latter who can always pay much more money than anyone else. The Admiral simply takes the money from both sides, and ultimately privileges Fortunatus after all ([74], p. 488).

By means of his money the protagonist receives the Admiral's full support for his plans to tour the countries further east, perhaps even up to China, and is well equipped ([74], p. 489), and this without running into any problems or conflicts because of their religious differences. In fact, money makes it possible in the first place to establish this good relationship, but there is no real problem anyway between the European merchants and the Sultan's court. In fact, we could identify this situation as the most transcultural one in all of the fifteenth-century German prose novels. But we know also from numerous pilgrimage accounts, such as by Felix Fabri or Arnold von Harff, how much traffic and commerce had brought together the representatives of the two world religions by the end of the fifteenth century ([85], see also note 7, "Introduction", pp. 93–120).

While Elisabeth and Eleonore had still elaborated their novels on the continuous military conflict between Islamic and Christian forces, which then allowed their protagonist to demonstrate their fighting skills, manly prowess, and leadership qualities, the anonymous author of *Fortunatus* pursued very different concepts, though he also located his text to a considerable extent within the framework of the Mediterranean world. However, here we observe a clear case of transculturality, as materialistic as it might be, since money proves to be a shared value on both sides of the religious divide. On his way home from the East, Fortunatus feels a great desire to stop first in Cairo to see the Sultan again and to thank him for all his help ([74], p. 492). He meets him, however, in Alexandria, and so also the Admiral, who is identified as his "guoten freund" ([74], p. 492; his good friend). After his own ship has returned to take him back home, and after all the merchandise has been sold quickly at low prices, the Sultan desires to invite Fortunatus to dine with him and to relate how he had fared in the Orient. As we learn, because of the letters of recommendation issued by the Sultan, the protagonist had been able to traverse all those foreign countries without any difficulties: "gar eerlich vnd schon von allen herren entpfangen waer worden / vnd wie ym all ander herren für vnnd für so grosse fördernus hetten gethon" ([74], p. 493; he had been received honorably and pleasantly by all lords, who then provided him with much support). Fortunatus himself emphasizes that his journey would not have been possible without those letters, thus underscoring how much the Sultan's authority and hence his personal sponsorship had mattered all over the eastern world ([74], p. 494).

After the dinner Fortunatus asks for the privilege to give a monetary gift to all the Mamluks and all other servants employed at court, which impresses the Sultan considerably. He praises the protagonist for his honorable behavior and then wants to demonstrate his own wealth, so he leads him to his treasury. But irrespective of all the gold and jewels, the true treasure consists of a magical cap that allows the person who puts it on his head to be transported magically to the location of his desire ([74], p. 496)—clearly another fairy-tale object and motif.

Fortunatus quickly realizes the enormous value of this object, and tricks the Sultan to place the hat himself on the visitor's head. He immediately wishes to be on his ship and can thus escape with the greatest treasure possible, and later adamantly refuses to return it despite various diplomatic efforts on the Sultan's part ([74], pp. 500–3). When his emissary Marcholando tries to negotiate with him regarding the hat, Fortunatus suddenly insists that there could never be any friendship between a Christian and a Muslim, and that the Sultan himself would never return the hat if he had stolen it from Fortunatus ([74], p. 503). Fortunatus treats the messenger very well, but he does not give in, which concludes this part of the narrative since the protagonist has no longer any interest to travel to the Holy Land or Egypt (ibid.). But the new conflict between Fortunatus and the Sultan is not based on any religious causes, but simply on their competition for this most valuable hat.

8. Conclusions

To conclude, we can observe how much *Fortunatus* was predicated on the global travel experience, on the localization of the central events in Cyprus and the eastern Mediterranean, and on the exchange between and contacts with the representatives of Christian societies in England, Italy, and Cyprus and the Near East. Fortunatus does not face any conflicts when he reaches Egypt, and with the Sultan's letters all political doors in the various Asian countries open up to him. Travel and mercantile activities, apart from tourism (already then) and diplomatic service made it fairly easy to traverse throughout the entire region and to reach even India. But Fortunatus returns to Cyprus, his real home, which the narrator projects as a most hospitable, welcoming, and international location in the eastern Mediterranean. For Fortunatus, both London and Constantinople could have been places where he might have faced, as an innocent victim, the death penalty. Alexandria and Cairo are important intermediate sites for further explorations, and Spain, Germany, Scandinavia, Flanders, the Balkans, Bohemia, and Poland are simply sites to be visited on the grand tour through Europe. Cyprus, by contrast, stands out as Fortunatus's country of origin and the desired place to settle. It is there where the Mediterranean and the transcultural meet and form a significant union.

In the other fifteenth-century examples, serious conflicts between Christians and Muslims dominate, but the appearance of large Islamic armies in Spain, Brittany, England, signify that the war between both cultures and religions was omnipresent. At the same time, despite the disappearance of

Humanities **2015**, *4*, 676–696

Byzantium after the fall of Constantinople in 1453, German authors continued to refer to that political unit long after that monumental event and regarded it as a major reference point in the imperial politics relevant for the German-speaking lands. Considering that we are dealing here with premodern novels, all examples demonstrate a fascinating openness toward the Mediterranean as a significant *locus operandi*, and they reflect on a phenotype of transculturality that was to develop considerably further in the following centuries. Even when the novelists project the foreign world, here mostly the Muslim-ruled countries, they consistently indicate their considerable interest in and awareness of the other cultures that by that time simply had to be reckoned with. Byzantium mattered just as much for western European authors and readers as Alexandria, Cairo, and Cyprus. While the historical chronicles might focus mostly on hostile relationships between the Arabic and the European world, the literary evidence, especially from the late Middle Ages, begins to paint quite a different picture [72,86].

By the same token, northwestern Spain, with Galicia, was suddenly just as important for German audiences as Armenia and Persia because major events crucial in the protagonists' lives take place there. Even if we were to claim that the degree of transculturality was still very low in late medieval German literature, these novels signal how much the foundations for a transcultural world view was increasingly established or already present in an early manifestation, and this in the *hinterlands* of the Mediterranean. The protagonists roam over much larger and much more concretely identifiable space, reflecting hence a significant "spatial turn" insofar as both Europe in specific geographic terms and the entire Mediterranean are now fully accessible irrespective of any religious or ethnic conflicts [87].

Conflicts of Interest: The author declares no conflict of interest.

References

1. Fernand Braudel. *Le Méditerranée et le Monde Méditerranéen à L'époquede Philippe II*. Paris: Armand Colin, 1949.
2. Gunther Hirschfelder. *Die Kölner Handelsbeziehungen im Spätmittelalter*. Veröffentlichungen des Kölnischen Stadtmuseums, X. Cologne: Kölnisches Stadtmuseum, 1994.
3. Peregrine Horden, and Nicholas Purcell. *The Corrupting Sea: A Study of Mediterranean History*. Oxford: Blackwell Publishers, 2000.
4. Klaus Rosen, ed. *Das Mittelmeer—Die Wiege der Europäischen Kultur*. Cicero-Schriftenreihe, 3. Bonn: Bouvier Verlag, 1998.
5. William V. Harris, ed. *Rethinking the Mediterranean*. Oxford: Oxford University Press, 2005.
6. Gobierno de Navarra, and Institución Príncipe de Viana, eds. *Itinerarios Medievales e Identidad Hispánica: XXVII Semana de Estudios Medievales, Estella, 17 a 21 de julio de 2000*. Pamplona: Gobierno de Navarra, Departamento de Educación y Cultura, 2001.
7. Michael Murrin. *Trade and Romance*. Chicago and London: University of Chicago Press, 2013.
8. Albrecht Classen, ed. *East Meets West in the Middle Ages and Early Modern Times: Transcultural Experiences in the Premodern World*. Fundamentals of Medieval and Early Modern Culture 14. Berlin and Boston: Walter de Gruyter, 2013.
9. Melitta Weiss Adamson. "Vom Arzneibuch zum Kochbuch, vom Kochbuch zum Arzneibuch: Eine diätetische Reise von der arabischen Welt und Byzanz über Italien ins spätmittelalterliche Bayern." In *Der Koch ist der bessere Arzt: Zum Verhältnis von Diätetik und Kulinarik im Mittelalter und in der Frühen Neuzeit. Fachtagung im Rahmen des Tages der Geisteswissenschaften 2013 an der Karl-Franzens-Universität Graz, 20.6–22.6.2013.* Mediävistik zwischen Forschung, Lehre und Öffentlichkeit 8. Edited by Andrea Hofmeister-Winter, Helmut W. Klug and Karin Kranich. Frankfurt a. M.: Peter Lang, 2014, pp. 39–62.
10. Jens Wollesen. "East Meets West and the Problem with Those Pictures." In *East Meets West in the Middle Ages and Early Modern Times: Transcultural Experiences in the Premodern World*. Fundamentals of Medieval and Early Modern Culture 14; Edited by Albrecht Classen. Berlin and Boston: Walter de Gruyter, 2013, pp. 341–88.
11. Giles Constable. *The Reformation of the Twelfth Century*. Cambridge: Cambridge University Press, 1996.
12. Rüdiger Arnzen, ed. *Words, Texts and Concepts Cruising the Mediterranean Sea: Studies on the Sources, Contents and Influences of Islamic Civilization and Arabic Philosophy and Science, Dedicated to Gerhard Endress on his Sixty-Fifth Birthday*. Orientalia Lovaniensia Analecta 139. Leuven: Peeters, 2004.

13. Charles Burnett. *Arabic into Latin in the Middle Ages: The Translators and Their Intellectual and Social Context.* Variorum Collected Studies Series 139; Farnham: Ashgate Variorum, 2009.

14. Mihran Dabag, Dieter Haller, Nikolas Jaspert, and Achim Lichtenberger, eds. *Handbuch der Mediterranistik: Systematische Mittelmeerforschung und disziplinäre Zugänge.* Mittelmeerstudien 8. Paderborn: Ferdinand Schöningh, 2015.

15. Larry J. Simons, ed. *Iberia and the Mediterranean World of the Middle Ages: Studies in Honor of Robert I. Burns, S.J.* Leiden, New York and Cologne: E. J. Brill, 1995.

16. Michel Mollat du Jourdin. *L'Europe et la mer.* Paris: Éditions du Seuil, 1993.

17. Nehemia Levtzion. "The Thirteenth- and Fourteenth-Century Kings of Mali." *Journal of African History* 4 (1963): 341–53. [CrossRef]

18. Roland Oliver, and Anthony Atmore. *Medieval Africa, 1250–1800.* Cambridge: Cambridge University Press, 2001.

19. Christian Halm, ed. *Deutsche Reiseberichte,* 2nd. revised and expanded ed. *Europäische Reiseberichte des Späten Mittelalters,* part 1. Kieler Werkstücke, Reihe D 5. Frankfurt and Berlin: Peter Lang, 2001.

20. Janet L. Abu-Lughod. *Before European Hegemony: The World System A.D. 1250–1350.* New York: Oxford University Press, 1989.

21. John M. Ganim, and Shayne Aaron Legassie, eds. *Cosmopolitanism and the Middle Ages.* The New Middle Ages; New York: Palgrave Macmillan, 2013.

22. Arturo Giraldez. *The Age of Trade: The Manila Galleons and the Dawn of the Global Economy.* Exploring World Histor; Lanham and Boulder: Rowman & Littlefield, 2015.

23. Sharon Kinoshita. "'Noi siamo mercatanti cipriani': How to do Things in the Medieval Mediterranean." In *Philippe de Mézières and His Age: Politics in the Fourteenth Century.* Edited by Renate Blumenfeld-Kosinski and Kiril Petkov. Leiden and Boston: Brill, 2012, pp. 41–60.

24. Brian A. Catlos. *The Victors and the Vanquished: Christians and Muslims of Catalonia and Aragon, 1050–1300.* Cambridge: Cambridge University Press, 2004.

25. Albrecht Classen. *Zur Rezeption norditalienischer Kultur des Trecento im Werk Oswalds von Wolkenstein (1376/77–1445).* Göppinger Arbeiten zur Germanistik 471. Göppingen: Kümmerle, 1987.

26. Alfred Noe. *Der Einfluß des Italienischen Humanismus auf die Deutsche Literatur vor 1600: Ergebnisse Jüngerer Forschung und Ihre Perspektiven.* Internationales Archiv für Sozialgeschichte der deutschen Literatur-Sonderheft 5. Tübingen: Max Niemeyer, 1993.

27. Sharon Kinoshita. "Locating the Medieval Mediterranean." In *Locating the Middle Ages: The Spaces and Places of Medieval Culture.* Edited by Julian Weiss and Sarah Salih. London: King's College London, Centre for Late Antique & Medieval Studies, 2012, pp. 39–52.

28. Eva R. Hoffman. "Pathways of Portability: Islamic and Christian Interchange from the Tenth to the Twelfth Century." *Art History* 24 (2007): 317–49. [CrossRef]

29. Brian A. Catlos. "Contexto social y 'conveniencia' en la Corona de Aragón: Propuesta para un modelo de interacción entre grupos etno-religiosos minoritarios y mayoritarios." *Revista d'Història Medieval* 12 (2002): 220–35.

30. David A. Wacks. *Framing Iberia: Maqamat and Frametale Narratives in Medieval Spain.* Leiden: Brill, 2007, pp. 10–13.

31. Mark T. Abate. "Islamic Spain: Al-Andalus and the Three Cultures." In *Handbook of Medieval Culture: Fundamental Aspects and Conditions of the European Middle Ages.* Edited by Albrecht Classen. Berlin and Boston: Walter de Gruyter, 2015, pp. 740–71.

32. Sharon Kinoshita. "Chrétien de Troyes's *Cligés* in the Medieval Mediterranean." *Arthuriana* 18 (2008): 48–61. [CrossRef]

33. Ernst Robert Curtius. *European Literature and the Latin Middle Ages.* Translated by Willard R. Trask. Bollingen Series, XXXVI. Original. 1948. Princeton: Princeton University Press, 1990.

34. De Claudio Galderisi, ed. *Translations Médiévales: Cinq Siècles de Traductions en Français au Moyen Âge (XIe–XVe Siècles).* étude et répertoire sous la dir. Turnhout: Brepols, 2011.

35. Hubertus Fischer. *Ritter, Schiff und Dame. Mauritius von Craûn: Text und Kontext.* Beiträge zur älteren Literaturgeschichte; Heidelberg: Universitätsverlag Winter, 2006.

36. William Crooke. "Der guote Gêrhart: The Power of Mobility in the Medieval Mediterranean." *Postmedieval: A Journal of Medieval Cultural Studies* 4 (2013): 163–76. [CrossRef]

37. Jonathan Hsy. "Mobile Language-Networks and Medieval Travel Writing." *Postmedieval* 4 (2013): 177–91. [CrossRef]

38. Dina Aboul Fotouh Salama. "Die Kolonialisierung des weiblichen Körpers in der spätmittelalterlichen Versnovelle '*Die heideninne*'." *Mediaevistik* 27 (2014): 59–90. [CrossRef]

39. Mark Taylor. "The Fortunes of Alatiel: A Reading of Decameron 2,7." *Forum Italicum* 35 (2001): 318–31. [CrossRef]

40. Sharon Kinoshita. "Ports of Call: Bocaccio's Alatiel in the Medieval Mediterranean." *Journal of Medieval and Early Modern Studies* 37 (2007): 163–95. [CrossRef]

41. Albrecht Classen. "The Crusader as Lover and Tourist: Utopian Elements in Late Medieval German Literature: From *Herzog Ernst* to *Reinfried von Braunschweig* and *Fortunatus*." In *Current Topics in Medieval German Literature: Texts and Analyses (Kalamazoo Papers 2000–2006)*. Göppinger Arbeiten zur Germanistik 748. Edited by Sibylle Jefferis. Göppingen: Kümmerle, 2008, pp. 83–102.

42. Steven D. Martinson, and Renate A. Schulz, eds. *Transcultural German Studies/Deutsch als Fremdsprache: Building Bridge/Brücken Bauen*. Jahrbuch für Internationale Germanistik Reihe A: Kongressberichte 94; Bern and Berlin: Peter Lang, 2008.

43. Maeda Ryozo, ed. *Transkulturalität—Identitäten in neuem Licht: Asiatische Germanistentagung in Kanazawa 2008*. Munich: Iudicium, 2012.

44. Bodo Gotzkowsky. "*Volksbücher*": *Prosaromane, Renaissancenovellen, Versdichtungen und Schwankbücher: Bibliographie der deutschen Drucke*. Part I: *Drucke des 15. und 16. Jahrhunderts*. Part II: *Drucke des 17. Jahrhunderts*. Bibliotheca Bibliographica Aureliana, CXXV and CXLII; Baden-Baden: Valentin Koerner, 1991 and 1994.

45. Albrecht Classen. *The German Volksbuch: A Critical History of a Late-Medieval Genre*. Studies in German Language and Literature, 15. Lewiston, Queenston and Lampeter: The Edwin Mellen Press, 1995.

46. Von Ertzdorff, and Xenia. *Romane und Novellen des 15. und 16. Jahrhunderts in Deutschland*. Darmstadt: Wissenschaftliche Buchgesellschaft, 1989.

47. Thomas Norbert. *Handlungsstruktur und Dominante Motivik im Deutschen Prosaroman des 15. und Frühen 16. Jahrhunderts*. Erlanger Beiträge zur Sprach- und Kunstwissenschaft, 37. Nuremberg: Verlag Hans Carl, 1971.

48. Klaus Grubmüller. *Die Ordnung, der Witz und das Chaos: Eine Geschichte der Europäischen Novellistik im Mittelalter: Fabiau-Märe-Novelle*. Tübingen: Max Niemeyer, 2006.

49. Sue Vice. *Introducing Bakhtin*. Manchester: Manchester University Press, 1997.

50. Klapuri Steinby, and Tintti Klapuri, eds. *Bakhtin and His Others: (Inter)Subjectivity, Chronotope, Dialogism*. London: Anthem Press, 2013.

51. Uwe Neddermeyer. *Von der Handschrift zum gedruckten Buch: Schriftlichkeit und Leseinteresse im Mittelalter und in der Frühen Neuzeit. Quantitative und qualitative Aspekte*. Buchwissenschaftliche Beiträge aus dem deutschen Bucharchiv München 61; Wiesbaden: Harrassowitz, 1998.

52. Jan-Dirk Müller, ed. *Romane des 15. und 16. Jahrhunderts: Nach den Erstdrucken mit Sämtlichen Holzschnitten*. Bibliothek der frühen Neuzeit 1; Frankfurt: Deutscher Klassiker Verlag, 1990.

53. Casey Hayes. "Herder's View of Culture and the Concept of Transculturality." In *Transcultural German Studies*. Edited by Steven D. Martinson and Renate A. Schulz. Jahrbuch für internationale Germanistik, A. Jahrbuch für internationale Germanistik: Reihe A, Kongressberichte 94; Bern and Berlin: Peter Lang, 2008, pp. 317–25.

54. Wolfgang Welsch. "Transculturality: The Puzzling Form of Cultures Today." In *Spaces of Culture: City, Nation, World*. Edited by Mike Featherstone and Scott Lash. London: Sage, 1999, pp. 194–213.

55. Bernd Fischer. "Transkulturelle Teilhabe." In *Transcultural German Studies*. Edited by Steven D. Martinson and Renate A. Schulz. Bern and Berlin: Peter Lang, 2008, pp. 55–72.

56. Bernd Fischer. "Herder Heute? Überlegungen zur Konzeption eines transkulturellen Humanitätsbegriffes." *Herder Jahrbuch* VII (2006): 175–93.

57. Rolf-Peter Janz. "Transkulturalität—In literaturwissenschaftlicher Perspektive." *Transkulturalität* 38 (2012): 19–28.

58. Steven Martinson. "Transcultural German Studies: Theorie und Literaturinterpretation." In *Transcultural German Studies*. Edited by Steven D. Martinson and Renate A. Schulz. Bern and Berlin: Peter Lang, 2008, pp. 73–84.

59. Frank Schulze-Engler, and Sissy Helff, eds. *Transcultural English Studies: Theories, Fictions, Realities*. Cross/Cultures 102; Amsterdam: Editions Rodopi, 2008.

60. *Der Roman von der Königin Sibille in drei Prosafassungen des 14. und 15. Jahrhunderts.* Mit Benutzung der nachgelassenen Materialien von Fritz Burg herausgegeben von Hermann Tiemann, Veröffentlichungen aus der Staats- und Universitätsbibliothek Hamburg 10. Hamburg: Dr. Ernst Hauswedell & Co., 1977.

61. Ute von Bloh. *Ausgerenkte Ordnung: Vier Prosaepen aus dem Umkreis der Gräfin Elisabeth von Nassau-Saarbrücken: "Herzog Herpin", "Loher und Maller", "Huge Scheppel", "Königin Sibille".* Münchener Texte und Untersuchungen zur deutschen Literatur des Mittelalters 119. Tübingen: Max Niemeyer, 2002.

62. Michael Angold. *The Fall of Constantinople to the Ottomans: Context and Consequences.* Harlow and New York: Pearson, 2012.

63. Eugene Webb. *In Search of the Triune God: The Christian Paths of East and West.* Columbia: University of Missouri Press, 2014.

64. Helmuth Kiesel. *»Bei Hof, bei Höll«: Untersuchungen zur Literarischen Hofkritik von Sebastian Brant bis Friedrich Schiller.* Studien zur deutschen Literatur 60; Berlin: Walter de Gruyter, 1979.

65. Adelbert Davids. *The Empress Theophano: Byzantium and the West at the Turn of the First Millennium.* Cambridge: Cambridge University Press, 1995.

66. Christian Gastgeber, and Falko Daim, eds. *Byzantium as Bridge between West and East: Proceedings of the International Confernce, Vienna, 3rd–5th May, 2012.* Denkschriften: Österreichische Akademie der Wissenschaften, Philosophisch-Historische Klasse 476. Veröffentlichungen zur Byzanzforschung 36; Vienna: Verlag der Österreichischen Akademie der Wissenschaften, 2015.

67. Jane E. Burns. "Magical Politics from Poitou to Armenia: Mélusine, Jean de Berry, and the Eastern Mediterranean." *Journal of Medieval and Early Modern Studies* 43 (2013): 275–301. [CrossRef]

68. David Nicolle. *Cross and Crescent in the Balkans: The Ottoman Conquest of South-Eastern Europe (14th–15th Centuries).* Barnsley: Pen & Sword Military, 2010.

69. Angel Nicolaou-Konnari. "Medieval Cyprus and Europe, from the Eleventh to the Sixteenth Century." In *Mapping Cyprus: Crusaders, Traders and Explorers; On the Occasion of the Exhibition Mapping Cyprus. Crusaders, Traders and Explorers, Centre for Fine Arts, Brussels, 22.06.—23.09.2012.* Edited by Lukia Loïzu Chatzegabriel. Milan: Cinisello Balsamo. Brussels: Bozar Books, 2012, pp. 25–68.

70. Rudolf Simek. *Monster im Mittelalter: Die phantastische Welt der Wundervölker und Fabelwesen.* Cologne, Weimar and Vienna: Böhlau, 2015.

71. Jean d'Arras. *Melusine; Or, the Noble History of Lusignan.* Translated by Donald Maddox, and Sara Sturm-Maddox. University Park: The Pennsylvania State University Press, 2012.

72. Meredith Cohen, and Fanny Madeline, eds. *Space in the Medieval West: Places, Territories, and Imagined Geographies.* Farnham and Surrey: Ashgate, 2014.

73. Margarete Köfler, and Silvia Caramelle. *Die beiden Frauen des Erzherzogs Sigmund von Österreich-Tirol.* Schlern-Schriften, 269; Innsbruck: Wagner, 1982.

74. Reinhard Hahn, ed. *Eleonore von Österreich: Pontus und Sidonia.* Texte des späten Mittelalters und der frühen Neuzeit 38; Berlin: Erich Schmidt, 1997.

75. Roger Crowley. *1453: The Holy War for Constantinople and the Clash of Islam and the West.* New York: Hyperion, 2005.

76. Matthias Thumser. "Türkenfrage und öffentliche Meinung: Zeitgenössische Zeugnisse nach dem Fall von Konstantinopel (1453)." In *Europa und die osmanische Expansion im ausgehenden Mittelalter. Zeitschrift für Historische Forschung: Vierteljahresschrift zur Erforschung des Spätmittelalters und der frühen Neuzeit.* Beiheft 20; Edited by Franz-Reiner Erkens. Berlin: Duncker and Humblot, 1997, pp. 59–78.

77. *L'Europa dopo la caduta di Costantinopoli: 29 maggio 1453: atti del XLIV Convegno Storico Internazionale, Todi, 7–9 ottobre 2007/Centro Italiano di Studi sul Basso Medioevo, Accademia Tudertina.* Spoleto: Fondazione Centro Italiano di Studi sull'Alto Medioevo, 2008.

78. Brian Catlos. "To Catch a Spy: The Case of Zayn Al-Dîn and Ibn Dhukân." *Medieval Encounters* 2 (1996): 99–113. [CrossRef]

79. Maribel Fiero, and John Tolan, eds. *The Legal Status of Dimmī-s in the Islamic West (Second/Eight–Ninth/Fifteenth Centuries).* Religion and Law in Medieval Christian and Muslim Societies; Turnhout: Brepols, 2013.

80. Albrecht Classen. "Die Rezeption des deutschen Volksbuchs *Fortunatus* in England: Thomas Dekkers *Old Fortunatus.*" *Neohelicon* XXII (1995): 289–311.

81. John Van Cleve. *The Problem of Wealth in the Literature of Luther's Germany.* Studies in German Literature, Linguistics, and Culture, 55. Columbia: Camden House, 1991.

82. Hannes Kästner. *Fortunatus—Peregrinator Mundi: Welterfahrung und Selbsterkenntnis im Ersten Deutschen Prosaroman der Neuzeit.* Rombach Wissenschaft—Reihe Litterae; Freiburg: Verlag Rombach, 1990.
83. Marjatta Wis. "Zum deutschen Fortunatus: Die mittelalterlichen Pilger als Erweiterer des Weltbildes." *Neuphilologische Mitteilungen* 63 (1962): 5–55.
84. Marjatta Wis. "Nochmals zum Fortunatus-Volksbuch: Quellen- und Datierungs probleme." *Neuphilologische Mitteilungen* 66 (1965): 199–209.
85. Albrecht Classen. "Traveler, Linguist, Pilgrim, Observer, and Scientist: Arnold von Harff Explores the Near East and Finds Himself among Fascinating Foreigners." In *Ain güt Geboren Edel Man: A Festschrift for Winder McConnell on the Occasion of His Sixty-Fifth Birthday. Göppinger Arbeiten zur Germanistik 757.* Edited by Gary C. Shockey, Gail E. Finney and Clifford A. Bernd. Göppingen: Kümmerle, 2011, pp. 195–248.
86. Suzanne Conklin Akbari, and Karla Mallette, eds. *A Sea of Languages: Rethinking the Arabic Role in Medieval Literary History.* Toronto, Buffalo and London: University of Toronto Press, 2013.
87. Jean-François Kosta-Théfaine, ed. *Travels and Travelogues in the Middle Ages.* AMS Studies in the Middle Ages 28. New York: AMS Press, 2009.

 *humanities*

Article

Joachim Heinrich Campe's Robinson the Younger: Universal Moral Foundations and Intercultural Relations

Claudia Nitschke

Modern Languages and Cultures, Durham University, Elvet Riverside, Durham, County Durham DH1 3JT, UK; claudia.nitschke@durham.ac.uk; Tel.: +44-191-334-3424

Academic Editor: Bernd Fischer
Received: 1 March 2016; Accepted: 6 June 2016; Published: 13 June 2016

Abstract: In his adaptation of *Robinson Crusoe*, Campe sets out to examine the legitimacy of his contemporary social reality (in Europe in the broadest sense) by tracing its origin back to the most basic roots conceivable. The experimental character of his book is emphasised and—to an extent—explicitly introduced through the frame narrative which constitutes Campe's most important addition to Defoe's story: Here the emergence of the rules and routines are extensively mooted by the father (who relates Robinson's story as a framed narrative) and his children who still have to internalise, grasp, and situate the moral rules around them and frequently offer divergent perspectives in the process. The frame narrative connects the moral "ontogeny" of the children to the "phylogenetics" of civilisation and suggests that both can be superimposed on one another. I will work with concepts that focus on the differentiation between "innate" moral characteristics and their social transformation on a cognitive, evolutionary level, from which Campe clearly deviates. However, his short-circuiting of the individual and the phylogeny leads to very similar specifications as laid out by, for instance, Moral Foundations Theory.

Keywords: Johann Heinrich Campe; Robinson Crusoe; Moral Foundations Theory

---

1. Introduction

"Was mich so in die Welt hinausgetrieben?—Will ich aufrichtig sein, so war der, der den ersten Anstoß dazu gab, ein alter Bekannter von uns Allen, und zwar Niemand anders als Robinson Crusoe." ([1], p. 244).[1]

With this succinct statement, Friedrich Gerstäcker, the famous German traveler and novelist, captured the profound and lasting impact that Daniel Defoe's *Robinson Crusoe* had made ever since its publication in 1719. Sixty years later, one of the most influential texts in the eighteenth century saw yet another re-iteration of its plot: The enlightened pedagogue Joachim Heinrich Campe wrote an adaptation for the "pleasant and useful entertainment of children" [2], following the purpose Jean-Jacques Rousseau suggested for Defoe's novel in his treatise *Émile*. This distinctly didactic overtone combined with the exotic elements of the story provide an insight into the specific "Germanization" of Robinson's fate [3]. Considered a veritable "bible for the bourgeois" [4], the novel indeed breaks down various ethical scenarios and rules, pertaining to both the moral entwinement with others and the "good life" as an ethical objective. The rules that materialise in the book at first seem predictable (especially in the heyday of Enlightenment); moreover, its foreign backdrop is tightly connected to the conventional colonial discourse patterns of the time. However, on closer

---

[1] "What drove me into the world? If I am to be honest, it was an old acquaintance that first initiated it, namely none other than Robinson Crusoe." My translation.

inspection the novel proves to be more complex than anticipated, as the second part of this article seeks to demonstrate: That, of course, does not change the fundamentally colonial slant of Campe's argument, but it demonstrates how authors at the end of the eighteenth and the beginning of the nineteenth centuries found multi-faceted answers to the challenges of colonial expansion in the age of Enlightenment.[2]

Robinsonades are often categorised as a sub-genre of the utopian novel. Johann Gottfried Schnabel's novel *Insel Felsenburg* [6] (*The Island Stronghold*, 1731–1743) offers a prime example of this classification, as the fourpartite novel combines shipwreck, insular isolation, and the conceptualisation of a utopian community far away from the war-ridden Europe of the eighteenth century. *The Island Stronghold*—at least in its first installment—presents a proper incarnation of the classic Utopia motif. The original Robinsonade, Defoe's *Robinson Crusoe*, focuses on the new beginning for the protagonist, primarily in terms of his introspection, his conversion to Christianity and the rebuilding of civisalisation (by means of tools and technical devices), in a constant fight against the forces of nature. Not only the conquest of nature, but also the conquest of self and the scale of human achievement have been read as utopian elements.

What has Campe's adaptation to offer beyond these ideas, which were routinely explored throughout the long eighteenth century, not least in Defoe's seminal novel? Campe himself found the material Defoe presented auspicious but objected to the dry delivery of the story. At first sight, the alterations Campe implemented seem geared toward making it more palatable to children for whom he foresaw the greatest pedagogical benefits. On closer inspection, his changes prove to have a far-reaching impact on the underlying argument. If read as (partially) utopian (or, by the same token, dystopian in certain respects), Defoe's text already interconnects personal growth with spatial isolation—in this sense it seems to anticipate aspects of a "temporal utopia" (as described by Reinhart Koselleck in reference to Louis-Sébastien Mercier's *L'an 2440*). Campe's appropriation of *Crusoe* brings out this aspect and fully aligns it with the idea of *Bildung* in the late eighteenth century ([3], p. 105). By means of an extensive frame narrative, in which the story is told and discussed with children, this pedagogical, evolutionary dimension comes to the fore. In view of the constant reflection and interpretation performed by the family and the children, Robinson's story presents less of an alternative reality and more of an illuminating experiment which doubles as a commentary on their coeval society.

With a particular focus on Wezel's *Robinson Crusoe* and Wilhelm *Meisters Wanderjahren* (1821, 1829) as a new type of literature, Torsten Hahn and Nicolas Pethes have argued that the idea of an open-ended experiment filled the void that providence had left [7]. Politically speaking, an "experiment" allowed for the notion of social governance to persist while also acknowledging a basic contingency of life. In clear contrast with these novels, the emerging social parameters in *Robinson the Younger* strike us as familiar as they resonate with the order in place in Europe. Furthermore providence is still an explicit and dominant concept in Campe's novel, although it mainly seems to be part of the overarching pedagogical message of *Bildung* and self-mastery: fearfulness is exposed and condemned as the main motivational source that is most likely to interfere with the principal notion of reason in the novel.[3] Just as in Wezel's and Goethe's novels, the professed uncertainty of the outcome is crucial for the ideological undertone of Campe's book and for what I claim to be its experimental character.[4] Campe sets out to examine the legitimacy of his contemporary social reality (in Europe in the broadest sense) by tracing its origins back to the most basic roots conceivable. Apparently he does not take the state of things *per se* for the best of all possible worlds: However, in his thought experiment it might emerge as such after a profound logical examination of its workings.

---

[2] In the late eighteenth century, new scientific approaches were often tied to these challenges, such as the budding discipline of anthropology and its integral assumption of a "unified, trans-temporal category of the human" ([5], p. 326).

[3] Robinson succeeds in mastering his fear and finds his unshakeable trust in God, which in turn provides him with equanimity required to cope with dangerous situation.

[4] Hahn and Pethes point out that the notion of an experiment is a fundamental element of utopias in any case ([7], p. 128).

In the following I seek to show how Campe's commentary is both highly affirmative and at the same time radically challenging in its intercultural outlook and its analysis of society. He dwells on processes of valuation themselves, thus, almost implicitly, tackling the premises of individual and collective moral engagement with the respective environment. While the 'formation of the German colonizer' ([3], p. 106) is indubitably crucial for the novel, the emphasis of my article lies exactly on Campe's attempt to focus on the activity of valuing which will here be understood and explored within the context of new cognitive research on issues of morality.

Campe's young Robinson has to grapple with two sets of values: one that is preordained by his Christian God, who is omnipresent in the novel, and another that actually emerges as the result of certain relational patterns of organism-environment interaction. This difference is vital. Campe's careful analysis of the human psyche differentiates between unchangeable constitutents and malleable components, which are the result of upbringing and education. It is this distinct focus on perfectibility—topical in the eighteenth century—which transforms the utopian notion of virtuous self-fashioning into an experiment. What Campe holistically conjures up is a zero hour in which the protagonist loses all the privileges of civilisation. While Defoe's Crusoe is able to salvage goods from the shipwreck, Robinson the Younger is marooned on the shores of a remote island without any possessions, let alone pets. All the same he manages to establish a routine, constructs tools and progresses through different technological stages to relative luxury and comfort. In view of Robinson's emerging daily routine Campe's narrative indeed converges with utopian concepts, as he develops a timeless blueprint for a "good life" (in an ethical sense) which proves straightforwardly transferable to eighteenth-century Germany. By establishing the new order on the island based on no other presupposition than its congruence with (human) nature and common sense Campe's novel follows an essential rule of utopian fiction. However, since the order on the island—again, derived from nature and extrapolated from reason—coincides with a significant number of laws, premises, rules and ideas of eighteenth-century Europe, as the father in the frame narrative is keen to emphasise, the outcome of the insular experiment broadly affirms the Western order that is in force. In this respect, Campe's *Robinson*—despite its proximity to utopian literature—clearly deviates from this genre.

The experimental character is emphasised and—to an extent—explicitly introduced through the frame narrative which constitutes Campe's most important addition to Defoe's story: here the emergence of the rules and routines are extensively mooted by the father (who relates Robinson's story as a framed narrative) and his children who still have to internalise, grasp, and situate the moral rules around them and therefore frequently offer divergent perspectives in the process. Although the outcome of the discussion is often predictable, the conversation is genuinely open-ended and dependent on an ostensibly judicious, unbiased exploration of the problem in question, thus duplicating the scrutiny (and problematic confirmation) of the Western social order in the framed narrative. Like Rousseau before, Campe follows the line of eighteenth-century conjectural, philosophical history with its "thrust [...] toward a more systematic treatment of the social" and presents his case study as moral science ([8], p. 171). The development of civilisation unfolds around Robinson's shipwreck, a virtual resetting event ([9], p. 19), which starts the process of civilisation afresh. *Vice versa*, the moral progression of the children is facilitated by the proper comprehension of this very phylogeny.

The frame narrative thus connects the moral "ontogeny" of the children with the "phylogenetics" of civilisation and suggests that both can be superimposed on one another, as they both follow the same explainable and logical rules. I am using these technical terms in inverted commas here, as they only conceptually resemble the biological terms. In the following I will work with concepts that focus on the differentiation between "innate" moral characteristics and their social transformation on a cognitive, evolutionary level, from which Campe clearly deviates.[5] However, his short-circuiting of the individual and the phylogenetic moral development leads to very similar specifications with regard to stability and change as laid out recently by "Moral Foundations Theory" [10], with which a group of social and cultural psychologists attempts to explain the origins of and variation in human moral reasoning on the basis of innate, modular foundations.

Highlighting this more elusive aspect by accentuating the above mentioned developmental perspective only means to bring out the ambivalence in Campe's novel more clearly: he heavily draws on characteristic colonial discourse patterns and topoi (savage, primitive, superstitious, illiterate, apolitical, child-like, *etc.* [11], p. 32), as Susanne Zantop has comprehensively shown [3]: Campe may admittedly foreground a dynamic concept of culture based on pedagogically guided transformation and change (which is distinctly German/European); he conceives of this process as strictly asymmetrical nonetheless. While the idea of a young German marooned on a remote island, who forges a friendship with the natives, seems to speak to the potential of transcultural hybridity, the novel concerns itself rather with basic processes of valuing which are unmistakably intended to justify the European order in place—just as the above mentioned experiment sets out to demonstrate. Thus the sphere on the island that opens up as an intercultural encounter zone cannot be perceived as reciprocal: only in view of peripheral aspects—for instance when it comes to merely technical know-how (Friday teaches Robinson how to ignite a fire)—Campe acknowledges a transcultural flow, *i.e.*, he concedes valuable knowledge (rendered unnecessary by the course the civilisation in Europe) to Friday, who is otherwise evidently the main recipient of worthwhile cultural input. While the novel defies the notion of transcultural hybridity proper (Friday is just transformed into a young European man), it still recognises the above-mentioned processual dimension of culture as civilisation—admittedly with a teleological bent. According to Campe's conventional narrative these different timelines of progress are ostensibly bound to culminate in enlightened Europe.

At the same time, Campe offers a very basic notion of human equality hidden beneath the layers of hierarchised cultural diversity: as I will demonstrate, this underlying idea of human equality helps to disabuse the children in the frame narrative from preconceived notions of superiority and encourages them to assess and evaluate moral actions within their original, culturally determined context. With these two different perspectives in place, Campe can highlight the—in his view—unquestionable dominance of Europe, whilst simultaneously embracing the inherent logic of other cultural orders: although the colonial discourse is the dominant tone in this novel, I will focus on this latter aspect in the following and argue that Campe is amenable to it, as he is able to identify basic and universally binding, meta-cultural core values (such as moral accounting and reciprocity), connecting humankind across all geographical and temporal barriers.

Ultimately, of course, these notions of diversity are the result of the (still) expanding colonial horizons of the eighteenth century, as the appreciation for different 'histories' (as in Johann Gottfried Herder's historism) had to be squared with the increasingly central idea of progress ([12], pp. 375–78). The transformative quality of this perspective indeed constitutes a subliminal, transcultural dimension of Campe's argument.[6]

2. History on a Small Scale

Based on the learning scenario in the frame narrative, Campe's novel—like its precursor *Robinson Crusoe*—contains many historically specific references that proceed from the parameters of European

---

[5]   With his notion of deep history Daniel Lord Smail problematises this concept by drawing attention to a problem connected with the premises of conjectural history: "Conjectural historians, concerned with the process, did not trouble themselves with origins. To make their schemes work, all they needed was a set of primitive or presocial conditions." ([9], p. 21).

[6]   In this sense, his argument resonates with central "fantasies of political origin" as for instance in Thomas Hobbes' *Leviathan*. Hobbes refers to the "savages" in America who still find themselves in the state of nature. Philip Manow elaborates on this "phylogenetic" perspective ([13], pp. 21–34).

law and morality, in particular natural law. As we know, Robinson's solitary existence eventually ends when he comes across indigenous people, saves and eventually befriends Friday. His encounter with Friday shows how the rights of the superior come into being. On entering Robinson's abode, Friday is duly impressed with the various products emanating from Robinson's incessant work:

"Hier machte der Wilde große Augen, da er die bequeme und ordentliche Einrichtung der Wohnung seines Erretters sahe, weil er so was schönes in seinem ganzen Leben noch nicht gesehen hatte. Es war ihm ohngefähr eben so dabei zu Muthe, als wenn ein Landman, der nie aus seinem Dorfe gekommen ist, zum erstenmahle in einen Pallast geführt wird." ([2], p. 203).[7]

Friday's wonder again throws into sharp relief the fact that Campe—following Defoe's material[8]—is actually retelling the story of civilisation. In view of Robinson's conspicuous excellence in all areas, Friday has no choice but to submit himself voluntarily to Robinson, especially, and I will return to this, as he owes him his life:

"Freitag (denn so wollen wir ihn nun künftig auch nennen) näherte sich ihm mit allen ersinlichen Zeichen der Ehrerbietung und der Dankbarkeit, kniete alsdan vor ihm nieder, legte seinen Kopf abermahls plat auf die Erde, und sezte eben so, wie er es das erstemahl gemacht hatte, seines Befreiers Fuß auf seinen Nakken. [...Robinson] gab ihm also durch Zeichen und Gebehrden zu verstehen, daß er ihn zwar in seinen Schuz genommen habe, aber nur unter der Bedingung eines strengen Gehorsams: daß er sich also müsse gefallen lassen, alles das zu thun oder zu lassen, was er, sein Herr und König ihm zu befehlen oder zu verbieten für gut erachten wurde. Er bediente sich dabei des Worts Katschike, womit die wilden Amerikaner ihre Oberhäupter zu benennen pflegen, wie er sich glüklicher Weise erinnerte, einmahl gehört zu haben. Mehr durch dieses Wort, als durch die damit verbundenen Zeichen, verstand Freitag die Meinung seines Herrn und äusserte seine Zufriedenheit darüber, indem er das Wort Katschike einige mahl mit lauter Stimme widerholte, dabei auf Robinson wies und sich von neuem ihm zu Füßen warf. Ja, um zu zeigen, daß er recht gut wisse, was es mit der königlichen Gewalt zu bedeuten habe, ergrif er den Spieß, gab ihn seinem Herrn in die Hand, und sezte die Spize desselben sich selbst auf die Brust, vermuthlich um dadurch anzuzeigen, daß er mit Leib und Leben in seiner Macht stehe. Robinson reichte ihm hierauf mit der Würde eines Monarchen freundlich die Hand zum Zeichen seiner königlichen Huld, und befahl ihm abermahls, sich zu lagern, um die Abendmahlzeit mit ihm einzunehmen. [...] Seht, Kinder, auf diese oder auf eine ähnliche Weise sind die ersten Könige in der Welt entstanden. Es waren Männer, die an Weisheit, an Muth und an Leibesstärke andern Menschen überlegen waren. Daher kamen diese zu ihnen, um sie zu bitten, sie gegen wilde Thiere, deren es anfangs mehr gab, als jezt, und gegen solche Menschen zu beschüzen, die ihnen Unrecht thun wolten.—Dafür versprachen sie dan, ihnen in allen Stükken gehorsam zu sein, und ihnen von ihren Heerden und von ihren Früchten jährlich etwas abzugeben, damit sie selbst nicht nöthig hätten, sich ihren Unterhalt zu erwerben, sondern sich ganz allein mit der Sorge für ihre Unterthanen beschäftigen könten." ([2], pp. 206–7)[9].

---

7 "Here the savage stared, to see the convenient and regular disposition of his deliverer's habitation, because he had never seen any thing so handsome in his life. He was nearly in the same frame of mind, as a country man, who has never been away from his village, when he sees a palace for the first time." ([14], p. 58).

8 Johann Karl Wezel, who published his adaptation of *Robinson Crusoe* in 1779, highlighted this aspect in Defoe's novel, when he explicitly stated that *Robinson* describes—if presented appropriately—human history on a small scale, a miniature painting of different states humankind had successively gone through ([15], p. XVII). Campe's and Wezel's rather different adaptations appear at almost the same time; *cf.* for the ensuing controversy and further context [16].

9 "Friday (for so we will call him for the future) drew near with all possible marks of respect and gratitude, then kneeled down before him, laid his head flat on the ground and placed his deliverer's foot on the neck, as he had done the first time. [...Robinson] gave him therefore to understand by signs and gestures, that he had indeed taken him under his protection, but only on condition of the strictest obedience: that he must therefore consent to door not to do, whatever he, his Lord and King should think proper to order or forbid him. In making him understand this, he made use of the word Katschike, a name, by which the Americans call their superious, which he luckily remember'd to have heard once. This word made Friday understand the meaning of his master, more than all the signs with which he accompanied it, and he expressed his satisfaction by repeating the word Katschike several times with a loud voice and by prostrasting himself again at his feet. Nay, to convince him that he knew very well, what royal authority was, he took hold of the lance, put it into his master's hands, and placed the point of it on his breast, probably to indicate, that his body and life were in his power. Hereupon

It is worth quoting this extensive passage, since it not only touches on a plethora of colonial stereotypes, but is as much a historical explanation as a reference to contractarianism—a veritable "social contract" which will be brought into play in its proper legal form at the end of the novel, when Robinson, figuratively speaking, passes on the sceptre to his fellow islanders (at that point, the governmental system is already in place, fully adapted to human strengths and weaknesses).

This scene evokes an archaic political ritual, bearing out the explicit claim that power relations came into being as a logical and natural consequence of physical and/or intellectual superiority. Following this premise of natural law, the episode prior to this alliance also complies with eighteenth-century moral requirements. As Robinson shies away from killing an enemy to protect his life in the long run (Friday, untouched by civilisation as it were, has to step in and slay the native, which he incidentally does without any hesitation), the scene dispels any suspicion that Campe's Robinson might act out of self-interest.[10] Robinson's impeccable actions and motivations prove instrumental in Campe's attempt to show rather than to postulate the realisation of legitimate power hierarchies. By the same token, these scenarios supply the reader with a logical, reasonable justification of power.

What follows is the quasi-enthronement of Robinson as the island monarch in whose jocular description the father and the children revel: "Robinson war also nunmehr ein wirklicher König, nur daß seine Herschaft sich nicht weiter, als über einen einzigen Unterthan und einige Lamas erstrekte; den Papagai mit einbegriffen."[11] ([2], p. 207).

Strikingly, these two young men—later portrayed as brothers, *i.e.*, as family—are very clearly conceptualised as ruler and subject on the island. Thus the European understanding of order is seamlessly imposed on them; the children in the frame narrative laugh at this as expected, however, the whole etiology determines that Campe indeed associates the beginning of civilisation proper with concepts of legitimate, "reasonable" power hierarchies. Replaying this historical genesis on an island in the sixteenth century—this is how the father dates the events on the island—lends it an air of teleology where "history" naturally culminates in Western civilisation.[12] In so doing, Campe allows for different strands of history, but he is also keen to highlight the European superiority which he again not so much postulates but quasi scientifically establishes by dint of Robinson's life on the island: the young castaway has to re-invent it from scratch, guided only by reason, necessity and a "natural" morality—all of these latter aspects belong to the experimental arrangement of the novel.

Campe also repeatedly emphasises Friday's childlikeness,[13] projecting the concept of family bonds onto the political realm in a way that was not uncommon in eighteenth-century Germany (especially in the reference to the *Landesvater*). The novel occasionally recognises that Friday might be better adapted to the life on the island, but it also clarifies that his mind (Verstand) is still less developed. In this sense, Robinson indeed serves as a well-meaning patriarch who loves, protects, and

---

ROBINSON kindly reached him his hand with the dignity of a monarch as a sign of his royal favour, and order'd him again to sit down, and take his supper with him. [...] Look ye, my children, the first kings in the world took their rise in this and the like manner. They were men, who surpast others in wisdom, courage and bodily strength. Therefore they came to them and begged their protection against wild beasts, of which there were anciently more than at present, and against such people as would wrong them.—For this they promised to obey them in every thing and to give them every year something of their flocks and fruit, that they might not be in the necessity of getting their own livelihood, but employ themselves solely with the care of their subjects." ([14], pp. 62–64).

10 Campe's effort to clarify the scenario morally becomes tangible in comparison with Wezel's Robinson in which Robinson pursues the natives intentionally to satisfy his need for a companion: "*Er wollte den Wilden auflauern, sie anfallen und ein Schlachtopfer ihrer Grausamkeit erlösen, damit der Errettete aus Dankbarkeit sein Freund würde und ihm den Weg nach dem festen Lande zeigte. [...] Man merkt, daß ihm die Leidenschaft diesen Grund eingab, denn er ist falsch.*" "He wanted to ambush the savages and save a victim from their cruelty, so that the saved victim would become his friend out of gratitude and would show him the way to the mainland. [...] One realises that passion inspired him to think of this as the reason for it is false." My translation.

11 "Robinson was now a real king, only that his dominion reached no further, than over a single subject and some lama's, the parrot included." ([14], p. 64).

12 This is obviously connected to the colonial discourse in Germany into which I cannot delve here, *cf.* ([17], pp. 19–21, 74–80).

13 This take again differs from Wezel, who extensively dwells on Franz' (who is the equivalent of Friday in this text) animal-like qualities, when he describes how Franz follows his master like a dog ([15], p. 195).

educates his subjects. The notion of the non-European as a "child" is a familiar trope in postcolonial discourse of course, however, in Campe's novel it serves another function as well: I will return to this notion of family as a master trope of power later; for now it remains notable that childhood is perceived as a form of immaturity that the adolescent is required (and, if taught and educated properly, bound) to overcome. In this sense the relation between Robinson and Friday is also determined by a temporal aspect (not in terms of their biological age, but rather their cultural stage) and supposed to balance itself out in the long run. As this trope is also famously an intercultural one, it ties together the "phylogeny" of mankind with the individual "ontogeny" which is insouciantly projected onto the status quo: The world presents itself to Robinson (and to the audience in the frame narrative 200 years later) as segmented into different historical-temporal layers, focussing on nations and ethnicities that find themselves at varying developmental stages. Automatically, the novel inculcates the reader with the importance of the Western world, as it defines the teleological endpoint of the journey on which Friday both studiously and successfully embarks. According to the text, the synchronisation of these different stages is conceivable (at least for young Friday, his father Thursday dies before they embark the ship to Europe) and can be achieved to a full extent, extinguishing almost all cultural differences.

3. Eighteenth-Century Law and Value Concepts

The discussions between the father and the children in the frame narrative extensively cover legally specific questions ranging from self-defence to the *jus litoris* (which entitles Robinson to take possession of the jetsam after the shipwreck). *Vis-à-vis* the notion of self-defence, the father re-emphasises the foundation of natural law, but also refers to the rare necessity to resort to it in Hamburg (viz. Holy Roman Empire of the German Nation):

"Allerdings, lieben Kinder, ist eine solche Nothwehr nach menschlichen und götlichen Gesezen recht, aber wohl gemerkt!—nur in dem einzigen Fal, wenn ganz und gar kein anderes Mittel zu unserer eigenen Rettung übrig ist. [...] Vergeßt nicht, lieben Kinder, Gott zu danken, daß wir in einem Lande leben, in welchem die Obrigkeit so gute Veranstaltungen zu unserer Sicherheit getroffen hat, daß unter hundert tausend Menschen höchst selten ein Einziger in die traurige Nothwendigkeit gerathen kan, von dem Rechte der Nothwehr Gebrauch machen zu müssen." ([2], pp. 201–2).[14]

The status quo is perceived as similarly exemplary with a view to "Wrecking"; Robinson, who is the owner of the island, has an obvious right to appropriate the jetsam. This notion also derives from a distinctly European context of property, which is presented as (ahistorical) common sense in the novel. Robinson's political power, prompting him to think of himself as a "proper king", not only emanates from what the novel understands as his intellectual and spiritual superiority, but also from a specific conceptualisation of property: *"Die ganze Insel war sein Eigenthum"* ([2], p. 307). While he specifies that the loyalty of his subjects originates in the fact that they all owe him their lives, the notion of the island (that is also frequented by cannibals) as his property harks back to Locke's extensive treatment of the property question in the *Second Treatise of Civil Government*.[15] The concept of self-ownership that extends to the products of one's labour permeates the entire novel and provides yet another layer of justification for the power relations depicted in the novel. The acquisition of power is perceived as a natural process that not only depends on innate superiority, but is also fundamentally connected with

---

[14] "To be sure, my dear children, such self-defence is just according to divine and human laws, but—observe me well! In this case only: when there is no other remedy so save ourselves. Whereas if we have an opportunity to escape, or to be protected by others, or to disable our pursuers from hurting us: any attempt upon his life is real murder, and is punish'd as such by the law. Don't forget to thank God, my dear children, that we live in a country, in which our superiors have made such good dispositions for our security, that scarce one man in a thousand can ever come in the melancholy necessity of fighting for his own preservation." ([14], p. 56).

[15] "27. Though the earth, and all inferior creatures be common to all men, yet every man has a *property* in his own *person*. [...] The *labour* of his body, and the *work* of his hands, we may say, are properly his. Whatsoever then he removes out of the state that nature hath provided, and left it in, he hath mixed his *labour* with and joined to it something that is his own, and thereby makes it his property." [18].

a humble work ethic (which Robinson decides to maintain even when he could delegate all work to his subjects).[16]

Many of the concepts are historically specific to the onset of modernity in Europe and closely tied to the discourses connected with it. However, as I said earlier, Campe's originality lies in the specific addition of the narrative frame, which focuses on the emergence, appropriation and production of rules. The father and the children in the frame narrative are eager to explore the moral dimension of every event that occurs: not only on the island, but also in the dialogues between grown-ups and children we encounter a second and decisive zero hour narrative, as the children go through different stages of evaluation when they are confronted with the various ethical dilemmas in their father's story. Again the insight the reader is supposed to gain from this is twofold: first, children prove to be adept in common-sense (and thus confirm it as "natural"); second, where they seem more susceptible to subjective perspectives led by personal preferences, the father forces them to probe and evaluate these false assumptions and—as a result of this rational and reasonable scrutiny of all relevant facts and premises—they prove happy to part with them. The conclusion they reach is thus in keeping with their natural instinct where it is compatible with the intersubjective morality of the family and not driven by unrationalised feelings.[17]

4. Individual and Collective Developmental History: Moral Foundations

In this sense, Campe's *Robinson the Younger* not only concentrates on a miniature version of the history of civilisation, but also explores the developmental aspect of moral standards.[18] In view of recent cognitive theories, Campe's approach seems "modern" in this respect, as he conceptualises morality as a form of "complex problem-solving—the reworking of a situation that has become problematic and has inhibited our ability to skillfully, meaningfully, and harmoniously navigate our social space", drawing on a constellation of "human capacities and propensities for making sense of our experience and engaging in problem-solving forms of inquiry." ([20], p. 160).

Robinson does not find himself at a proper neutral point of course: he enters his adventure with a primary understanding of values endorsed by his devout parents and transcendentally substantiated by God. While everything related to human power is in need of an explanation and a reasonable justification, Campe deems Christian morality an axiom for his exploration, as God holds unlimited moral authority over people. It is striking nonetheless that Robinson's relation to God is metaphorically predicated on the notion of paternal guidance and protection, dovetailing with Campe's approach to power. Cognitive theories have engaged with the premises of morality by analysing its evolution but also by searching for universal, quasi-biological (or biologically evolved) patterns. Although the answers to these questions are still tentative, they conspicuously coincide with parts of Campe's analysis. Georg Lakoff's and Mark Johnson's thesis that virtually all our abstract moral concepts are structured metaphorically is a long-established theory in the area of cognitive studies [21,22]. They have not only suggested that conceptual metaphors are omnipresent in our quotidian life and shape the way we think. Proceeding from the principal idea that the human mind is intrinsically embodied, they have also introduced a 'philosophy in the flesh', concluding that "virtually all of our abstract moral concepts are structured metaphorically." ([22], p. 290). At the same time, they propose that the range of metaphors relating to morality is limited, as basic moral metaphors are rooted in bodily experience and social interactions: "We have found that the source domains of our metaphors for morality are typically based on what people over history and across cultures have seen as contributing to their well-being." ([22], pp. 290–91).

---

[16] This notion goes hand in hand with a specific take on nature. *Cf.* [19].

[17] *Cf.* also Wezel's above quoted, identical comment of the narrator: "*Man merkt, daß ihm die Leidenschaft diesen Grund eingab, denn er ist falsch.*"

[18] As such it differs from other adaptations of Defoe's novel, as they lack the specific layout of Campe's dialogical frame narrative.

Indeed when we examine the text more closely, we can see how Robinson's realm is borne by bodily projections (encapsulating above mentioned ideas of labour and property) which emanate from various forms of bodily well-being: Robinson strives for (and achieves) security, safety, and comfort for him and others, which is intricately interwoven with his ethical principles. All these categories relate back to "basic possessions, bodily movement, and freedom from the infliction of pain" ([22], p. 329): Campe's Robinson aspires to the "freedom from the infliction of pain" accordingly—nature appears as particularly threatening, and, as the protection mechanisms that civilisation has developed (shelter, clothes, *etc.*) are unavailable to him at first, he has to recreate them. His remarkable trajectory begins by reacquainting himself with basic necessities—aspiring to the absence of pain and harm, well-being, physical intactness.

He experimentally formulates his life rules over the course of the novel, for instance when he decides that he ought to maintain his daily routine borne by moderation and diligence, even though Friday (as his "subject") could relieve him of all physical labour.

Morever, the novel isolates two distinct principles of "moral accounting" which coincide with the definition given by Lakoff and Johnson, who understand moral action as something that gives "something of positive value" (*i.e.*, to save Friday's life, provide him with shelter and food *etc.*) ([22], p. 293); *vice versa*, immoral action is something of negative value (*i.e.*, eating enemies without necessity). In addition to this first principle, the second principle adds that there is a moral imperative to pay one's debt and the failure to do so is in turn immoral (Friday's unconditional loyalty derives from this second principle).

The novel in fact introduces various forms of basic moral accounting schemes which extend beyond Christian concepts. Although there are examples for altruism and forgiveness (*i.e.*, when the mutineers arrive on the island), the most common principle of moral accounting in the novel is reciprocity in the sense of moral debt as it underpins the relationship between Robinson and Friday.

In so doing the novel attempts to develop ideas of power, rights, and duties as abstract "second-order metaphorical concepts" from very concrete cases of debts and credits.

This brings us back to the above-mentioned moral initiation which Robinson has experienced in his Christian family home. We can see how his Christian devotion is clearly modeled upon a father-child relationship. Lakoff and Johnson suggest that morality might "be based on models of family" and thus also connected to immediate, human experience. When Lakoff and Johnson tentatively conclude: "To think of morality in general as some form of family morality requires another metaphor, in which we understand all of humanity as part of one huge family which has traditionally been called the 'Family of Man'. This metaphor entails a moral obligation, binding on all people, to treat each other as we ought to treat our family members." ([22], p. 317).

Campe conforms with this statement as he indeed casts his protagonists in different roles that conspicuously correspond with roles within a family. Friday might enter Robinson's life as a subject (*i.e.*, as Robinson rules as a Landesvater, as a child), but, in the course of the novel, he evolves and becomes his nominal brother. With this evolutionary dimension hierarchies can be devised on a very basic notion of equality as human beings. Casting the "savages" as children not only coincides with a specific colonial discourse pattern, it also chimes with core ideas of development and *perfectibilité*. Enlightenment ideas about childhood and education follow a similar notion, when they consider the immaturity (and thus inferiority) of children to be temporary.[19] Both discourses are intrinsically connected, as the European "ontogenetic" take on childhood provides the moral blueprint for the colonial "phylogenetic" development: Campe's frame narrative proves indispensable for this perspective.

---

[19] *Cf.*, for instance, Karl Ludwig Pörschke: "Es findet zwischen Eltern und Kindern ebenso wenig als zwischen Bürgern [Ungleichheit statt...], denn die Eltern befehlen dem Kind nur in seinem Namen das, was das Kind selbst sich bei voller Vernunft befehlen würde." [23]. "There is no inequality between parents and children, nor is there between citizens, for the parents command their child only what the child would command herself if she were fully mature." My translation.

Friday becomes a paramount example of such developmental achievement, not without implying a national superiority on Robinson's part (owed to some sort of "phylogenetical" evolution as well, which cannot fully be achieved by the people who join Western civilisation late). The asynchronicity that Campe alludes to is both validating in general terms, as Campe is quite clear that even the 'savages' are fellow human beings, and condescending in a concrete respect, for instance, when the father labels the "Wilden" as only "*menschenähnliche*" "*Geschöpfen*" ([2], p. 187),[20] who resemble "wild beasts" ([2], p. 188) given their brutish and "stupid" ([2], p. 187) upbringing. What the "savages" need is proper education that builds on and fully develops their humanity: cannibalism derives from ignorance ([2], pp. 225–26), but is nevertheless tied to ethical rules, as 'only' enemies are eaten. Although this of course does not validate the abhorrent practice as such, the specification implies that even 'savages' follow rules of moral accounting (enemies are paying their debt with their own flesh) and are quite upset if accused that they would harm the innocent (who are debt free). Whilst forming a fairly inclusive concept of humanity and drawing attention to these crucial nuances, Campe offers a harsher view of their state of civilisation and confidently promotes his European ideas as binding and fully-fledged. Thus, Campe's *Robinson* affirms the civilised society in place, presenting the bourgeois values implemented by Robinson as natural and perfectly adapted for survival,—even and specifically—in competition with other *modi vivendi*. By dint of his "micro-history" of civilization Campe is nonetheless forced to put European values up for discussion (even if they ultimately re-emerge uncontested). The urge to perform an analysis of the origin of the power relation and the question of its legitimacy is revealing as it indirectly formulates the need of justification in the first place. Political theory was exploring these questions throughout the centuries—with special rigour since the Renaissance—but Campe goes one step further and shows the inherently evolutionary quality of the moral valuing processes (and thus their degree of changeability).[21]

Against this background, I will now investigate Campe's reflections on 'innate' and taught values. Robert McCauley has proposed a distinction between maturational naturalness and practiced capacities. For him maturational naturalness describes natural cognition whose acquisition does not depend on any form of explicit instruction, specifically structured learning environments, artifacts, inputs that are particular to a culture or (even) on inputs that are culturally distinctive. Maturational natural actions are undertaken spontaneously and a few of them feature general forms that are shared by other species ([24], p. 29).

McCauley famously uses this specification to explore "why religion is natural and science is not". Maturationally natural capacities are in this sense theories with which humans are typically equipped and which influence their implicit cognition. In his book *Morality for Humans* Mark Johnson extends this definition to maturationally natural values which are of interest here. Johnson follows John Dewey in the notion that valuing presents a more appropriate term than value, as it emphasises the dynamic situation between organism and environment. He sees the preferential directness which aims for certain states of organism-environment interaction as an evaluative process which can be "selectively and abstractly described as that organism's value, as long as we refrain from turning those 'values' into abstract entities." ([20], p. 52).

With his specific adaptation of Defoe's novel for children, Campe promotes both the relational, interactive and the dynamic nature of valuing: we observe Robinson's journey on which he not only builds a material existence, but on which he also defines and expands on rules which are brought into being as necessary; Campe might emphasise divine providence and reason specifically, however, what bestows legitimacy on Robinson's actions is the fact that they coincide with 'values' that are indeed shared (or are potentially shareable) by everyone, even the 'savages'. Only if Robinson meets this very

---

[20] "Men; but no, only of such creatures, as have the mere shape of man" ([14], p. 36).
[21] He not only suggests that a legitimate form of government has to be "natural" and comply with reason, but he also draws a distinct line between nature and nurture, when he describes an underlying universal human understanding of morality, displayed even by "savages" on remote islands.

premise, learning and readapting is possible. He can influence the process of valuing and its evaluative results, but he cannot interfere with the 'blueprint' that is shared by all human beings. Friday's innocent comment about his ignorance in view of cannibalism ("I didn't know yet that it was wrong" ([2], p. 250) can be adduced as evidence for this twofold value spectrum Campe introduces and with which he indeed draws a distinction between cultural manifestion and inherent, *i.e.*, maturationally natural value: as such the concept of self-defence also formulates an exception from the explicit rules Robinson knows (for instance, the fifth commandment). It is important that the "savages" are by no means disqualified by their killing, as Campe recognises that they behave in correspondence with their own culturally learned practices. As they "only" harm their enemies, Campe also accentuates the relevant rule which cannot be infringed on: the immorality of harming the "innocent" within a complex moral accounting scheme of reciprocity which happens to bear on the elaborations on self-defence as well. Admittedly, this discourse is not Campe's invention; he models his thoughts on Robinson Crusoe's scruples, as longwindedly portrayed by Defoe [25]. As opposed to Defoe, Campe however offers a confident solution to this inconclusive and arduous examination of conscience by tying the question of "self-preservation" closely to the educational frame narrative in which the father—in reference to contemporary law—rationally decides that self-defence constitutes no crime.

In addition to this, Campe's entelechical concept of humanity historicises the anthropological concept he espouses with regard to maturational values; by focusing this process on the Western world he immobilises the dynamic (that he suggests for Robinson within the parameters of the zero hour narrative) on a historical level and thus caters to both a liberation narrative of the *conquistadore* and the highly complacent notion of a "German special path": "Imperceptibly but all the more powerfully, *Robinson the Younger* helped propagate the myth of the benign, efficient, and restrained German colonizer, a myth that would permeate not just nineteenth-century, but also a good part of twentieth-century German literature." ([3], p. 120).

While this aspect proves highly ideological, Campe's novel indirectly gives an answer to the question of how other nations can be converted to other cultural practices (in particular if the latter prove to be more "reasonable"): all human beings are fundamentally the same in view of certain maturationally natural values (a "family of man"). He shows himself as aware of the—at times counter-intuitive—complexity of these maturationally natural values and is keen to explore the origin(s) of and variation in human moral reasoning with a clear focus on "innate" foundations. In the debate between young Christel and her father about cannibalism Campe consequently differentiates between cultural values and innate instincts connected with it by proceeding from a widely accepted moral rule echoing throughout human history: absence of harm:

"Christel. O das hätten sie doch auch wohl wissen können, daß das nicht hübsch sei! Vater. Und woher, lieber Christel, hätten sie das denn wohl wissen können? Christel. O das weiß ja das kleinste Kind, daß es nicht recht ist, einen umzubringen, um ihn aufzuessen! Vater. Aber woher weiß denn dieses das kleinste Kind? Nicht wahr, weil es frühzeitig belehrt worden ist? [...] Vater. Und wenn's nun nicht belehrt worden wäre? Wenn sogar seine Eltern und andere erwachsene Menschen, die es liebte und ehrte, ihm von früher Kindheit an immer vorgesagt hätten, daß es etwas sehr schönes sei, seine Feinde zu ermorden und aufzuessen? [...] nicht wahr, dan würd' es wohl schwerlich einem Kinde jemahls einfallen, das Gegentheil zu vermuthen? Es wurde vielmehr, sobald es groß genug dazu wäre, mit schlachten und mit verzehren helfen. Und das war der Fall worin diese armen Wilden sich befanden. Wohl uns, daß Gott uns nicht unter ihnen, sondern von gesitteten Eltern hat lassen geboren werden, die uns frühzeitig lehrten, was recht und unrecht, was gut und böse sei!" ([2], p. 303).[22]

---

[22] The English translation curiously replaces young Christel with a male child, Christopher: "Oh, they might very well have known, that such actions are not good! Father. And how could they have known that, my dear Christopher? Christopher. Why, the least child knows, that it is not right, to kill and eat people! Father. But whence does the least child know that? Because it has been told so, is not it true? Christopher. Yes. Father. Now we'll suppose, it had not been taught so? Suppose, even its parents and other grown people, whom the child loved and honour'd, had from its infancy always told it, that it

In contrast to his daughter, the father identifies very general "foundations" of morality. He thus ensures that the violation of specific rules suggested by Western civilisation does not qualify the 'savages' as immoral per se. While Christel indirectly suggests that right and wrong are hard-wired into everyone's psyche as a fixed moral premise,[23] the father emphasises the role of education and customs, even when it comes to actually killing and ingesting people. This radical take on learned values stresses rather than undermines the above mentioned distinction Campe emphatically draws; first of all, he is keen to underscore that the "savages" "only" kill and eat their enemies (thus still following a basic norm of moral accounting, albeit within an—according to Campe—false framework of culturally learned values). Campe acknowledges that there are different moral foundations whose varying priorities, if colliding, define distinct, cultural approaches. Based on links between evolutionary theory and anthropological observations Jonathan Haidt arrives at a similar conclusion in view of the political spectrum nowadays, determining five moral foundations[24] on which different political attitudes rely in different ways, all of which appear in Campe's *Robinson*: "care/harm" as a moral foundation (which "evolved in response to the adaptive challenge of caring for vulnerable children" ([10], p. 178), revolves around protection and an "innate" aversion towards violence (as Christel explicitly points out). "Fairness/cheating" ([10], p. 178) presents a response to exploitation, as it provides us with a sense for persons who prove trustworthy partners for collaboration and reciprocal altruism (as becomes visible in Friday's and Robinson's friendship). "Loyalty/betrayal" which "evolved in response to the adaptive challenge of forming and maintaining coalitions" ([10], p. 178) is evoked throughout Campe's novel as one of the primary values, especially when it comes to parent-child relations. Campe also addresses the foundation "authority/subversion" ([10], p. 179) in his political reflections (see above) and of course also in view of filial respect and submission whose violation provides the starting point for the story in the first place, as Robinson goes to sea against his parents' better judgement, thus disrespecting their legitimate authority. Finally "sanctity/degradation" ([10], p. 179)—evolved as a response to the adaptive challenge of potentially compromised food—is a recurrent proof for the inferiority of the cannibalistic "savages".

Although his reflections and descriptions relate to Haidt's pluralistic scenario, Campe offers a conclusive hierarchy of these foundations (whose legitimate existence he discerns and accepts) insofar as he insists that Christian values, as implemented in the eighteenth century, embody a perfected version of morality. Ultimately, it is this customary (*i.e.*, pedagogically inculcated) viewpoint, a kind of moral shortcut, that Christel confidently assumes, at first oblivious to the more complex developmental, moral scenario to which the father has to alert her eventually.

In this particular dialogue he also reiterates one of the uncontested "values" that seem omnipresent in the novel: the bond between parent and child. For Campe, in his capacity as pedagogue, the parent-child relation is the vital moral interface. Built on devoted filial trust as the most important moral reflex, proper values can be learned and developed, *i.e.*, they take on a certain cultural shape.

---

was something very good, to murder one's enemies and to eat them? Christopher. Nay then—Father. Then a child would hardly ever get a contrary idea, is not it true? Such a child would rather, as soon as it was big enough, begin to assist the rest in killing and eating. And that was the case with these poor savages. Happy for us, that God almighty has not suffer'd us to be born among them, but of civilized parents, who taught us from our infancy, what is right and wrong, good and bad!" ([14], pp. 202–3).

23 This coincides with the resurgence of the idea that men as such possess a moral faculty, as elaborated on by Marc Hauser: "Moral judgements are mediated by an unconscious process, a hidden moral grammar that evaluates causes and concequences of our own and other's actions. [...] I show that by looking at our moral psychology as an instinct—an evolved capacity of all human minds that unconsciously and automatically generates judgements of right and wrong—that we can better understand why some of our behaviours and decisions will always be construed as unfair, permissible [...]" ([26], p. 2). Johnson argues persuasively that it is heuristically not necessary to assume a prexistent moral faculty inherent in humans that underpins their intuitive judgements. ([20], pp. 137–62).

24 Haidt later also includes the foundation "liberty and oppression" as a likely candidate for the moral foundations, which, maybe not surprisingly, is missing from Campe's otherwise comprehensive compilation. Given the utopian context Campe is more concerned with legitimate authority and illegitimate rebellion (mutiny).

It is their filial and parental loyalty that stands out as the crucial maturationally natural value in Campe's moral universe, as it promises change, development, and perfectibility.

Campe's stance chimes with the potent concept of education and *Bildung* in the eighteenth century. By the same token, this specific scenario admittedly also seems a great concession to the malleability of human essence and potential in the eighteenth century, as the individual does not command autonomously over her/his own individuality: Campe concedes that society and its rules assume an important role in forming a person.

His twofold approach to "values" and the valuing process interestingly appears—despite all displayed determination to prove the superiority of the West with recourse to reason—indeed to be in line with the results of *Moral Foundation Theory*, which also focuses on the phenotypical diversity of values and the naturally maturational sameness of certain underlying patterns. Moral Foundation Theory follows Gary Marcus' specification of innateness in that it acknowledges that "nature bestows upon the newborn a considerably complex brain, but one that is best seen as prewired—flexible and subject to change—rather than hardwired, fixed, and immutable." ([27], p. 12).

In keeping with Marcus' concept of "innateness", *Moral Foundation Theory* emphasises that nature provides a first draft, which is then revised by experience: "The genes (collectively) write the first draft into neural tissue, beginning in utero but continuing throughout childhood. Experience (cultural learning) revises the draft during childhood, and even (to a lesser extent) during adulthood." ([28], p. 8). This notion of a first draft and its manifold realisations as a pluralistic take on morality stands out in Campe's novel, even though he renders this very notion conspicuously less explosive by integrating it in the progress achieved by the civilising process,[25] simply by providing a clear moral destination in the present.

While Campe thus assumes a common humanity by "relegating some peoples to the past moments of a European humanity's historical becoming" (as Chad Wellmon implies for Kant ([5], p. 432)), his theories prove to be pertinent to another important aspect of these anthropological/ethnological/colonial discourses: *i.e.,* the debate around human rights and their reach which started to unfold around 1800. In a pedagogical manual intended for his daughter (*Paternal Advice for my Daughter*, [29]) Campe stresses that she is both human and female, but has to conform to the limits of the latter definition which he acknowledges to be artificial, *i.e.,* socially imposed. However, beneath this schizophrenic imposition on female behaviour, it reveals the same potential for unconditional inclusion,[26] as Friday's fate shows. To Campe women and "savages" clearly are (or have the potential to be) full-fledged humans in the *moral* sense and are eligible to enter the realm where human rights—as envisaged by the eighteenth century—apply: this is one of the subliminal outcomes of his social experiment which draws so much explicit attention to Western superiority. In this sense Campe's novel is not only revealing with regard to the question of concrete morality; it is also an illuminating attempt to determine the moral rules and properties of humanity in the eighteenth century, when a clear look at the diversity of different cultures and norms actually preempted any clarity of such definition.

Conflicts of Interest: The author declares no conflict of interest.

---

[25] Campe's notion of a civilising process indeed reminds the reader of Norbert Elias' reflections on psychogenesis and sociogenesis in his eponymous work *The Civilising Process* (*Über den Prozeß der Zivilisation*).

[26] Campe's French adaptation of Sophie von La Roche's *Erscheinungen am See Oneida* (*Appearances at Lake Oneida*, 1798) is quite striking in this context. La Roche's protagonist Emilie also encounters Natives Americans, 'savages', however, "analyzing her own reaction leads Emilie to empathize with the Native Americans. She sees similarity between their situation and her own with respect to the obstacles they both face on their path to knowledge." ([30], p. 122). Campe "deleted La Roche's arguments for equal education and her critique of colonial projects" ([30], p. 130). Against this backdrop, Campe's very specific conglomerate of progressive educational thoughts and distinct, sometimes conspicuous, sometimes subliminal disenfranchisement becomes even more tangible.

References

1. Friedrich Gerstäcker. "Geschichte eines Ruhelosen." *Gartenlaube* 16 (1870): 244–47.
2. Joachim Heinrich Campe. *Robinson der Jüngere, zur Angenehmen und Nützlichen Unterhaltung für Kinder, Alwin Binder and Heinrich Richartz.* Stuttgart: Reclam, 2000.
3. Susanne Zantop. *Colonial Fantasies. Conquest, Family, and Nation in Precolonial Germany, 1770–1870.* Durham and London: Duke University Press, 1997.
4. Wolfgang Promies. "Kinderliteratur im späten 18. Jahrhundert." In *Deutsche Aufklärung bis zur Französischen Revolution 1680–1789, Rolf Grimminger, Hansers Sozialgeschichte der Deutschen Literatur vom 16. Jahrhundert bis zur Gegenwart Bd. 3.2.* Munich: Hanser Verlag, 1980, pp. 765–831.
5. Chad Wellmon. "Poesie as Anthropology. Schleiermacher, Colonial History and the Ethics of Ethnography." *The German Quarterly* 79 (2006): 423–42. [CrossRef]
6. Johann Gottfried Schnabel. *Insel Felsenburg,* 2nd ed. Edited by Volker Meid and Ingeborg Springer-Strand. Stuttgart: Reclam, 1994.
7. Nicolas Pethes, and Torsten Hahn. "Das zweifache Ende der Utopie: Literatur als Gesellschaftsexperiment in Wezels *Robinson* und Goethes *Wanderjahren*." In *Literarische Experimentalkulturen: Poetologien des Experiments im 19. Jahrhundert.* Edited by Marcus Krause and Nicolas Pethes. Würzburg: Königshausen und Neumann, 2005, pp. 123–48.
8. Mark Salber Phillips. *Society and Sentiment: Genres of Historical Writing in Britain, 1740–1820.* Princeton: Princeton University Press, 2000.
9. Daniel Lord Smail. *On Deep History and the Brain.* Berkeley, Los Angeles and London: University of California Press, 2008.
10. Jonathan Haidt. "The Righteous Mind." In *Why Good People Are Divided by Politics and Religion.* London: Penguin, 2012.
11. Pramod K. Nayar. *The Postcolonial Studies Dictionary.* Oxford: Wiley Blackwell, 2015.
12. Reinhart Koselleck. "Fortschritt." In *Geschichtliche Grundbegriffe. Historisches Lexikon zur Politisch-Sozialen Sprache in Deutschland. Volume 2.* Stuttgart: Klett-Cotta, 1975.
13. Philip Manow. *Politische Ursprungsphantasien. Der Leviathan und Sein Erbe.* Konstanz: Konstanz University Press, 2011.
14. Johann Heinrich Campe. *Robinson the Younger from the German.* Hamburg: C.E. Bohn, 1781.
15. Daniel Defoe, and Johann Karl Wezel. *Robinson Krusoe.* 2 vols. Edited by Neu Bearbv. Leipzig: Verlag der Dykischen Buchhandlung, 1779–80.
16. Reiner Wild. "Die aufgeklärte Kinderliteratur in der Literaturgeschichte des 18. Jahrhunderts. Zur Kontroverse um die Robinson-Bearbeitung zwischen J.H. Campe und J.C. Wezel." In *Aufklärung und Kinderbuch, Dagmar Grenz.* Pinneberg: Renate Raecke, 1986, pp. 47–78.
17. Urs Bitterli. *Die "Wilden" und Die "Zivilisierten". Grundzüge Einer Geistes- und Kulturgeschichte der Europäisch-Überseeischen Begegnung.* Munich: C.H. Beck, 1991.
18. John Locke. *Second Treatise of Government: An Essay Concerning the True Original, Extent and End of Civil Government.* Edited by Richard H. Cox. Wheeling: Harlan Davidson, 1982, p. 18.
19. Hans-Edwin Friedrich. "Nützliche oder grausame Natur? Naturkonstruktion in der spätaufklärerischen Robinsonade (Campe, Wezel)." In *Erschriebene Natur. Internationale Perspektiven auf Texte des 18. Jahrhunderts.* Jahrbuch für Internationale Germanistik. Reihe A, Kongreßberichte, 66. Edited by Michael Scheffel. Bern: Peter Lang, 2001, pp. 289–308.
20. Mark Johnson. *Morality for Humans: Ethical Understanding from the Perspective of Cognitive Science.* Chicago: University of Chicago Press, 2014.
21. Georg Lakoff, and Mark Johnson. *Metaphors We Live by.* Chicago: Chicago University Press, 1980.
22. Georg Lakoff, and Mark Johnson. *Philosophy on the Flesh: The Embodied Mind and its Challenges.* New York: Basic Books, 1999.
23. Karl Ludwig Pörschke. *Vorbereitung zu Einem Populären Naturrechte.* Königsberg: Friedrich Nicolovius, 1795.
24. Robert N. McCauley. *Why Religion Is Natural and Science Is Not.* Oxford: Oxford University Press, 2011.
25. Daniel Defoe. *Robinson Crusoe,* Critical edition. Edited by Michael Shinagel. New York: Norton, 1975.
26. Marc Hauser. *Moral Minds. How Nature Designed Our Universal Sense of Right and Wrong.* New York: HarperCollins, 2006.

27. Gary Marcus. *How a Tiny Number of Genes Creates the Complexities of Human Thought.* New York: Basic Books, 2004.

28. Jesse Graham, Jonathan Haidt, Sena Koleva, Matt Motyl, Ravi Iyer, Sean P. Wojcik, and Peter H. Ditto. "Moral Foundations Theory: The Pragmatic Validity of Moral Pluralism." Available online: http://www-bcf. usc.edu/~jessegra/papers/GHKMIWD.inpress.MFT.AESP.pdf (accessed on 29 January 2016).

29. Joachim Heinrich Campe. *Väterlicher Rath an meine Tochter. Ein Gegenstück zum Theophron. Der erwachsenern weiblichen Jugend gewidmet.* Braunschweig: Verlag der Schulbuchhandlung, 1791.

30. Stephanie M. Hilger. *Gender and Genre: German Women Write the French Revolution.* Newark: University of Delaware Press, 2015.

 *humanities*

Article

Transcultural Literary Interpretation: Theoretical Reflections with Examples from the Works of Gotthold Ephraim Lessing and Johann Wolfgang Goethe

Steven D. Martinson

Department of German Studies, University of Arizona, Tucson, Arizona 85721, USA;
martinso@email.arizona.edu

Academic Editor: Bernd Fischer
Received: 22 April 2016; Accepted: 27 June 2016; Published: 30 July 2016

Abstract: The present contribution explores the topic of literary interpretation from a transcultural perspective. We employ two dramas by Gotthold Ephraim Lessing (*Die Juden* and *Nathan der Weise*) and one by Johann Wolfgang Goethe (*Iphigenie auf Tauris*) as models for the investigation of intercultural and transcultural readings of literary texts. We first consider the epistemologies of Johann Martin Chladenius and Johann Gottfried Herder in order to distinguish between intercultural and transcultural studies. As a field of inquiry, transcultural literary studies does not employ one particular approach or advocate one specific method since it seeks to create new knowledge by opening up literary texts. For the first time, the article differentiates clearly between intercultural and transcultural studies and offers a clearer definition of transcultural spheres or spaces than has been advanced before. The critique of Karl-Josef Kuschel's reading of Lessing's *Nathan der Weise* opens up the literary-dramatic text to new possibilities. The field does not focus on what cultures do with human beings but with what different human beings do with culture. In sum, the transcultural dimensions of literary texts foster transcultural mentalities. They also have the potential to identify shared experiences and to develop common understandings while respecting the authenticity of difference.

Keywords: intercultural; transcultural; transcultural literary interpretation; Johann Martin Chladenius; Johann Gottfried Herder; Gotthold Ephraim Lessing; *Nathan der Weise*; Johann Wolfgang Goethe; Karl-Josef Kuschel

---

Im Zuge des kulturtheoretischen Übergangs von 'Inter' zu 'Trans' verlagert sich das kulturwissenschaftliche Interesse also von der althergebrachten Frage, was unterschiedliche *Kulturen* mit den Menschen tun, zur neuen Frage, was unterschiedliche *Menschen* mit den Kulturen tun.

(—Friedrich Schulze-Engler ([1], p. 46))

1. Introduction

The topic of transculturality raises a number of intriguing questions. First of all, what are transcultural fields and how are they unique? What phenomena do they identify, and what is their potential for cultivating greater understanding ("Verstehen") and even agreement ("Verständigung") among peoples of different cultures worldwide? What is transported from one location to another, and what is left behind, lost, or forgotten? What structures emerge when one culture passes through another and both cultures are transformed? Transcultural studies as a field of inquiry does not employ one particular approach or subscribe to one specific methodology. It is a way of seeing and opening up the world. Transcultural literary interpretation focuses first and foremost on literary texts which are rich sources for the creation of meaning.

Regarding our procedure on this topic, we first engage in a critical analysis of intercultural and transcultural studies. The second part of the contribution is devoted to the interpretation of several selected literary texts written in German. There is a distinct political component of the concept of the transcultural we are advancing here. Because transcultural fields are receptive to many different cultures, they encourage understanding, rapprochement, and agreement by appreciating not only differences but also commonalities.

2. Defining the Terms: "Inter-" and "Transcultural"

The prefixes "inter" and "trans" denote that the words "intercultural" and "transcultural" are not synonymous. In order to clarify the distinction, we turn to theories of knowledge that were first circulating in the German eighteenth century.

2.1. Intercultural Studies: Epistemology

Johann Martin Chladenius's theory of knowledge serves as one of the starting points of intercultural studies and Intercultural Germanics. Chladenius's *Einleitung zur richtigen Auslegung vernünftiger Reden und Schriften* [2] has had a profound effect on hermeneutic studies including the work of the twentieth-century philosopher, Hans-Georg Gadamer (although he was not uncritical of Chladenius, e.g. in his *Wahrheit und Methode* (Truth and Method, [3], see also [4]). In brief, Chladenius holds that people have different perceptions of the same object. In his *Einleitung*, Chladenius defined his concept of a "Sehepunkt" (point of view) in terms of space and time, as the location of our eye ("der Ort unseres Auges"), especially as regards our distance from an object ([2], paragraph 309). Every person has his or her own image of something and no other. By virtue of Chladenius's concept of the "Sehepunkt", it appears that no two people share the same point of view. In his masterful study of literary hermeneutics, *Introduction to Literary Hermeneutics*, Peter Szondi sees that Chladenius's "theory of 'point of view'" relates not to the historicity of the understanding of texts but to the changing ideas about the subject matter treated in the texts [5].

Chladenius believed that it is not only possible but necessary to determine an author's intention in order to fully understand a text. He does not seem to have been aware of the possibility, if not the need, to reflect critically on the reliability of the intention when studying the text. As Hans-Georg Gadamer [*Truth and Method*] would make clear, when engaging in an exegesis ("Auslegung"; literally: a laying out) of a text, the reader needs to account for one's presuppositions (and biases), accounting for the play of one's own subjectivity which necessarily affects one's reading [3].

The founder of Intercultural Germanics, Alois Wierlacher, adapted Chladenius when describing the Other ("das Fremde") as "das aufgefasste Auge" (the construed eye) ([6], p. 207). Instead of the term "Sehepunkt," Wierlacher employs the word "Blickwinkel" (angle of vision) which, he believes, is an apt signifier for the complex condition and position of the human being to whom belong one's history, ways of thinking, language, everyday knowledge, cultural memory, professional knowledge, knowledge of the world, and one's cultural identity ([6], p. 309). Wierlacher maintains that intercultural phenomena comprise a "Modus kooperativer Selbstaufklärung" since self-enlightenment itself first takes place through the self-distancing in self-conscious awareness of the other ("das Fremde"). Politically, Wierlacher maintains that, as a "Modus der Kulturauseinandersetzung," interculturality conflicts with a narrow, aesthetic "geisteswissenschaftlich" (Gadamerian) concept of culture that has dominated official German political institutions ([6], p. 276, fn. 4). Intercultural Germanics shares with the hermeneuticist Hans-Georg Gadamer the idea that understanding ("Verstehen") means to comprehend things differently. However, Wierlacher does not share Gadamer's conviction that understanding presupposes consent ("ein tragendes Einverständnis"; [6], p. 271). Whereas the primary object of study in intercultural studies is difference, transcultural studies seeks to understand the permeation of two or more cultures and the results of such interaction. Literary texts reflect and comment on these processes in and through their representations.

Like Wierlacher, Bernd Thum locates "the center of intercultural hermeneutics and research [in] the plurality of, and difference between cultures" [7]. Because Intercultural Germanics focuses on the tensions in opposing themes ("Gegenthemen"), such as between the foreign and the "other" ("das Fremde") and one's own ("das Eigene") ([6], pp. 267–68), the field has a difficult time moving beyond encounter ("Begegnung") and its analyses of difference and conflict. The key objective of Intercultural Germanics is to do justice to the cultural diversity of interests in German and German-speaking countries and the need for transcultural understanding ("Leitziel interkultureller Germanistik ist, der kulturellen Vielfalt des Interesses am Deutschen und den deutschsprachigen Ländern sowie dem Bedarf an transkultureller Verständigung besser gerecht zu werden als es bisherige Modelle von Germanistik vermochten," [8], p. IX). Unlike Transcultural German Studies [9], however, given its roots in the study of German as a Foreign Language, Intercultural Germanics remains focused largely on Germany. Wierlacher's employment of the adjective "transkulturell" in his definition of the key objective of "intercultural" studies should make us pause. Interculturalists have not differentiated clearly between the fields. They may desire better relations between people(s), but their primary focus is on one's own ("das Eigene") versus the other ("das Fremde"). The problem here is not that differences are clarified but that they are reinscribed once such knowledge is attained.

The relation between intercultural and transcultural studies does not constitute a binary opposition between two distinctly different fields of activity since the latter depends on the former for its meaning. One of the practical values of transcultural studies consists in the formation of common understandings and purposes that shared experiences create while respecting the authenticity of differences. Transcultural studies draws upon the knowledge intercultural research establishes but this field of inquiry goes far beyond it. The intercultural flows into the transcultural. The knowledge that is now at one's disposal creates a field of activity in which the permeation and intermixing of cultures of all sorts are understood not in their particularity but in their reciprocal relations.

2.2. Transcultural German Studies: Epistemology

Transcultural German Studies draws upon the work of Johann Gottfried Herder. In his essay, *Vom Erkennen und Empfinden der menschlichen Seele* (On the Cognition and Sensation of the Human Soul), Herder argues that cognition is sparked by the inner state of the powers of sensation, which he terms "der innere Sinn" [10]. For Herder, sense is more basic than sight for the advancement of knowledge. This point is particularly interesting in the light of Herder's determinations about the cultures of far-off places around the world in his monumental work, *Ideen zur Philosophie der Geschichte der Menschheit* (Ideas on the Philosophy of the History of Humankind, [11]). Whereas hermeneutics renders the unintelligible intelligible, with the aid of the inner sense, the imperceptible is made perceptible. Feeling is the most predominant of all human senses. It is the most fundamental faculty of the soul that collects perceptions ("Vorstellungen") in their external relations. Humanity signals the noble education ("edle Bildung") of the human being which develops finer senses and lends our drives their purpose [12]. In retrospect, because Chladenius valued reason above all else, he did not consider the possibility of shared experience. As Herder's essays suggest, shared experience is cultivated through the "inner sense" that is common to all human beings.

2.3. Contemporary Understandings of the Transcultural

Wolfgang Welsch first provided a theoretical framework for transcultural studies. The study of culture, he argued, must take into account the permeation of cultures ("die gegenwärtige Durchdringung der Kulturen", [13], pp. 334–35) and the external networks of cultures ("die externen Vernetzungen der Kulturen"; [13], p. 336). Theoreticians of transcultural studies understand cultures to be multilayered, interactive, and fluid. In fact, the phenomenon of flow is one of the field's main objects of study. Transcultural spheres emerge in the interface between cultural, linguistic, literary, and social phenomena. The intermingling of different cultures in the widest sense form transcultural spheres that move beyond differences and the storm and stress of initial encounters. Transcultural studies' main task is to determine the nature, function, and development of shared spaces and places through which process differences are recognized and shared concerns, commonalities, and understanding, if not always agreement, are first realized. The following questions are pivotal: What results when, after initial encounters and conflict, cultures permeate each other? Are not these differences transformed? Moreover, if so, in what ways? The effects of transcultural interaction become apparent when strong contrasts and differences are transformed into new and emerging unities. Such interaction is not only visible in literary texts but also acted out in them. What do we see in them and how does our "inner sense" comprehend them?

Transcultural studies move beyond the encounter and opposition between one's own and another's culture. For the German Americanist Heinz Antor dialogue first makes possible the initial contact between different positionings in hybrid, transcultural spheres ([14], p. 33). As we have proposed, the chief characteristics of transcultural spaces consist in the mutual reciprocity of different cultural elements in which individual cultures retain the authentic forms ([15], p. 75). Friedrich Schulze-Engler has suggested that "transcultural studies do not focus on what culture does with human beings but what different human beings do with culture" (in [14], p. 46). This is a fundamental distinction.

A transcultural sphere, space, or place is ever active. It is revealed not simply by the intersection of two or more cultures. The formation and transformation that inhere in transcultural spheres presupposes that both one's "own" and the "other" change. The reciprocity that the intermixing and permeation of cultures entails also means that the one does not dominate the other. The eighteenth-century German philosopher Immanuel Kant was one of the first to characterize the nature of a transcultural space without naming it. In his *Anthropologie in pragmatischer Hinsicht* (Anthropology from a Pragmatic Point of View, 1798 [16]), Kant called for thinking differently. A new way of thinking emerges when pluralism opposes egoism. A person no longer attempts to grasp the entire world in one's self but considers oneself to be "simply" ("bloß") a world citizen ("Weltbürger": "Dem Egoism kann nur der *Pluralism* entgegengesetzt werden, d. i. die Denkungsart: sich nicht als die ganze Welt in seinem Selbst befassend, sondern als einen bloßen Weltbürger zu betrachten und zu verhalten," [16] in [17], p. 92, fn. 35.) On the transcultural plane, a person shares a space in which people begin to "speak" a more common language. In the open spaces of transcultural spheres, human beings recognize their differences and, through their very interaction with each other, begin to understand what they may have in common while at the same time retaining their uniqueness. Proponents of transculturality are not interested in sameness (which is static) but in a distinctiveness and sense of commonality that are perpetually active and creative. Politically, whereas intercultural spaces are often marked by conflict, transcultural spheres are characterized by differentiated unities that promote peace and worldwide cooperation. (As Helge Bonholt and Gerhard Rupp have seen, "The phenomenon of space-time-compression, for example, produces a global, common present and a virtual togetherness, or community of people in the most diverse locations" ([18], p. 166). Like Alois Wierlacher, however, they blur the distinction between intercultural spaces and transcultural spheres.

2.4. Transcultural Literary Interpretation

We have suggested before that it is worth considering how cultures of all kinds are tied to, further developed, and transformed through permeating, mixing, and intersecting with other cultures. To what extent does the new research field of Transcultural German Studies produce new ways of interpretation ([15], p. 76, fn. 7)? How does the transcultural study of literary texts function, what can it ascertain, and what insights might it offer into the nature of human interaction and life in general? We here seek to illustrate how transcultural literary interpretation can open up a literary text and show how it can be of interest and even relevance for one's own times. The study of transcultural phenomena can be especially helpful when analyzing the multiple genres/forms that converge in and conjoin literary texts.

In this paper, we return to eighteenth-century "Germany" to disclose intercultural and transcultural dimensions of three literary texts by two German dramatists. In Gotthold Ephraim Lessing's *Die Juden* (The Jews) ([19], Vol. 1) we seek to illuminate the operation and limits of the intercultural encounter between a Jewish traveler and a Christian baron. Our second reading explores the realization and operation of transcultural dimensions in Lessing's *Nathan der Weise* (Nathan the Wise) ([19], Vol. 9) while engaging in critical analyses of major contributions to the current secondary literature. Finally, we interpret Johann Wolfgang Goethe's *Iphigenie auf Tauris* (Iphigenia in Tauris; [20], Vol. 5) in the light of both intercultural and transcultural literary interpretation arriving at a new reading of this classical German text.

3. Gotthold Ephraim Lessing's *Die Juden*

As Hugh Barr Nisbet has seen, Lessing's *The Jews* is the first wholly positive portrayal of a Jew in German drama ([21], p. 95). The comedy was the result of considerable reflection on the suppression that Jews were experiencing and continued to suffer. One of Lessing's projects of enlightenment consists in showing that, as true human beings, Jews are capable of good works and possess nobility of soul.

The play begins with a Traveler (a Jew) rescuing a (Christian) Baron from robbers and possibly being killed. The dramatic irony is that we readers/spectators know that the thieves are two servants under the baron's employ. In the course of the action, the two idiotic bandits disclose information that convicts them. Time and again, they voice their prejudice against Jews. The fact that they openly express their bias in the Traveler's presence magnifies the problem of hatred against Jews.

Although the dramatist Lessing exposes the foolishness of discrimination, the intercultural conflict between "nations" (Jews and Christians) remains unresolved in the end. The last exchange between the baron and the Traveler exposes the lack of connection and understanding. BARON: "O wie achtungswürdig wären die Juden, wenn sie alle Ihnen glichen!" (Oh, how dignified Jews would be if they were all like you!) ([19], Vol. 1, p. 487). TRAVELER: "Und wie liebenswürdig die Christen, wenn sie alle Ihre Eigenschaften besäßen!" (And how amiable Christians would be if they all had your attributes!) ([19], Vol. 1, p. 488). The divide between the Christian and the Jew is narrowed but not bridged. The comic effect of *The Jews* is generated primarily by the servant-thieves whose criminal antics are ridiculed. These stock figures of Saxon comedy, among whom the thief Martin Krumm is the most foolish of the lot, are laughed off the stage. Importantly, already early in his career as a writer of literature, Lessing began to transition from evoking ridicule ("Verlachen") in comedy to cultivating genuine laughter ("Lachen"), good humor. This shift in emphasis led Lessing to write one of his most successful comedies, *Minna von Barnhelm*. In the serious comedy ("ernsthafte Komödie") audiences begin to reflect critically, also self-critically on their prejudices and insensitivity to one's fellow human beings. In *The Jews*, Lessing began with the clash between people of different religious and cultural orientations, drawing attention to the inhumanity of prejudice. One of Lessing's greatest contributions to German drama culture is having created literary characters with whom the audience might actually identify. For one thing, the text makes it clear that every country is populated by good and bad people ("daß es unter allen Nationen gute und böse Seelen geben könne"; [19], Vol. 1, p. 461). Even Lessing's main character, the Jewish Traveler, is not without blemish for, as he is given to say, if a Jew deceives, it is usually a Christian who is responsible for having made him do it ([19], Vol. 1, p. 454; see also [22]).

Lessing's drama challenges readers/audiences to take both others ("das Fremde") and themselves ("das Eigene") into consideration when interacting. To this extent, an intercultural reading of the play can be most fruitful for it encourages enlightened critical self-reflection. At the same time, the baron is impressed with the Traveler. He admires the love he has for his fellow man and his magnanimity. Out of gratitude for having rescued him the baron offers his daughter in marriage. But when he discovers that the Traveler is a Jew, he exclaims what a cruel fate it is to discover that his rescuer should be a Jew. The Traveler's servant, Christoph, is stunned. Although his actions can hardly be characterized as Christian-like, Christoph charges that his employer, a Jew, has insulted all of

Christianity by having him in his employ ([19], Vol. 1, p. 487). The Traveler reminds Christoph as well as the other "Christians" that he cannot expect him to think any better than the rest of the common Christian horde ([19], Vol. 1, p. 487). Reminding his servant that he had rescued him from his miserable situation in Hamburg, Christoph returns the silver box that the thieves had stolen from the Baron, calls the Traveler an honest man, and pledges to stay with him. After all, Christoph notes, a Christian would have given him a kick in the ribs and no box! Later, in *Nathan the Wise*, Lessing would express his concern about the treatment of Muslims by Christians. As the protagonist's sister, Sittah, states: "Ihr Stolz ist: Christen sein; nicht Menschen" (Your pride is to simply be a Christian, not a human being) *Nathan*, Act II, Scene 1; [19], Vol. 9, p. 461).

In conclusion, an intercultural reading of Lessing's *The Jews* discloses the effects of unresolved cultural-religious conflict and the ambivalence that the interactions between "Christians" and the Jewish Traveler create when enmity and distrust prevail.

4. From Intercultural to Transcultural: Lessing's *Nathan der Weise* (1779)

Unlike intercultural encounters, transcultural spaces are not dominated by a specific group or directed by one particular interest. The transcultural sphere is observable in the fluid nature of literary texts. The flow from the intercultural into the transcultural creates new forms, such as the dramatic poem, Lessing's *Nathan the Wise*. As the borders between people of different cultures and religious persuasions shift and flow, so do the forms that literary texts assume. Through language, literary texts explore, critique, and even reconstruct reality through their representations and the contours of the forms they take.

Literary texts reflect countless examples of hybridity in both the forms they take as well as in the nature of their representations. This is especially true of German literature around 1800 during the "Second Age of Discovery" when the world opened up to frequent sea journeys and continental land expeditions. The pioneering work of Karl S. Guthke in this area is indispensable for our knowledge of cultural-historical developments around 1800, in particular his *Die Erfindung der Welt. Globalität und Grenzen in der Kulturgeschichte der Literatur*, where he explores the ideas that "die Welt wird global, wird neu erfunden als global" (the world becomes global and is rediscovered as being global) and, importantly, for our study, "[g]lobales Bewußtsein kann sogar den Verhältnissen der nächsten Nähe entspringen, wenn die alltägliche Begegnung mit dem Fremden durchdacht wird" (global consciousness can even stem from everyday local connections when one considers one's everyday encounters with the foreign) ([23], pp. 3–4; see also [24,25]). The "hybridity" that results include the intermingling of "Lebenswelten" inside and outside of Germany and German-speaking countries and cultures, that is, locally, regionally, and globally as well as between and within other languages. Lessing's *Nathan der Weise* is a mixed, i.e., hybrid form of drama, a dramatic poem ("ein dramatisches Gedicht") as the subtitle of the piece reads. Lessing's classical drama also draws upon several literary forms such as the parable. The play is one of the first to underscore the need for tolerance, ethical right, divine purpose, and deeds. In terms of its content, the work also presents and works with the hybrid character of the multi-, inter-religious family. The play begins with the near-death experience of Recha, the protagonist's adopted daughter, and the growing "love" relationship between her and her rescuer, the Christian knight Templar. A tragedy is averted when it is revealed that they are actually brother and sister. The hybrid nature of the multi- and interreligious family is evident also in Nathan's adoption of a Christian girl and the kinship between Saladin and the Templar. As an adopted daughter, Recha is a link in the expansion of the family.

According to Karl-Josef Kuschel, there is no other work in the history of German literature like this drama which, on the one hand, mirrors the potential for conflict among Judaism, Christianity, and Islamism while, on the other hand, offering a model for reconciliation among Jews, Christians, and Muslims ([26], p. 131). The play is also the first work in the history of German literature to present a Jew, a Christian, and a Muslim on the German stage in the same piece, and positively so ([26], p. 132). Kuschel's main thesis consists in the idea that Lessing pursued his interest in an Islamic humanity against strict orthodoxy and that he also intervened in inner-Islamic discourses for the sake of a positive tie between Islam and humanity ("Menschlichkeit") ([26], p. 133). Kuschel points out that Lessing also appreciated the fact that the historical Sultan Saladin was praised not only for his faith and power but also for his tolerance. He argues strongly that Saladin was endowed with reason, morality and humanity not in spite of Islam but through Islam and his faith as a Muslim ([26], p. 134).

In her contribution to the 2006/2007 *Lessing Yearbook*, Barbara Fischer objected to Kuschel's claim that Lessing's *Nathan* is pro-Muslim ("ein promuslimisches Stück" ([27], p. 135)) and that the ring parable is an Islamic message is forced. She asks why Lessing did not let Saladin tell the ring parable rather than Nathan. We do not have to wait until the twentieth century to hear from Muhammed Salim Abdullah, upon whom Kuschel draws, in order to answer the question. Lessing was the son of a Lutheran pastor and highly knowledgeable of the Christian protestant tradition. Monika Fick reminded us of the Christian heritage in which Lessing was raised and continued to be actively engaged, in particular the "(Erb)-Sünde-Gnade-Erlösungszusammenhang" of his writings ([28], p. 415f.)). Lessing's vociferous disagreement with Pastor Johann Melchior Goeze (senior pastor of the St. Katharina Church in Hamburg), who Lessing knew personally, in the *Anti-Goeze* ([19], Vol. 9) and the *Axiomata* ([19], Vol. 9) confirms that his primary concern was for the messages and practices of the Christian religion. For literary scholars, as Fischer reiterates and Karl S. Guthke had made vividly clear, even given Lessing's considerable knowledge of the region, in *Nathan der Weise*, the dramatist and theater critic employs "the East" only as a backdrop. In short, the story is still told from a Western perspective ([27], p. 106).

As a follow-up to that discussion, in 2012, Kuschel published the results of his thorough-going investigation of Lessing's references to Islam. (Barbara Fischer was not able to respond. She was killed in 2010 in an automobile accident.) The Catholic theologian advances the idea that Lessing was engaged in a strategic re-evaluation of despised minority religions (including Judaism). Lessing voiced his consternation that people would call Muslims a barbaric folk ([29], p. 23). We should add that with the establishment of university professorial chairs in Orientalist studies in the course of the eighteenth century, the idea of Islam as an anti-Christian, demonic power was questioned by closer study and historical differentiation. Kuschel suggests that, like Christianity and Judaism, Islam is "a natural religion based on reason" ([29], p. 32). As such, it is not a fall from faith but stands in line with the belief in the one, true God found in the Jewish-Christian Bible: "Der Islam ist somit kein Abfall vom Glauben, sondern steht in Kontinuität mit dem in der jüdisch-christlichen Bibel grundgelegten Glauben an den einen und wahren Gott" (Therefore, Islam is not a fall from faith but is contiguous with the belief in the one, true God that is fundamental to the Jewish-Christian Bible) ([29], p. 32).

Given their recognition of, and faith in one God (*regula fidei*), all three may be seen as natural religions in which reason and revelation inform one's understanding of the Godhead. Perhaps the real point of contention is Kuschel's tendency to conflate the different understandings of God that the three world religions espouse. The strength of Kuschel's understanding consists in his appreciation of Lessing's widening of the view of the Islamic world and his call for tolerance. To be sure, Fischer recognizes that there is "a common tradition revealed in the Torah, the New Testament, and the Qur'an, and all scriptures teach common interreligious ethics" ([27], p. 107). Most importantly, Lessing's drama promotes the common goal of practicing humane humanity, i.e. "Menschlichkeit", which takes place only in the transcultural sphere. We observed that no two people in *Die Juden* attained this level of interpersonal communication.

Lessing was also concerned with the question of what constitutes truth. In the famous ring parable in *Nathan the Wise*, none of the three sons possesses the truth. Instead, they are instructed to act as if they owned the true ring. Action is more efficacious than reasoning. Although often overlooked, there is a close tie between the ring parable and the palace parable in Lessing's responses to Pastor Goeze: In *Eine Parabel nebst einer kleinen Bitte, und einem eventualen Absagungsschreiben an Herrn Pastor Goeze, in Hamburg* (A Parable Along With a Small Request, and Possibly a Rejection Letter to Herr Pastor Goeze, in Hamburg, ([19], Vol. 9, pp. 39–52, a fire breaks out in a palace. The intellectuals gather around to think about what one should do, but they fail to act. Fortunately for them, it is a false alarm and all are spared. The message is clear. Action requires both commitment and practical engagement (for a fine discussion of this topic, see [30]).

Kuschel portrays Saladin positively, all-too positively. Doing so leads him to claim that Saladin's (and his sister Sittah's) basic understanding is identical to that of the ideal Jew and ideal Christian ([31], p. 38). To be sure, unlike many of his contemporaries, Lessing did not see in the prophet Mohammed an accomplice of the devil. We agree with Kuschel that, in *Nathan the Wise*, Lessing created a model for how personal interrelations between peoples of these different religions can be established in the awareness of deeply enmeshed conflicts ([31], p. 39). At first glance, Jews, Christians, and Muslims appear to belong to antagonistic worlds. However, it becomes apparent that a different relationship may lie on the horizon brought about by the realization that they all belong to an original unity and as such share a single community of destiny ([31], p. 41).

Upon examining contemporary performances of *Nathan der Weise*, Barbara Fischer concluded, and rightly so, that "[b]y propagating Lessing's eighteenth-century interest in the multiplicity of signification at the time of growing transnational communities, global migration, and hybrid identities, directors [of dramas] from diverse cultural and religious backgrounds can help audiences to identify commonalities by—at the same time—pointing out differences" ([27], p. 110). Fischer's conclusion extends from the point of intersection between intercultural and transcultural literary studies.

There is no question that Kuschel's reading of Lessing's dramatic poem is of relevance in our post-9/11 age. His contributions to interreligious dialogue worldwide have been very influential. In the light of our discussion, the "interfaith" relationships that Lessing draws in his dramatic poem operate within a transcultural sphere of activity, which, while fostering tolerance and humanity, retain the authenticity of their most basic religious convictions. But Kuschel's argument regarding the roots of the idea and practice of submission to God in Jewish, Christian, and Islamic religious cultures seems forced. We are to believe that the key word, "Ergebenheit in Gott" (submitting oneself to God) has not only Jewish-Christian but above all ("vor allem") Muslim roots and that by using the adjective, "gottergeben" (surrending oneself to God) Lessing was thinking about the core of Islam ([26], pp. 185 and 186, respectively). The commentators to the ninth volume of the Deutscher Klassiker Verlag's edition of Lessing's works ([19], Vol. 9), Klaus Bohnen and Arno Schilson, refer the reader back to Lessing's theological *Auseinandersetzungen* with Pastor Goeze. Here, Lessing repeatedly raises the question of the inner truth ("innere Wahrheit") of faith vs. the letter ("Buchstabe") of the Bible. The editors also include Lessing's Reimarus fragments which emphasize the *feeling* of divine bliss ([19], Vol. 9, p. 1269). In this play, however, it is Nathan, the Jew, and neither the Christian nor the Muslim who conveys the judge's advice in the ring parable. Let the sons practice unbiased love and without prejudice. The strife over which one of them has the genuine of the three rings. If there is rivalry, then it must be in achieving the highest virtues of what the ring symbolizes. Humility, forbearance, and benevolence will aid them in this and submission to the will of God.

However, a common link between the representatives of world religions in this play is not only submission to God but also the practice of love. Kuschel emphasizes the fact that truth and falsehood are determined according to the new criterion of mutual interaction with and for each other before God in the spirit of love ([31], p. 171; see also [32]). It would seem that the transcultural spirit of love is the true source of tolerance for vs. the toleration of differences. From this perspective, Kuschel's main point rings true. The most basic dimension of human existence is submission to God, out of which concrete action in the world is first established and made meaningful; [31], p. 182).

Nathan the Wise moves beyond the encounters of intercultural relations. The permeation and intermixing of Islam with Christianity and Judaism creates a transcultural space in which Christians, Jews, and Muslims embrace each other as members of a larger, extended family while retaining the authenticity of their religious convictions. What is shed in the move from the intercultural to the transcultural is not faith but that letter of the law advanced by institutions of religion. In this drama that law is represented by the Patriarch of the (Eastern) Orthodox Church whose extreme orthodoxy works against interfaith dialogue and the improvement of relations between human beings.

Kristlieb Adloff's recent contribution to scholarship deserves special attention. For Adloff, the distinctive component of the drama is the space between the Jew, the Christian, and the Muslim. "'Der Christ ist *zwischen* uns, zwischen Jude und Muslim', sagt Saladin, und dieses 'Zwischen' ist das reizvolle Gelände, in dem sich das Drama bewegt" (The Christian stands between us, between Jew and Muslim,' says Saladin, and this 'between' is the appealing terrain in which the drama moves; [33], p. 124). Adloff argues that the ring parable occurs within this "in-between" space. As such, the dramatic action cannot suspend the different forms of positive religions into a universal religion ([33], p. 124). But they do not really need to since they already converge transcultural spaces.

Although he does not say so, Adloff seems to have embraced Homi Bhabha's idea of "in-betweenness". Bhabha has argued that an intervening space (interstice) emerges in the interface between cultural differences ([34], p. 2). The gaps, or "in-betweenness" of "third" spaces produce forms of culture that interrogate established borders in and between race, gender, and class. Adloff further argues his point, in part in disagreement with Kuschel, as follows:

> Der Wahrheitsstreit ist im Ernst zu führen, nicht so sehr als 'interreligiöser Dialog' zwischen den Religionen, dessen unbestreitbarer Nutzen sich auf Abbau von Vorurteilen und die Möglichkeit mitmenschlicher Begegnungen erstreckt, sondern in jenem gerade für das Christentum so bezeichnenden 'Zwischen', wo sich zeigt, was innerhalb der jeweiligen religiösen (bzw. areligiösen) Existenz strittig *bleiben* muss. Dieser—hoffnungsvolle—Streit erhält Kraft und Glanz von einer Utopie her, von einem Gerichtstag 'über tausend tausend Jahre' (III/7, Z. 23), an dem ein letzter Spruch den Streit beenden wird, kein St. Nimmerstag, wo doch bei Gott tausend Jahre wie ein Tag sind (Ps 90,4). Utopie bedeutet hier nicht, dass die Gegenwart einer imaginären Zukunft geopfert würde.

> (The controversy about truth is to be taken seriously, not so much as an 'interreligious dialogue' between religions, whose indisputable benefit encompasses the dismantling of prejudices and the possibility of humane encounters, but in that 'Between' [space] which is so characteristic of Christianity, showing what must *remain* contentious within religious (and areligious) existence. This—hopeful—controversy contains the power and luster of a utopia, of a judgment day 'over the course of thousands and thousands of years' (III,7, l. 23), on which a final utterance will end the fight, not a St. Neversday [St. Nimmerstag], as, with God, one day is like a thousand years (Ps. 90, 4). Utopia here does not mean that the present would be sacrificed to an imaginary future).

> ([33], p. 125)

The maintenance of such narrow spaces continues to activate contestation in the political sphere. In transcultural studies, however, a "third" space is not the in-betweenness but a field of reciprocity and mutual permeation that conjoins opposing walls. In Lessing's *Nathan the Wise*, the space between the Muslim, the Christian, and the Jew ("Zwischen") is bridged by the mutual embrace and the creation of an extended family. We certainly agree with Adloff that, in *Nathan the Wise*, we are shown that the bridge to the future is built on a groundwork of friendship ([33], p. 125). The reader/spectator may sense that there is an urgency to building bridges. Nathan expresses this strongly when he beseeches the Templar: "Wir müssen, müssen Freunde sein" (We must be friends) (Act II, Scene 5, l.532; [19], Vol. 9, p. 533).

To be sure, intercultural studies show and underscore the value and importance of tolerance. Transcultural studies already presuppose and being with acceptance of others. According to Monika Nenon [35], friendship is more than tolerance for an(other) which of itself may not withstand the test of cruel reality. Hence, Nathan works for the Templar's friendship and, in the case of his friend, Saladin, participates in a duel between death and life. In friendship, a bond is achieved, a ring is forged. A transcultural field of activity is evident here as a model for human interaction and the necessary action required to actualize that model. Words are not enough: "Hier brauchts That!" (Here, deeds are required!) ([19], Vol. 9, p. 127).

In sum, in *Nathan the Wise*, initially strong contrasts and differences are transformed into new and emerging unities that retain the distinctness (authenticity) of difference, in this case, the different belief structures of Jews, Christians, and Muslims. In the transcultural sphere, all three religions are united in their submission to God and the action that flows from love of humanity. Given its positive reception and recurrent performances worldwide today (as examples, performances of Lessing's *Nathan der Weise* are planned for 2016 at the Blackbird Theatre in Vancouver, British Columbia, Canada and the Pearl Theatre in New York City), Lessing's *Nathan the Wise* has become a part of not simply a specific cultural or even collective memory but of worldwide transcultural memory.[1]

5. Goethe's Iphigenie auf Tauris (1790)

In his classical drama, *Iphigenia in Tauris* [20], Johann Wolfgang Goethe, filled the ancient Greek myth of Agamemon and Clytemnestra and the fate of their oldest daughter, Iphigenia, with a new and modern content to explore relations between natives and foreigners.

Early in his work on the intercultural, Wierlacher offered a perceptive analysis of Goethe's dramatic writing. Wierlacher placed the disposition toward foreigners, that is, the intercultural, at the center of his analysis of Goethe's classical drama. Wierlacher begins with line 76 where the protagonist, Iphigenia, asks King Thoas's confidant, Arcas, "Kann uns das Vaterland die Fremde werden?" (Can our fatherland become the foreign?) Wierlacher contends that the absolution of Iphigenia's brother, Orestes, constitutes the turning point in Iphigenia's relationship to the foreign ([37], p. 67). Her fate lies in King Thoas's foreign ("fremde") hand ([20], l. 1185). Wierlacher also addresses the ties between the language of the drama and the legal discourse of Goethe's place and time regarding the law of nations (*Völkerrecht*). From his intercultural perspective, Iphigenie treats Thoas as a natural citizen ("Rechtssubjekt"; [37], p. 72). The dramatist sanctions a new custom of universal friendship toward foreigners vs., in a nut shell, xenophobia. Thoas does not refuse Iphigenie's plan to resolve the conflict between the king and her brother and his friend, for "through the acceptance of a valid pledge," as is contained in the *Landrecht für die Preußischen Staaten* (General Provincial Law of the Prussian States Allgemeines; 1794), a contract is sealed ([37], p. 72)). The fact that the *General Provincial Law* (which granted legal status to Jews) was not written until well after the writing of Goethe's drama does not seem to bother Wierlacher.

Goethe himself actually went so far to claim that as a member of the highest administrative body in Weimar, he could see even more clearly than Nathan and his creator (Lessing) that the human being must first become a citizen of a country before that person can become a subject of humanity in general ([37], p. 73). However, from a transcultural view, which places human rights (*Menschenrechte*) over the law of nations, perhaps it is the other way around. Without the "inner sense" of humane humanity advanced by Herder, any such law can only be stated. It is up to people to actualize it and put it into action. Recalling Friedrich Schulze-Engler [1], the field of transcultural studies does not dwell on the question of what culture does with human beings but what different human beings do with culture.

Although agonizing at times, positive social changes occur when Iphigenia is driven by the fates, passes through Taurus, and returns to her homeland, i.e., original culture. What has occurred now that one culture has permeated and intermixed with another culture? Furthermore, what is the result of their interaction? Goethe's classical drama shows that there is a significant shift in individual cultural practices in the direction of humane humanity (*Menschlichkeit*) and peace. According to ancient law, King Thoas is required to execute strangers who land on the island. Because Iphigenia's brother, Orestes, and his friend, Pylades, have transgressed the cultural-political border of Taurus, they must be killed. There are two important results of the power of Iphigenia's humanity. First, even though Thoas has the right and the intention to marry the (foreign) priestess, Iphigenia refuses and is able to avert a

---

[1] A dissertation in progress on this topic is by James Howell, entitled *Alexander von Humboldt and (Trans)Cultural Memory* [36].

forced marriage when she exclaims, "Ich bin so frei geboren wie ein Mann." (I am as free born as any man) ([20], Vol. 5, p. 609, l. 1858). Second, Iphigenia and Orestes succeed in convincing the king to let them return to their homeland. Iphigenia's high and noble soul ("hohe Seele") and pure childlike trust in a noble man (ll. 2143–2145) speaks to Thoas's heart. (For an account of the noble soul and the ethics of politics in Goethe's administrative and literary-dramatic work, see [38]). Iphigenia also asks the king not to simply ban them from his land but, rather, give them his blessing ([20], Vol. 5, pp. 618–19, ll. 2153b–2155a). To be sure, Iphigenia had not wished to be separated from her homeland, "Denn ach mich trennt das Meer von den Geliebten/ Und an dem Ufer steh ich lange Tage,/ Das Land der Griechen mit der Seele suchend" (For, oh, the sea separates me from my loved ones/And I have been standing for many days on the shoreline/Seeking with my soul the land of the Greeks) ([20], Vol. 5, p. 555, ll. 10–12). Spoken, as they are, at the beginning of the drama, the words express the suffering of separation and, now with equal force, apply to the foreign culture. "Leb wohl und reiche mir/Zum Pfand der alten Freundschaft deine Rechte" (Farewell and extend to me/your rights as a pledge of ancient friendship) ([20], Vol. 5, p. 619, ll. 2172–2173). Thoas has the final word, and it is a word of humanity ("Menschlichkeit"): "Lebt wohl!" It is now clear that all three of the Greeks' understanding of a foreign culture has changed. They are now allowed to return to their homeland. Thoas remains at home, but he too has been transformed: "By speaking the truth, Iphigenia not only exposes deception but destabilizes the power constellation. Moral authority usurps political authority and virtuous behavior effects change. The re-formation of society succeeds without recourse to violence" ([38], p. 211, fn. 18). With regard to related scholarship on Goethe's classical drama, Nicolas Boyle sees that it is the human heart that unites the divine world and the world of human moral attitudes. The new "gospel" of humanity is rooted in the human spirit) ([39], p. 450). One of the best contributions on the subject is by T. J. Reed who underscores Iphigenia's ethical integrity and ethical doubt she senses when fleeing with her brother, Orestes, and his friend, Pylades ([40], pp. 211 and 213, respectively).

Given Thoas' experiences, perhaps the law of the land will change and foreigners accepted into Tauris. Perhaps the practice of humanity can effect change in the political public sphere. At least, this was the hope of the German eighteenth century.

6. Conclusions

The transcultural dimensions of literary texts cultivate transcultural mentalities. Thinking transculturally promotes a "Lebenspraxis" that includes all "others." By exposing the reader to the presence of transcultural dimensions in literature and having him or her engage in a discussion of it, minds begin to be trained to think transculturally. In the eighteenth century, the activity of "Bildung" (education/cultivation) became an integral part of the perpetual process of enlightenment that Kant theorized and others practiced in the writing and staging of literature in one's own language.

While Lessing's *The Jews* ends with the gap between the Christian Baron and the Jewish Traveler, the latter drama concludes with the commonality between the three main representatives of Judaism, Islamism, and Christianity regarding submission to God. The authenticity is retained in that each understands the nature of God differently. In both of Lessing's dramas, we observe a physical transcultural space on stage that engages us no longer as spectators but as participants in the action. At the end of *Nathan the Wise*, the characters embrace each other as members of an extended family. While in this piece recipients consider the relations between world religions, the same kind of structure can adhere in relations between cultures and nations, at which point the transcultural and the transnational share common ground. With respect to Goethe's drama, *Iphigenia in Tauris*, a transcultural reading discloses how transcultural communication can effect both personal and political change. While the story begins with the storm and stress of crossing borders and its consequence, it ends with reconciliation through mutual understanding. In Goethe's drama, it is not resignation to the will of God but the cultivation and practice of one's own humanity that overcomes the barriers between human beings and political institutions.

Conflicts of Interest: The author declares no conflict of interest.

References

1. Friedrich Schulze-Engler. "Von 'Inter' zu 'Trans': Gesellschaftliche, kulturelle und literarische Übergänge." In *Inter- und Transkulturelle Studien. Theoretische Grundlagen und interdisziplinäre Praxis.* Edited by Heinz Anton. Heidelberg: Carl Winter, 2006, pp. 41–53.
2. Chladenius. *Einleitung zur richtigen Auslegung vernünftiger Reden und Schriften.* Leipzig: Lanckisch, 1742, Photomechanischer Nachdruck der Ausgabe. Mit einer Einleitung von Lutz Goldsetzer. Düsseldorf: Stern-Verlag Janssen, 1969.
3. Hans-Georg Gadamer. *Truth and Method,* 2nd ed. Edited by Joel Weinsheimer. Translated by David Marshall. New York: Continuum, 2004, First published as *Wahrheit und Methode. Grundzüge einer philosophischen Hermeneutik.* Tübingen: J. C. B. Mohr, 1960.
4. Christoph Friedrich. "Johann Martin Chladenius: Die allgemeine Hermeneutik und das Problem der Geschichte." In *Klassiker der Hermeneutik.* Edited by Ulrich Nassen. Paderborn: Schöningh, 1982, pp. 43–75.
5. Peter Szondi. *Introduction to Literary Hermeneutics.* Translated by Martha Woodmansee. Foreword by Joel Weinsheimer; New York: Cambridge UP, 1995.
6. Alois Wierlacher. "Interkulturalität. Zur Konzeptualisierung eines Rahmenbegriffs interkultureller Kommunikation aus der Sicht interkultureller Germanistik." *Jahrbuch Deutsch als Fremdsprache* 26 (2000): 263–87.
7. Bernd Thum. "Auf dem Wege zu einer interkulturellen Germanistik." *Jahrbuch Deutsch als Fremdsprache* 11 (1985): 334, quoted by H.-J. Schulz. "Identity or Alterity: American Germanistik and Hermeneutics." In *Challenges of Germanistik. Traditions and Prospects of an Academic Discipline. Germanistik weltweit? Zu Theorie und Praxis des Disziplinrahmens.* Edited by Eitel Timm. Munich: iudicium, 1992, p. 15.
8. Alois Wierlacher, and Andrea Bogner, eds. *Handbuch interkulturelle Germanistik.* Stuttgart: J. B. Metzler, 2003.
9. *Transcultural German Studies/Deutsch als Fremdsprache. Building Bridges/Brücken bauen.* Steven D. Martinson, and Renate A. Schulz, eds. Bern: Peter Lang, 2008, [=*Jahrbuch für internationale Germanistik* (Kongreßberichte A, 94)].
10. Johann Gottfried Herder. *Vom Erkennen und Empfinden der menschlichen Seele. Bemerkungen und Träume.* Riga: J.F. Hartknoch, 1778.
11. Johann Gottfried Herder. *Ideen zur Philosophie der Geschichte der Menschheit.* Riga: J.F. Hartknoch, 1784–91.
12. Hans Adler. "Herder's Concept of Humanität." In *A Companion to the Works of Johann Gottfried Herder.* Edited by Hans Adler and Wulf Köpke. Rochester: Camden House, 2009, pp. 93–116.
13. Wolfgang Welsch. "Transkulturalität. Zwischen Globalisierung und Partikularisierung." *Jahrbuch Deutsch als Fremdsprache* 26 (2000): 327–51.
14. Heinz Antor, ed. *Inter- und Transkulturelle Studien. Theoretische Grandlagen und Interdisziplinäre Praxis.* Heidelberg: Carl Winter, 2006.
15. Steven D. Martinson. "Transkulturelle German Studies." In *Transcultural German Studies/Deutsch als Fremdsprache. Building Bridges/Brücken bauen.* Edited by Steven D. Martinson and Renate Schulz. Bern: Peter Lang, 2009, pp. 72–83.
16. Immanuel Kant. *Die Anthropologie in pragmatischer Hinsicht.* Königsberg: Friedrich Nicolovius, 1798.
17. John McCarthy. *Crossing Boundaries: A Theory and History of Essay Writing in German, 1680–1815.* Philadelphia: UP Pennsylvania, 1989.
18. Helge Bonholt, and Gerhard Rupp. "Leseentwicklung im Zeitalter der Globalisierung. Der Beitrag von literarischem Lesen zur interkulturellen Erziehung und zur Ausbildung von Toleranz." In *Nathan und seine Erben. Beiträge zur Geschichte des Toleranzgedankens in der Literatur. Festschrift für Martin Bollacher.* Edited by Oxana Zielke. with the assistance of Thorsten Meier; Würzburg: Königshausen & Neumann, 2005, pp. 163–95.
19. Gotthold Ephraim Lessing. *Werke und Briefe in zwölf Bänden.* Edited by Wilfried Barner, Klaus Bohnen, Gunter E. Grimm, Helmuth Kiesel, Arno Schilson, Jürgen Stenzel and Conrad Wiedemann. Frankfurt: Deutscher Klassiker Verlag, 1985–2003, vol. 3.

20. Johann Wolfgang Goethe. *Iphigenie auf Tauris, Egmont, Torquato Tasso. Dramen 1776–1790, Vol. 5. Sämtliche Werke. Briefe, Tagebücher und Gespräche.* 40 vols, Edited by Dieter Borchmeyer. Frankfurt a. M.: Deutscher Klassiker Verlag, 1988.

21. Hugh Barr Nisbet. *Gotthold Ephraim Lessing. His Life, Works, and Thought.* Oxford: Oxford UP, 2013.

22. Agnes Kornbacher-Meyer. *Komödientheorie und Komödienschaffen Gotthold Ephraim Lessings.* Berlin: Duncker & Humboldt, 2003, pp. 216–17.

23. Hans S. Guthke. *Die Erfindung der Welt. Globalität und Grenzen in der Kulturgeschichte der Literatur.* Tübingen: Francke, 2005.

24. Hans S. Guthke. *Lessings Horizonte. Grenzen und Grenzlosigkeit der Toleranz.* Göttingen: Wallstein, 2003.

25. Hans S. Guthke. *Der Blick in die Fremde. Das Ich und das Andere in der Literatur.* Tübingen: Francke, 2000.

26. Karl-Josef Kuschel. "Sei keinem Jud' und Muselmann zum Trotz ein Christ. Gotthold Ephraim Lessing im Spannungsfeld von Judentum, Christen und Islam." In *Karl-Josef Kuschel "Gott liebt es sich zu verstecken." Literarische Skizzen von Lessing bis Muschg.* Ostfildern: Matthias-Grünewald-Verlag, 2007.

27. Barbara Fischer. "To Each His Nathan: On the Theological Instrumentation of Lessing." *Lessing Yearbook* 35 (2006/2007): 103–12.

28. Monika Fick. *Lessing-Handbuch. Leben—Werk—Wirkung*, 2nd ed. Stuttgart: J. P. Metzler, 2004.

29. Karl-Josef Kuschel. "'Strategische Aufwertung': Lessings Bilder vom Islam im Zeitalter der Aufklärung." In *Islam in der deutschen und türkischen Literatur.* Edited by Michael Hofmann. Paderborn: Schöningh, 2012, pp. 19–46.

30. Beate Allert. "About a Burning Building in Eco and Lessing, or: How to Process Messages." *Lessing Yearbook* XXIV (1997): 57–86.

31. Karl-Josef Kuschel. *"Jud, Christ und Muselmann vereinigt"? Lessings Nathan der Weise.* Düsseldorf: Patmos, 2004.

32. Daniel Müller Nielaba. *Die Wendung zum Bessern. Zur Aufklärung der Toleranz in Gotthold Ephraim Lessings "Nathan der Weise."* Würzburg: Königshausen & Neumann, 2000.

33. Kristlieb Adloff. "'Und doch ist Gott!': Religionskritik und theo-poetische Utopie in Lessings *Nathan der Weise.*" In *Lessing im Kontext des europäischen Theaters. Vortragsreihe der Lessing-Akademie (8. März-19. April 2012).* Edited by Helmut Berthold. Wolfenbüttel: Lessing-Akademie, 2012, pp. 109–27.

34. Homi Bhabha. *The Location of Culture.* London: Routledge, 2004.

35. Monika Nenon. "Brücken der Freundschaft in Lessings frühen Komödien." In Proceedings of the Tucson Lessing Conference; Edited by Steven D. Martinson and Richard E. Schade. *Lessing Yearbook.* 2006/2007, 37, pp. 93–101.

36. James Howell. Alexander von Humboldt and (Trans)Cultural Memory. Ph.D. dissertation, University of Arizona, in progress.

37. Alois Wierlacher. "Ent-Fremdete Fremde—Goethes *Iphigenie auf Tauris* als Drama des Völkerrechts." In *Architektur interkultureller Germanistik.* Edited by Alois Wierlacher. Munich: iudicium, 2001, pp. 58–76.

38. Steven D. Martinson. "Toward an Ethical Politics: Johann Wolfgang Goethe, Administrator and Writer or Classical Dramas." *Euphorion. Zeitschrift für Literaturgeschichte* 109 (2015): 193–234.

39. Nicolas Boyle. *Goethe: The Poet and the Age. Volume I: The Poetry of Desire.* Oxford: Clarendon Press, 2000.

40. T. J. Reed. "Iphigenie auf Tauris." In *Goethe Handbuch. Vol. II: Dramen.* Edited by Bernd Witte, Theo Buck, Hans-Dietrich Dahnke, Regine Otto and Peter Schmidt. Stuttgart: J. P Metzler, 1996.

 *humanities*

Article

Recasting the Significant: The Transcultural Memory of Alexander von Humboldt's Visit to Philadelphia and Washington, D.C.

James F. Howell

Department of German Studies, University of Arizona, 9720 N. Oak Shadows Pl., Tucson, AZ 85737, USA;
jfhowell@email.arizona.edu

Academic Editor: Bernd Fischer
Received: 1 May 2016; Accepted: 27 June 2016; Published: 1 July 2016

Abstract: Alexander von Humboldt was internationally known as a world traveler, having collected data and analyzed samples from five of the world's seven continents. He spoke several languages fluently, and split most of his adult life between the cosmopolitan centers of Berlin and Paris. The great deal of time Humboldt spent in Latin America, along with his staunch belief in human equality, led to his reverence in those countries. Indeed, Humboldt was a world citizen in the truest sense of the word. But what of the United States? What claim can this nation make to the heritage and legacy of the world-exploring baron? A brief stop in Philadelphia and Washington, D.C. at the end of Humboldt's expedition to the equatorial regions of the Americas seems to suffice. This short stay, along with the Humboldt-Jefferson correspondence, constitutes the great American link in Humboldt studies, a link whose nature and importance has, over the years, received an exaggerated amount of attention from authors writing for an American audience. The following analysis, using the tools of transcultural memory studies, investigates why this relatively insignificant event in a long and storied life assumes an inflated role in current accounts of the life and work of Alexander von Humboldt.

Keywords: Alexander von Humboldt; cultural memory; transcultural memory; Thomas Jefferson; Founding Fathers

---

1. Humboldt's Arrival in the United States

On 24 May 1804, Alexander von Humboldt arrived in Philadelphia, marking the beginning of his one and only visit to the United States. Between his arrival and departure on June 30th of the same year, Humboldt traveled between Philadelphia and Washington, D.C., meeting with scientists and dignitaries at every stop. Humboldt was the talk of the new republic, indeed the world, after the completion of his five-year scientific and ethnographic survey of South and Central America. During his almost six weeks in the United States, Humboldt's inquisitive hosts received him warmly, and he returned the warmth, remarking that the time spent in Washington and Philadelphia was "the most delightful of [my] life" ([1], p. 24), and that he considered himself from then on to be "half an American" ([2], p. ix). Although Humboldt did enjoy his stay in the United States and appreciated the connections he made there, he wrote very little about this pleasant and short detour in his long and storied travels. When later summarizing the final phase of his voyage, Humboldt merely remarked that he sailed from Havana to Bordeaux "by the way of Philadelphia" ([1], p. 30). This succinct characterization seems almost unthinkable when compared to recent textual depictions of Humboldt published in the United States.

With the notable exception of Mary Louise Pratt's volume *Imperial Eyes: Travel Writing and Transculturation*, Humboldt and his work have experienced an overwhelmingly positive reception in the United States over the past 25 years. In addition to this general positivity, another hallmark of

American Humboldt literature is the aforementioned visit to Philadelphia and Washington, D.C. in the late spring of 1804. Recently, writers in the United States have interpreted this short stay not merely as a cornerstone of Humboldt's influence on American culture during the nineteenth century, but also as a defining moment in the Prussian baron's life and intellectual career. Although Humboldt's visit and his connection to the Founding Fathers certainly did not damage his notoriety in the United States during the course of the nineteenth century, it is problematic to overemphasize the relevance of these encounters. Indeed, the connections and correspondence Humboldt initiated with numerous American scientists and artists in Paris and Berlin *after* 1804 were more important in terms of his impact on American science and exploration. Contrary to the representations in many current accounts, the most probable source of the respect and popularity Humboldt enjoyed in the United States came from the translation and publication of the first several volumes of his magnum opus, *Kosmos*. This work was an international sensation, and within the United States its impact was felt and celebrated by the likes of Ralph Waldo Emerson, Walt Whitman, Henry David Thoreau, and Edgar Allan Poe. Why, then, does this brief and marginally relevant chapter in a life otherwise overflowing with acquaintances and accolades take such a central role in America's modern understanding and representation of Alexander von Humboldt? This investigation will demonstrate the ways in which Humboldt and his visit to the United States are currently presented to American audiences, as well as analyze the transcultural and mnemonic processes involved in the reintroduction of Alexander von Humboldt to American cultural memory.

2. Framing Humboldt's Visit

One need not look far to find the narrative centrality of Humboldt's visit in contemporary American texts. Humboldt's presence on the eastern seaboard and his subsequent relationship with the Founding Fathers represent the starting point, the turning point, or the conclusion of American accounts of his life and works. Aaron Sachs, the author of *The Humboldt Current: Nineteenth-Century Exploration and the Roots of American Environmentalism*, begins his work with the following harrowing and adventurous account: "It would have been easier to sail straight back to Europe. Politics and weather both favored the conservative course: to make the detour from Havana to Philadelphia, his ship would be forced to brave a British naval blockade and risk a dangerous stretch of water at the beginning of hurricane season" ([3], p. 1). Here, Humboldt's visit to the United States serves as the introduction to Humboldt and his biography. Only later does the reader learn in full detail from Sachs about Humboldt's background and accomplishments. The explorer's scientific influence and contributions to American environmentalism—Sach's central themes—initially assume a secondary role to the establishment of Humboldt's true credentials: his connection to the founders, and thereby to the founding, of the new republic. This association bestows a level of authenticity and indigeneity to the influence Humboldt exercised on the imagination and training of early American explorers and scientists. Humboldt impacted the American intellectual tradition not only through books and articles as a distant European scholar; rather by highlighting and prioritizing the dangerous passage from Havana to Philadelphia and the subsequent stay in the United States, Humboldt's story becomes, in part, an American story.

Laura Dassow Walls, author of *Passage to Cosmos: Alexander von Humboldt and the Shaping of America*, employs Humboldt's visit to Philadelphia and Washington, D.C. as a turning point in the narrative of Humboldt's biography, as well as in her own investigation. Although Walls' account of Humboldt's life does not begin with his time in Philadelphia and Washington, D.C., these events are afforded special attention and are represented in a way reminiscent of Sach's narrative. As seen in the following selection, Walls frames Humboldt's decision to brave the Bahama Strait in familiarly courageous and daring terms: "Beyond the 'moral obligation' he felt to see the world's lone functioning republic, there was every reason to avoid the detour. Humboldt was desperate to get himself, his friends, and his collections safely home to Paris. [...] Heading north risked losing everything they had with them to the British blockades of U.S. ports—assuming his ship was spared by the notorious Atlantic storms" ([2], p. 99). This dramatic account of Humboldt's fateful decision to visit the United States initiates the second half of Walls' analysis, in which she begins to shift her focus away from Humboldt's biography and onto his influence on nineteenth-century American literary culture. Although Humboldt's fame in English-speaking North America would truly blossom with the first translations of *Kosmos* in 1845, Walls, among others, claims that the seeds had already been planted in the late spring of 1804.

Gerard Helferich, in his work *Humboldt's Cosmos: Alexander von Humboldt and the Latin American Journey that Changed the Way We See the World*, utilizes Humboldt's brief stopover in the United States to frame the remainder of the explorer's biographical narrative after having completed his American travels. The twelfth and final chapter of Helferich's book bears the title of "Washington, Paris, and Berlin" [4]. This condensation of the final two-thirds of Humboldt's life is indeed noteworthy, as it seemingly gives his time spent in Washington equal weight to his years spent living and working in Paris (1807–1827) and in Berlin (1827–1859). It should, of course, be noted that the biographical narrative crafted by Helferich focuses on Humboldt's experiences in South and Central America, and therefore leaves little space for details regarding his life prior to and following the years 1799–1804. Considering, however, the fact that the vast majority of Humboldt's scientific engagement and literary activity took place following his return to Europe, Helferich's choice is truly remarkable. It suggests that visiting the United States and encountering Thomas Jefferson profoundly affected Humboldt and his legacy in a way equal to the composition of *Kosmos*, the Russian Expedition of 1829, or participation in the nineteenth-century scientific discourses centered in Paris. These accounts make it clear that visiting the United States was no mere fancy for Humboldt on his return journey; indeed, American authors go to great lengths to suggest that some kind of imperative was at work, compelling Humboldt to look upon this new republic with his own eyes, and meet the men and women who brought it about.

Perhaps the most interesting use of Humboldt's visit to frame a biographical narrative is employed by David McCullough in his essay on Humboldt entitled "Journey to the Top of the World." McCullough, like Sachs, begins his account with Humboldt's arrival in the United States in May of 1804; unlike Sachs, however, McCullough does not reveal Humboldt's identity until the reader has been introduced to a well-known cast of American characters. All the reader knows of the "aristocratic young German" on the first page is that he had "come to pay his respects to the president of the new republic, Thomas Jefferson, a fellow 'friend of science,' and to tell him something of his recent journeys through South and Central America. For the next several weeks he did little else but talk, while Jefferson, on their walks about the White House grounds; or James Madison, the secretary of state; or the clever Mrs. Madison; or Albert Gallatin, the secretary of the treasury; or those who came to dine in with the president or to do business with him, listened in awe" ([5], p. 3). Only after the reader is securely ensconced in the thoroughly American context does McCullough reveal on the second page that "The young man's name was Humboldt, Alexander von Humboldt—Friedrich Wilhelm Karl Heinrich Alexander von Humboldt—or Baron von Humboldt, as he was commonly addressed" ([5], p. 4). Although not even lasting six weeks, Humboldt's presence in the newly established United States and his subsequent relationship with the Founding Fathers constitute an axis around which current American historical narratives revolve.

3. Humboldt and the Founding Fathers

Recent American accounts associate Humboldt's imperative to visit the United States with his desire to meet and consult with one particular Founding Father. As Joyce Appleby succinctly puts it in her volume *Shores of Knowledge: New World Discoveries and the Scientific Imagination*: "The purpose of this final leg of their voyage was to meet the president, Thomas Jefferson [...]" ([6], p. 224). Sachs echoes Appleby's assertion in more detail: "If any particular person in the young Republic could have quieted Humboldt's wanderlust for a more prolonged period, it would probably have been Thomas Jefferson himself. President not only of the nation, but also of its foremost Philosophical Society, Jefferson seems to have been the real object of Humboldt's visit to the United States" ([3], p. 3).

Humboldt had introduced himself to Jefferson in a letter, expressing his interest in discussing some of his paleontological finds from the Andes with the president. He soon found in Jefferson a gracious and intellectually equal host. As David McCullough states: "But there they were in Washington for several days, two of the most remarkable men of their time, fellow spirits if ever there were, talking, talking endlessly, intensely, their conversation having quickly ranged far from fossil teeth" ([5], p. 4). The representation of Jefferson in many of these texts appears as a personification of the new nation itself, an embodiment of its growth, curiosity, and potential. And in accordance, Humboldt's correspondence with Jefferson has come to symbolize in many cases Humboldt's continued interest in and preoccupation with the United States. As Helferich explains: "The two men would correspond for many years, and Jefferson's high regard for Humboldt is obvious in his letters. [...] The friendship, rooted in their shared political philosophy and common love of science, would endure for more than twenty years, until Jefferson's death in 1826" ([4], p. 299). As will later be argued, however, this epistolary connection proves to be tenuous at best.

Jefferson is not the only Founding Father with ties to Humboldt, a fact that is continually underlined in the American investigations of the last 25 years. The best example of this connection between Humboldt and the revolutionary generation is provided by Walls in *Passage to Cosmos*. Like McCullough and Sachs, Walls mentions in detail Humboldt's relationship with James and Dolley Madison. Unlike her counterparts, though, Walls goes on to discuss Humboldt's consultations with other, lesser-known Founding Fathers, such as Dr. Benjamin Rush: "Over several visits with the famous physician Benjamin Rush—the obstinate and passionate reformer who had ridden to the First Continental Convention with John Adams and signed the Declaration of Independence next to Benjamin Franklin—Humboldt shared his speculations over the moral influence of New World gold and silver" ([2], p. 105). A textual connection emerges among Adams, Franklin, and the signing of the Declaration of Independence through Rush and his interactions with Humboldt. Walls again emphasizes this connection to Franklin when she notes Humboldt's activities in Philadelphia: "The members of the American Philosophical Society, the premier learned society of the United States (founded by Benjamin Franklin in 1743), adopted Humboldt as one of their own, voting him to full membership at their next meeting. [...] It was probably in the fine new building of the Library Company of Philadelphia (founded by Franklin in 1731) that Humboldt shouted for joy when he read the announcement that his irreplaceable manuscripts had arrived safely home" ([2], p. 101). Here the reader is presented with Humboldt's connection to Franklin expressed either in his membership in an organization, or in a joyous, yet merely probable, event. Some of these connections are tenuous at best, but perhaps the most interesting is the way in which Walls creates a textual connection between Humboldt and George Washington: "One day the party set off for Mount Vernon, where the visitors drank in the view while [Charles Wilson] Peale mourned for the good old days when he sat and drank with George Washington. Peale introduced Humboldt to Billy Lee, the last of Washington's slaves, who had been granted freedom and an annuity in his will" ([2], pp. 102–3). In this passage, Walls not only connects Humboldt to the central figure among the Founding Fathers, she also connects him to the most problematic and divisive element of their legacy. The establishment of such a link to the Founding Fathers and the complexities of American slavery is remarkable, to be sure, as Humboldt was a lifelong abolitionist and an ardent opponent of the slave trade in the Americas.

4. The Constitution of Convention

Perhaps the most intriguing elevation of Humboldt's visit to the United States and his relationship with Thomas Jefferson comes in the form of two recent books written by European authors for American audiences. The first volume, *Humboldt and Jefferson: A Transatlantic Friendship of the Enlightenment* by Sandra Rebok, a European scholar working out of the Spanish National Research Council in Madrid, appeared in 2014, and fits neatly into the mold of American Humboldt literature. In Rebok's account, the reader again finds Humboldt's imperative to visit the United States: "From Cuba they initially intended to return to Europe and thus conclude their expedition, but instead they took the Spanish ship *Concepción* to Philadelphia and added five weeks in the United States to their journey. As we will see, this unplanned visit would assume a special importance in Humboldt's life" ([1], p. 11). The special importance alluded to by Rebok takes the form of Humboldt's subsequent friendship and correspondence with Jefferson. Rebok identifies this relationship as being of extreme importance to both men, as well as being an exemplar of enlightened, transatlantic discourse in a cosmopolitan age. According to Rebok, Humboldt's experience in the United States and his connection to its founders was indeed formative: "He had met the Founding Fathers and architects of the first independent nation on the American continent, and he had seen for himself the functioning of the first republican institutions in the New World. This was the realization of ideals he passionately embraced" ([1], p. 31).

Although Rebok's text is irreplaceable as perhaps the most detailed and thoroughly researched account of Humboldt's visit to Philadelphia and Washington, D.C., it contains information that undermines the supposedly strong epistolary connection between Humboldt and Jefferson celebrated in the title, as well as the overall importance of Humboldt's detour to the United States. Rebok notes that Humboldt was perhaps one of the most prolific letter writers of his day, penning an estimated fifty thousand letters in his lifetime. Jefferson, although not nearly reaching Humboldt's total, still drafted some nineteen thousand letters. The number of extant letters written by the two men to one another, however, totals a mere fourteen: eight letters from Humboldt to Jefferson, and six letters from Jefferson to Humboldt ([1], pp. 53, 54). This sum certainly bespeaks neither a close and enduring friendship nor a passionate connection to an idealized state; rather it seems much more to be a sign of general good will and respectful interest on the part of both men. It is telling, for instance, that many of the succinct letters were written when the two correspondents sent, received, or requested each other's publications as a gift. Even a brief correspondence and the polite exchange of written materials can, to be sure, have a profound impact on a person's life or an intellectual environment, but there simply is no evidence in the extant textual record to suggest that such was the case between Humboldt and Jefferson. In the end, Rebok's focus seems to be at times misplaced and her study, although thoroughly researched, faces many of the same interpretational issues experienced by her American counterparts.

The second work on Humboldt by a European author for an American audience is Andrea Wulf's *The Invention of Nature: Alexander von Humboldt's New World*, published in 2015. In this—the most recent and best-selling work on Humboldt to appear in the United States over the last several decades—all of the previously mentioned American Humboldt conventions can be found. Echoing the suspenseful depictions of the stormy passage from Havana to Philadelphia crafted by Walls and Sachs, Wulf provides the following riveting account:

> It was as if the sea were about to swallow them. Huge waves rolled on to the deck and down the stairway into the belly of the ship. Humboldt's forty trunks were in constant danger of flooding. They had sailed through a hurricane and for six long days the winds would not stop, pounding the vessel with such force that they could not sleep or even think. The cook lost his pots and pans when the water came gushing in, and was swimming rather than standing in his galley. No food could be cooked and sharks circled the boat. The captain's cabin, at the ship's stern, was flooded so high that they had to swim through it, and even the most seasoned sailors were tossed across the deck like ninepins. Fearing for their lives, the sailors insisted on more brandy rations, intending, they said, to drown drunk. Each wave that rolled towards them seemed like a huge rock face. Humboldt thought that he had never been closer to death ([7], p. 94).

And all of this so that Humboldt could see with his own eyes the new country that supposedly embodied his most heartfelt political and philosophical beliefs, as well as "meet Thomas Jefferson, the third President of the United States. For five long years, Humboldt had seen nature at its best—lush, magnificent and awe-inspiring—and now he wanted to see civilization in all its glory, a society built as a republic on the principles of liberty" ([7], p. 95). Wulf also reminds the reader that it is not only Jefferson with whom Humboldt made a connection while in Philadelphia and Washington, D.C. Madison and Gallatin are also featured prominently in the narrative, along with other luminaries of the early republic. Most notably, Wulf employs a familiar literary tactic, which allows Humboldt to forge associations with Founding Fathers in absentia. In a scene reminiscent of Walls' account, Wulf describes how "Humboldt travelled to Mount Vernon, George Washington's estate, some fifteen miles south of the capital. Though Washington had died four and a half years previously, Mount Vernon was now a popular tourist destination and Humboldt wanted to see the home of the revolutionary hero" ([7], p. 101). Another way in which Wulf recapitulates American Humboldt literary convention is in her representation of the Jefferson-Humboldt correspondence. In the twelfth chapter of *The Invention of Nature*, "Revolutions and Nature: Simón Bolívar and Humboldt," Wulf presents the correspondence between Humboldt and Jefferson as a constant back and forth, in which the finer points of the Latin American independence movements were discussed in detail. With no further point of reference provided by Wulf, the Humboldt-Jefferson correspondence appears to be *the* primary source material for the political debates of the age. This implicit characterization is unfortunate, as the Latin American struggles for independence were only explicitly thematized in four letters, and often in passing. In Wulf's narrative, however, this was a passionate and important exchange, in which "the former American president, Thomas Jefferson, bombarded Humboldt with questions [...]" ([7], p. 148). In truth, a handful of questions spread out over a small number of short letters hardly constitutes a bombardment. As previously noted, the exchange of each other's written works was the primary purpose of the Humboldt-Jefferson correspondence. Here again, an otherwise thoroughly researched and responsibly constructed narrative of Humboldt's life and work overemphasizes a relatively minor event and the significance of a handful of encounters.

5. The Transcultural Synthesis of Memory

Why is it then that so much recent scholarship and popular writing published in the United States inflates the significance of Humboldt's visit to Philadelphia and Washington, D.C.? Although one might easily make charges of Americentrism or intellectual imperialism, processes of cultural memory and cultural integration are actually at work. For example, Sachs writes somewhat wistfully that: "It is tempting to wonder what Humboldt might have contributed to American politics had he moved to Washington and become an advisor to presidents instead of kings" ([3], p. 104). This statement does not advocate the explicit appropriation or annexation of Humboldt into American culture; rather it expresses much more a desire to share in Humboldt's cultural and scientific legacy. Instead of appropriation, the talk should be of incorporation. This process of incorporation can be at times a bit cumbersome and problematic, as evidenced by the exaggerated accounts in the selections above; but it is also the process by which a culture's memory adapts and reconfigures itself, so as to include a new element.

In the field of cultural memory studies, an element such as Alexander von Humboldt is best identified as a memory site. This terminology should not be understood as referring to a specific site of historical action; rather memory sites can take any number of forms, including, but not limited to, places, people, events, periods, and ideas. This distinction is essential, as cultural memory studies do not investigate actual past events per se; rather the investigation focuses on how actors in the present create representations and knowledge of the past and to what purpose. Although cultural memory "operiert [...] in beiden Richtungen: zurück und nach vorne," and "rekonstruiert nicht nur die Vergangenheit, es organisiert auch die Erfahrung der Gegenwart und Zukunft" ([8], p. 42), this is a concept that functions exclusively in the present. In other words, the remembering individual, and thereby the culture to which it belongs, is always present and active, while the event being remembered "is of the past and thus absent" ([9], p. 4).

In considering cultural memory as a process of the present, it is important to keep in mind the distinction between history and the past. History is the product of the collection and analysis of textual records of every kind, with the aim of reconstructing a realistic and accurate representation of things that have taken place. The past is also "eine kulturelle Schöpfung" ([8], p. 48), but it is not the locus of thoughtful scholarly reflection as history is thought to be; rather the past serves as a necessary, cognitive point of reference and satisfies "das kollektive Bedürfnis nach Sinnstiftung" ([10], p. 13). The past, unlike the material collections and institutions of history, "ensteht überhaupt erst dadurch, daß man sich auf sie bezieht" ([8], p. 31). In other words, the past, along with the memory sites into which the past is divided, serves as a means of orientation that guides cultural actors in the present.

If cultural memory is differentiated thus from history, the Age of Discovery or Charlemagne are as much points of reference as the Alamo or Auschwitz; and they therefore constitute memory sites "nicht dank ihrer materiellen Gegenständlichkeit, sondern wegen ihrer symbolischen Funktion. Es handelt sich um langlebige, Generationen überdauernde Kristallisationspunkte kollektiver Erinnerung und Identität, die in gesellschaftliche, kulturelle und politische Üblichkeiten eingebunden sind und die sich in dem Maße verändern, in dem sich die Weise ihrer Wahrnehmung, Aneignung, Anwendung und Übertragung verändert" ([10], p. 18). And these sites, much like the cultural memory they constitute, are contextually specific. Alexander von Humboldt memory sites exist in numerous cultures, but each Humboldt memory site interacts with each culture in a specific manner. The German Humboldt, for instance differs from the Venezuelan Humboldt, and each fulfills a different role in the respective cultures.

What then are the ways in which cultural memory functions? How is it that some things are remembered and celebrated while others are not? These questions get to the very heart of the representation and use of Alexander von Humboldt in recent American texts, as they highlight the role of forgetting in the processes of cultural memory. In addition to the aforementioned themes and conventions that pervade contemporary American Humboldt literature, Humboldt's absence from twentieth and twenty-first-century American culture forms a cornerstone of almost every Humboldt narrative published in the United States. As Sachs notes following his depiction of Humboldt's rough passage from the Caribbean to the Delaware River: "As far as the twenty-first century memory of Alexander von Humboldt is concerned, he may as well have gone down with his ship: many people have never even heard of him" ([3], p. 2). Helferich concurs with Sachs, in that "[a]lthough many North Americans have a vague sense of Humboldt's name [...] most would be hard pressed to give particulars" ([4], p. xx). The name might seem familiar to many Americans, considering the number of places and natural phenomena that have been named after Humboldt; but even this, as Appleby concludes, does not protect against cultural amnesia: "What astounds today is how little Humboldt is remembered. [...] Few great men have had their reputations fade so quickly, just leaving his name on a bay, peak, lake, current, sinkhole, penguin, lily, orchid, and oak whose namesake few remember" ([6], p. 229). This is truly astounding to McCullough, who reflects on the fact that Humboldt's "was a journey that would capture the imagination of the age, but that has been strangely forgotten in our own time. It is doubtful that one educated American in ten today could say who exactly Humboldt was or what he did, not even, possibly, in Humboldt, Iowa, or Humboldt, Kansas" ([5], p. 5). Some authors, such as Walls, do not merely lament the level of American ignorance regarding Humboldt. Indeed, she sees it as a deficiency in America's understanding of its own history that is in desperate need of correction: "That U.S. American literary and cultural studies have remained oblivious to Alexander von Humboldt is a scandal exactly equivalent to analyzing Romanticism without Goethe, naturalism without Darwin, modernism in ignorance of Einstein, or postmodernism without Heisenberg" ([2], p. x). American authors not only bemoan this absence, it serves as the stated *raison d'etre* for their work. The reintroduction of Humboldt to American culture and the recovery of Humboldt's "environmental thinking" will allow for a host of progressive cultural advances, including "a global debate over capitalism and imperial power" ([2], p. 9). Wulf alone slightly breaks with convention and reminds the American reader that not the entire world has forgotten Humboldt in the same way: "Though today almost forgotten outside of academia—at least in the English-speaking world—Alexander von Humboldt's ideas still shape our thinking. And while his books collect dust in libraries, his name lingers everywhere" ([7], p. 7).

Fittingly enough, these images of dusty libraries and tomes of neglected toponyms allude to Aleida Assmann's groundbreaking work on the role of forgetting in the processes of cultural memory. Assmann has identified two types of memory that shape a culture's understanding and representation of itself, and that are constantly engaged in dynamic interaction with one another. There is the active, or functional, memory of a culture, which is comprised of the memory sites being synthesized and utilized by a culture on a constant basis; and the stored, or saved memory of a culture. The functional memory of a culture can be thought of as a kind of canon that is continually invoked by cultural actors as a means of orientation and reference. No memory site in the functional memory of a culture may be assured of continued thematization, however, "[d]enn Kanonisierung bedeutet obendrein auch die transhistorische Selbstverpflichtung zu wiederholter Lektüre und Deutung. So bleiben die Bestände des Funktionsgedächtnisses trotz der Bewegung beschleunigter Innovation auf den Lehrplänen der Bildungsinstitutionen, auf den Spielplänen der Theater, in den Sälen der Museen, den Aufführungen der Konzerthallen und Programmen der Verlage. Was einen Platz im Funktionsgedächtnis einer Gesellschaft hat, hat Anspruch auf immer neue Aufführung, Ausstellung, Lektüre, Deutung, Auseinandersetzung" ([11], p. 56).

In contrast, the archived memory extant within a culture should be understood much more as "a storehouse for cultural relicts," in which memories "are not unmediated; they have only lost their immediate addressees; they are de-contextualized and disconnected from their former frames which had authorized them or determined their meaning" ([12], p. 99). The contents of a culture's stored memory have not lost any of their productive power; rather their creative energy has gone from kinetic to potential. To be sure, there is a constant back and forth between a culture's stored and functional memory; and this continual deactivation and reactivation "entsteht dadurch, dass die Grenze zwischen Funktions—und Speichergedächtnis nicht hermetisch ist, sondern in beiden Richtungen überschritten werden kann. Aus dem vom Willen und Bewusstsein ausgeleuchteten 'aktiven' Funktionsgedächtnis fallen beständig Elemente ins Archiv zurück, die an Interesse verlieren; aus dem 'passiven' Speichergedächtnis können neue Entdeckungen ins Funktionsgedächtnis heraufgeholt werden." ([11], p. 57). The dynamic relationship between the two forms of cultural memory provides cultural actors with an almost unlimited set of memory sites with which to work. In turn, cultural actors select, activate, and modify these memory sites based on their current needs and aspirations.

Taking all of this into consideration, the textual representations of Humboldt in the United States can be understood as an appeal to the reading public to reincorporate the Humboldt memory site into the functional memory of American culture. Time and again, these American and European authors decry Humboldt's absence as a loss, and advocate for him and his place in science to be venerated much as they were in the nineteenth century. This advocacy lays bare many of the ways in which cultural memory functions, and provides a fascinating look into the constitution of memory sites in a contemporary context. Beyond even this utility, however, the Humboldt memory site provides unprecedented insight into the potential of transcultural memory and transcultural influences on cultural memory. This investigation contends that the confluence of Humboldt representation in the literary works of American and European authors indicates the initiation of a transcultural memory site. The depictions of Humboldt in North America and Europe, and more importantly, the cultural motivations and aspirations behind those depictions, have aligned to such an extent that a transcultural space has been created in which multiple cultures can communicate about pressing needs and concerns while drawing on common points of reference. Rebok's *Humboldt and Jefferson* and Wulf's *The Invention of Nature* demonstrate this transcultural coordination most clearly, as both exemplify the ease with which textual representations of Humboldt, and the memory sites they constitute, flow back and forth from European and North American cultural discourses.

Most certainly, the litmus test of any element within cultural memory is its importance and relevance to the current conditions and needs of a given culture. Fittingly, the majority of recent Humboldt texts published in the United States and Europe present Humboldt either as a climate change activist *avant-la-lettre*, or an embodiment of Enlightenment ideals and their potential. By connecting Humboldt as securely as possible to the pantheon of the Founding Fathers and the Olympus of the early republic, these contemporary authors elevate his relevance in a way that might affect the reaction of current audiences on both sides of the Atlantic to the issues often associated with him, be it global warming or enlightened discourse. The texts investigated here demonstrate an effort, whether conscious or subconscious, coordinated or uncoordinated, toward reincorporating Humboldt back into America's active cultural memory. As Andrea Wulf states in the epilogue of *The Invention of Nature*, "now is the time for us and for the environmental movement to reclaim Alexander von Humboldt as our hero" ([7], p. 337).

Conflicts of Interest: The author declares no conflict of interest.

References

1. Rebok, Sandra. *Humboldt and Jefferson: A Transatlantic Friendship of the Enlightenment.* Charlottesville: University of Virginia Press, 2014.
2. Walls, Laura Dassow. *The Passage to Cosmos: Alexander von Humboldt and the Shaping of America.* Chicago: University of Chicago Press, 2009.
3. Sachs, Aaron. *The Humboldt Current: Nineteenth-Century Exploration and the Roots of American Environmentalism.* New York: Penguin Books, 2007.
4. Helferich, Gerard. *Humboldt's Cosmos: Alexander von Humboldt and the Latin American Journey that Changed the Way We See the World.* New York: Gotham Books, 2004.
5. McCullough, David. "Journey to the Top of the World." In *Brave Companions: Portraits in History.* New York: Simon and Schuster, 1992, pp. 3–19.
6. Appleby, Joyce. *Shores of Knowledge: New World Discoveries and the Scientific Imagination.* New York: W.W. Norton & Company, 2013.
7. Wulf, Andrea. *The Invention of Nature: Alexander von Humboldt's New World.* New York: Alfred A. Knopf, 2015.
8. Assmann, Jan. *Das kulturelle Gedächtnis: Schrift, Erinnerung und politische Identität in frühen Hochkulturen.* München: C.H. Beck, 2007.
9. Huyssen, Andreas. *Present Pasts: Urban Palimpsests and the Politics of Memory.* Stanford: Stanford University Press, 2003.
10. François, Etienne, and Hagen Schulze. "Einleitung." In *Deutsche Erinnerungsorte.* Edited by Etienne François and Hagen Schulze. München: Verlag C.H. Beck, 2001, vol. 3, pp. 9–24.
11. Assmann, Aleida. *Der lange Schatten der Vergangenheit: Erinnerungskutlur und Geschichtspolitik.* München: C.H. Beck, 2006.
12. Assmann, Aleida. "Canon and Archive." In *A Companion to Cultural Memory Studies.* Edited by Astrid Erll and Ansgar Nünning. Berlin: De Gruyter, 2010, pp. 97–108.

Article

Re-discovering Alessandro Spina's Transculture/ality in *The Young Maronite*

Arianna Dagnino

Department of French, Hispanic and Italian Studies, The University of British Columbia, Vancouver, BC V6T 1Z1, Canada; arianna.dagnino@ubc.ca; Tel.: +1-778-984-3734

Academic Editor: Bernd Fischer
Received: 16 February 2016; Accepted: 4 June 2016; Published: 9 June 2016

Abstract: Alessandro Spina, *né* Basili Shafik Khouzam, was born in Benghazi in 1927 into a family of Maronites from Aleppo and spent most of his life between Libya and Italy, speaking several languages and writing in Italian. He may be described as the "unsung" writer of Italian colonial and post-colonial past in North Africa. Spina's oeuvre—collected in an omnibus edition, *I confini dell'ombra. In terra d'oltremare* (Morcelliana)—charts the history of Libya from 1911, when Italy invaded the Ottoman province, to 1966, when the country witnessed the economic boom sparked by the petrodollars. The cycle was awarded the Premio Bagutta, Italy's highest literary accolade. In 2015, Darf Press published in English the first instalment of Spina's opus with the title *The Confines of the Shadows. In Lands Overseas*. Spina always refused to be pigeonholed in some literary category and to be labeled as a colonial or postcolonial author. As a matter of fact, his works go beyond the spatial and imaginary boundaries of a given state or genre, emphasizing instead the mixing and collision of languages, cultures, identities, and forms of writing. Reading and re-discovering Spina in a transcultural mode brings to light the striking newness of his literary efforts, in which transnational lived life, creative imagination, and transcultural sensibility are inextricably interlaced.

Keywords: transculturality; transcultural novels; world literature; Italian literature; Libya; colonialism; mobility; identity; unbelonging; translation

1. Introduction

Writers with a neo-nomadic penchant, with complex cultural orientations, or engaged in transnational exchanges have become increasingly visible in the past decades. Such authors eschew former narrow identitarian labeling, such as (im)migrant, colonial, postcolonial, ethnic, Commonwealth, or minority writers and can no longer be considered to belong primarily to a single (or original) national framework. In a previous study [1], I explored what makes a writer a "transcultural" writer in this age of growing transnational movements taking place on many levels, from people and groups to global media and cultural products. The definition I came up with may well apply to writers of past ages as well as to Alessandro Spina, a contemporary Syrian author who became a naturalized Italian citizen. Indeed, Spina can be included in that loose category of writers "on the move" whose sense of identity and belonging—rooted in a complex mix of linguistic and cultural declinations—takes multiple trajectories and reflects itself in their narratives. In this article, I set out to reveal Spina's transcultural disposition, its development through cultural encounters and processes of "transpatriation" ([1], p. 4), and its re-enactment in the form of transcultural narratives. For this purpose, I will analyze in detail Spina's novel *The Young Maronite* [2] and expose its relation with the author's lived experience, acquired transcultural sensibility, and extended body of work.

2. From Transculturation to Transculture/ality

My use of the term "transculture/ality", which expands Fernando Ortiz's [3] original notion of "transculturation" by combining Mikhail Epstein's concept of "transculture" ([4], p. 49) and Wolfgang Welsch's concept of "transculturality" [5], provides this article with its theoretical framework. We can think of transculturality [5] as the analytical model through which one can give account of the cultural dynamics and the creative expressions happening in highly mobile individuals "out of the narrow national and regional boundaries" ([6], p. 45). And we can think of "transculture" as "the freedom of every person to live on the border of one's 'inborn' culture or beyond it" ([7], p. 334). Thus, transculture/ality ([1], pp. 113–14) rests on the idea that individuals may find a mode of identity formation as well as of creative expression which goes beyond the conventions and obsessions of identity politics and the exclusive dimension of national identity. What makes cultures interesting, as Edward W. Said stated ([8], p. 15), is not their purity but their reciprocal enmeshing, mutual influences, and constant processes of borrowing and border-crossing (even when they are witnessing unbalanced power relations).

Working at the level of the individual, transculture/ality takes on a plurality of forms (as many forms as there are individuals); as such, it is a dimension which can be accessed by multiple entry points and engaged in different ways and circumstances. This transcultural dimension, or "transplace" ([1], p. 199), may be understood as an all-inclusive space of subjective consciousness and cultural possibilities which does not deny the formative importance of native cultures—and, to some extent, their accompanying worldviews—but at the same time allows an openness to the reception, integration, and negotiation of other cultures. I suggest that those writers who inhabit the transplace have previously undergone a "transpatriation" process ([1], p. 4). This process, which is the result of physical and symbolic movement through and embedding in deep and diverse cultural contexts, allows individuals to adopt new ways of self-identification. While leading to the formation of multifaceted identities, it also facilitates the development of a transcultural lens, "a perspective in which all cultures look decentered in relation to all other cultures, including one's own" ([9], p. 312). Calling this process of becoming transcultural "transpatriation" emphasizes the importance of moving beyond one's own culture, as well as of overcoming—or, better, "unlearning"—ways of identity formation strongly dependent on ethnicity, nationality, locality, or religious affiliation.

Finally, transculture/ality may lead to or may work in conjunction with its ensuing ethical (rather than ideological) stance: "a will to interact starting from the intersections rather than from the polarities and differences, a consciousness of the transcultural that is in us to better comprehend and accept what is outside of us, a vision that privileges flexibility and fluidity, movement and ongoing exchange, the constant re-negotiation of identity" ([6], p. 44). Though individualist in perspective, transculture/ality should not, however, be seen as a (somewhat natural) extension of the traditional liberal understanding of the individual. A transcultural disposition is rather to be seen as a socially mediated "process of subjectivity" that disengages itself from the conventional concept of individualism and asserts the difference-in-unity of mankind—that is the undeniable singularity, fluidity, but also interrelatedness of any self-constituting being as part of a "collective enterprise" ([10], p. 7).

To summarize, transculture/ality provides individuals: (a) a mode of identity formation; (b) a dimension of cultural belonging and artistic expression (the transplace); (c) an analytical tool to better capture the interplay between culture/s and the works of a globalizing imagination; and (d) a strategy of cultural resistance to the exclusive dimension of national/ethnic identity, to the homogenizing pressure (including the standardization of literary taste) imposed by corporate global culture, and to the isolating effects of current multicultural policies. As Epstein claims, in relation to our present, transculture "differs from both leveling globalism and isolating pluralism" ([7], p. 327).

3. What is a Transcultural Writer and what is a Transcultural Novel?

In a nutshell, a transcultural writer is a writer who, by undergoing a transpatriation process, has developed a transcultural sensibility and expresses it through her or his writing. It is impossible to measure and thus quantify aspects such as sensitivities, imaginaries, or outlooks in a literary work. Nevertheless, these impalpable elements are revealed (and thus made detectable) in the choice of themes, characters, voice, setting, as well as in the use of dialogue, plot construction, or language performed by individual authors. Those writers who move outside their own native cultures or homelands tend to defy conventional categorizations: as with their works, their complex and fluid nature seems to dispel any attempt to pin them down, to fit them into any kind of defining box, even the most flexible and sophisticated one.

The main question thus becomes: Can we think of Spina in terms of a transcultural writer? In my book *Transcultural Writers and Novels in the Age of Global Mobility* ([1], p. 183), I came up with an initial list of elements that exemplify the tight connection between lived experience and creative/fiction narratives on the transcultural frontier. Those authors who, by virtue of their transnational and culturally errant status, write across cultures or with an eye to the dynamics of cultural encounters and negotiations, tend to: (a) set their novels in more than one country. Most importantly, though, foreign settings (but foreign to whom? we might ask) are not used as exotic stereotypes functional to the growing market of global mass fiction—the so-called "postcolonial exotic" [11]; (b) create characters coming from more than one cultural background or who are immersed in more than one culture; (c) display a proliferation of narrating voices and tell a story from "a multiplicity of perspectives" ([12], p. 257); (d) work in more than one linguistic code and narrative genre, thereby creating texts characterized by a mix of linguistic/cultural spaces and genres; (e) write in a way and express things in such a way that it is difficult for a reader to understand (or infer), without knowing their complex biographies, to what nationality/cultural community/ethnic group they belong; in other words, they tend to undermine "habitual classification of literary texts in terms of national or regional literatures" ([12], p. 251).

These elements tend to be common features of transcultural prose fiction; yet, they do not need to be present at the same time in the same novel for it to be defined as transcultural. The next section of this article therefore reviews some of these constitutive transcultural elements in order to analyze to what extent they inhabit Spina's lived experience and literary output. For the purpose of illustration, and due to space limits, this will be done by focusing on a close reading of Spina's novel *The Young Maronite*, published for the first time in Italian in 1971 with the title *Il giovane maronita* [13].

Before applying myself to the task, though, I wish to make a preliminary remark. As writers, readers, or critics, we are all somewhat defined by our own cultural and historical specificity, which—in addition—often changes with time and circumstances. We are all situated in time, space, and culture. Sharing the view that identities are inherently multiple in nature and constantly shifting, is not a new concept, although it has been interpreted and assumed differently according to different locations, intellectual contexts, and time periods. The way I/we may interpret a work of fiction through a transcultural lens is certainly influenced by our *Zeitgeist*, characterized by increased global mobility and cultural flows. Moreover, my perspective is inevitably situated in my being one of those scholars and creative writers living in the West and able to freely move across countries, cultures, and languages. As Said clarifies, "the real intellectual is a secular being" and as such is situated in society whereby his or her "morality" is influenced by "where it takes place, whose interests it serves, how it jibes with a consistent and universalist ethic, how it discriminates between power and justice, what it reveals of one's choices and priorities" ([14], p. 120).

With Said's warning in mind, what follows is not meant to be a celebration of what some might perceive as privileged lifestyles or elitist literary attitudes and theorizations, but as an effort to analyze the combined effects of transnational mobility and cultural globalization in the development of a specific form of transcultural writing. At the dawn of what Peter Burke sees as a "new form of cultural order", what mostly matters is the need to find new interpretive keys and theoretical frameworks, together with a new terminology, that may prove better suited to the analysis of an emerging transcultural literature ([15], p. 115). What follows is just an attempt in this direction.

4. Alessandro Spina, World Literature and his Own Time

Alessandro Spina, *né* Basili Shafik Khouzam, was born in Benghazi in 1927 into a family of Maronites from Aleppo, Syria and spent most of his life between Libya and Italy, speaking several languages (including Arabic, French and English) and mostly writing in Italian. He might be described as the "unsung" writer of Italian colonial and post-colonial past in North Africa. In 2007, the Italian publisher Morcelliana managed to publish his works in an omnibus edition, *I confini dell'ombra. In terra d'oltremare* [16]. A year later, the cycle, which comprises six novels, a novella and four collections of stories, was awarded the Premio Bagutta, Italy's highest literary accolade. This recognition, however, was not enough to put Spina on Italy's literary map: till today, only a limited number of readers, scholars, and literary critics know and have studied his work. In 2015 and three years after Spina's death, the poet André Naffis-Saheli produced the English translation of the first instalment (containing three novels—*The Young Maronite*, *The Marriage of Omar*, and *The Nocturnal Visitor*) of *The Confines of the Shadows* [17]. Hopefully, this will help to let Spina's genius out of the limiting bottle of Italian national literature and reach its due place into the wider realm of world literature.

In its broad generalization, world literature encompasses literary texts which are coming from different cultural and linguistic traditions and are able to cross national and cultural borders. David Damrosch views world literature as constituted by "all literary works that circulate beyond their culture of origin, either in translation or in their original language" ([17], p. 4). From the viewpoint proposed by Debjani Ganguly, this also means thinking of world literature as a literary territory "where the journeys are multi-linear and where literary capital can be found in works that are locally inflected and have both regional and global purchase" ([18], p. 26). In this light, the terrain of world literature has grown to progressively include a greater number of those transcultural works which by crossing borders and by going beyond their countries of origin challenge a way of studying literatures grounded in national traditions.

Spina's oeuvre is a colonial epic that charts the history of Libya from 1911, when Italy invaded the Ottoman province, to 1966, when the country witnessed the economic boom sparked by petrodollars. The first instalment is set during the initial Italian conquest and early occupation of the Ottoman province and it covers the years from 1911 to 1927. The other two instalments focus on the brief golden age of the Italian colony, in the 1930s, and on the period of independence leading up to Gadhafi's bloodless coup against King Idris in 1969. The dramatic social and political transformations the country went through in less than a century reverberate to this day and are a stern reminder of the multiple issues (from ethnic rivalry to lack of internal power structures) that any colonial conquest leaves in its wake.

Spina's body of work is intimately rooted in the transpatriation process he underwent, affecting the way he saw and fictionally described the world around him. As a writer, Spina always refused to be pigeonholed in some literary category; most of all—and rightly so—he refused to be labeled as a colonial or postcolonial author. Indeed, his works look past the spatial and imaginary boundaries of a given nation, ethnic group, or genre, emphasizing instead the mixing and collision of languages, cultures, identities, worldviews, and forms of writing. In doing so, they foster a more nuanced understanding of the complexities of identity-formation processes, especially when these happen in diverse transnational and cross-cultural frameworks.

5. Transcultural Elements in Spina's *The Young Maronite*

The Young Maronite is the opening novel in Spina's Cyrenaican saga. The novel is an existential and cultural examination of identity set against the backdrop of Italy's colonial past, in a time when Ottomans, Arabs, Berbers, and Italians found themselves, willy-nilly, living under the same north African sky and, most often than not, under the same roofs. It almost starts like a sort of dark Oriental tale, with a disfigured ogre (a powerful merchant) and his 12-year-old new wife; it develops into the tragic story of two young lovers; and it reaches its climax by plunging itself into the midst of modern Libyan history, exposing the "forgotten" pages of Italian colonization in Northern Africa.

Spina was particularly critical of the silence with which both Italian political factions—the left and the right—always carpeted the country's colonial crimes. During the first phase of the Libyan occupation, starting from 1929 and onwards, more than 100,000 people were deported to several concentration camps in Eastern Libya to deny the rebels the support of the local population. Tens of thousands died in those camps, mainly of disease and starvation ([19], p. 48).

In *The Young Maronite* Spina is mostly interested in analyzing the moment in which Europeans crossed the Mediterranean again after the time of the crusades and the social disruption this new age of invasion caused. The Italian presence in Libya and in the Horn of Africa produced a distinct, although rather sparse, Italian colonial literature [20] and an even more limited post-colonial literature. Although Italy's influence in the African continent extends well beyond the brief timespan of the former Italian Empire, the "writing back" by authors from Ethiopia, Libya, Somalia, or Eritrea has been small in comparison to that coming from the English-, French-, and Spanish-speaking areas of other former European colonial empires [21]. Within a literary context, the Italian post-colonial aftermath has certainly more to do with those writers who in the last two decades immigrated to Italy from its former colonies thus contributing to the establishment of an Italian (im)migrant literature. According to Ali Mumin Ahad, "for writers from Mussolini's 'place in the sun', Italian literature is marked by the absence of any authentically post-colonial form of expression proper to itself, as it cannot rely on any interest in post-colonial studies understood as a form of artistic expression that is at one and the same time critical reappraisal and analysis of the present-day consequences of the colonial past both in Italy and in the former colonies" ([21], p. 4). As Ursula Lindsey states, "Spina was a product of the Italian colony—he owed it his education and his inspiration, what he called his *destino*" [22]. As such, his interest as a writer lay in capturing "the twisted logic of colonialism past and present, which to justify itself first insists on a fundamental difference between 'us' and 'them', and then insists on annihilating that difference" [22].

I will now proceed by discussing in more detail some of the fundamental transcultural elements of *The Young Maronite*.

5.1. Transnational Locations

The year is 1912 and Italy has just begun its colonial enterprise in North Africa, wrestling Libya's eastern province of Cyrenaica from the Ottoman Empire. The story unfolds in the harbor city of Benghazi. From time to time, however, the narration shifts to Italian locales. Some of the most intriguing and revealing dialogues take place in a villa and at a theatre club in an undefined location in Lombardy. These are the settings in which Italian grand dames discuss the newly acquired colony and its future with Colonel Romanino, who is on a mission to find a suitable *buen retiro* for his friend and brother in arms Captain Martello. In the course of the narrative, several references are also made to Istanbul—the city where two other characters (Hajji Semereth Effendi and "the Venetian") spent a previous chapter of their lives—and to Sicily, the island to which Libyan soldiers who had enrolled in the Italian colonial Infantry (Fanteria Libia) were sent for their training. Despite this territorial heterogeneity, Spina is not prone to use foreign locations as exotic stereotypes but rather as settings best suited to the issues he intends to address and the themes he set out to develop. In the case of the *Young Maronite*, the writer is keen to explore issues related to patriotism, nationalist propaganda, cultural stereotyping, honesty/duplicity, multiple selves, loyalty, belonging, and sense of estrangement.

5.2. Characters Endowed with a Cross-Cultural Background and Destiny

The main character in the first act of Spina's Cyrenaican saga is undoubtedly Émile Chebas, a young and ambitious merchant from Aleppo who has just landed in Benghazi with his first cargo of goods from Alexandria. Once we get through the first pages, however, we quickly realize that other characters are as much relevant to the story as the young Maronite. The first one is the rich and powerful Turkish merchant Hajji Semereth Effendi, an imposing figure whose somber past makes him somewhat "larger than life" ([2], p. 27). Readers soon learn that prior to his fall in disgrace—leading to his exile in the backwater of Benghazi—Hajji was a high public officer of the Ottoman Empire in Istanbul. Another central character of the novel is Captain Martello, an Italian army officer who goes missing in Africa. Despite (or maybe precisely because of) his disappearance at the very beginning of the book, his ghost looms over the colonial horizon like a haunting moral compass. Another seemingly marginal character, the Venetian—a repudiated woman of Italian origin who followed Hajj from Istanbul as a housekeeper—plays a fundamental role in the way the plot develops towards its tragic end.

One cannot but notice how the various cultural and linguistic features most of the characters display reflect their author's hybrid identity and transnational destiny. On several occasions, in Spina's works we encounter protagonists who, more or less consciously and/or willingly, are engaged in getting accustomed and, possibly, adapting to changing geographies, perspectives, and socio-cultural contexts. In *The Young Maronite* in particular, Spina gives us insightful accounts of how individuals react when another culture poses a challenge to their identity. Most revealingly, he lingers on those characters more prone to steer away from common and debilitating group dynamics based on the "us and them" dichotomy. In this regard, Colonel Romanino's comment while conversing with Signora Ferrara is exemplary: "You're afraid ... of individual logic and experience. But our last hopes rest precisely on the individual. This is the moment to love Salvation more than the Motherland" ([2], p. 33).

5.3. A Proliferation of Points of View

Readers get often lost in Spina's plurivocal mazes. The author is a master at aptly shifting the point of view from one character to the other. One is never certain from which visual angle the story is being seen and from which perspective is being narrated. We move on shifting sands here. Nothing is given for granted nor for certain. Each personality represents a fascinating and complex conundrum. Most of the characters in the *Young Maronite* discover that their identity is not what it seems to others and is never so clear-cut as the others would like it to be. This contributes to enriching the inner complexity and contradictory nature of the narrative and to generating a destabilizing effect. It is as if the author's plural identities and points of view were dispersed among his characters, with their multiple voices, making it impossible to distinguish a single, reliable authorial standpoint. This aspect resonates with Brian Castro's reasoning when discussing with Karen Barker the voice assumed by his culturally hybridized characters: "Their métissage opens up a multiplicity of views and worlds which are not only new to homogenous cultures but which embody an open secret, an overt mystery which is ungraspable by those cultures, not because it is a mystery per se in the end, but because uniform cultures are so blind" ([23], p. 246).

Hajji, for example, is perceived by the local community as a man whose words and opinions always sound "ambiguous" ([2], p. 38) despite the fact that his life deeds will show he is, after all, a man of integrity who answers his own inner moral compass, even when this means falling and being chased from paradise ([2], p. 64). In the eyes of the reader he may appear a real "monster"—an adjective used by the same author to describe him ([2], p. 41)—who has no scruples in marrying a terrified 12-year-old girl, who—although repelling him—will become the youngest of his four wives. But who is the real monster in the end? Is it Hajji Semereth, who agrees to let his child bride grow into a woman before claiming his husband's rights and who is even willing to cover up her infidelity with the young and handsome Ferdinando (an orphan whom Hajji had rescued from a destiny of misery)? Or is it Hajji's nephew, who—going against Hajji's wish to forgive and save the two lovers—decides to kill them and thus avenge the family's honor? De facto—and according to the group logic of the natives—forgiving such a sacrilege "might unleash a host of terrible consequences: there would be less to fear from Ferdinando's [and Zulfa's] death than from his absolution. The world would become drearier and gloomier, but at least it wouldn't be turned upside down" ([2], p. 64).

In a similar fashion, we are exposed to Captain Martello's ambivalent disposition and identity dualism. The Italian officer is not only portrayed as the military representative of a colonial power, the aggressive agent of an expeditionary force. He is also someone who feels uncomfortable in his role as a colonizer, someone who is fascinated by the unknown Other and naively tries to develop a connection, finding only rejection and silence among the natives. He is a man torn between his sense of duty as an imperial military officer and his desire to get to know and be embedded in another culture. The dignity and the humanity that transpire from the enemy (for example, the troubling event of the Turkish soldier who kisses the beautiful face of a dead Italian young lieutenant) nurture the captain's respect towards his opponents and thus throw him in a state of doubt in regard to the whole colonial enterprise. According to the discerning description given by Signora Ferrara, Captain Martello is a man who, despite having a past "so similar to ours . . . has been to mysterious places where he's made new acquaintances or been dramatically deprived of certainties so familiar to us" ([2], p. 33). Later on, a fellow officer will confirm Signora Ferrara's shrewd reflection on the captain's unacknowledged wish to force his way into Libyan culture and his subsequent emotional derangement: "But what estranged him from us? Encountering a world governed by different laws, the legitimacy of such a society, the irredeemable sin of our attempt to destroy it? It's as if he'd stumbled into an opera house for the first time in his life and was confronted with a reality that followed its own rules: Instead of sitting back and enjoying the show, he suffered an identity crisis and could no longer draw any comfort from being a spectator" ([2], p. 216).

In one way or another, most of the characters in the novel are made to feel outsiders, and most of the time in more than one way. If it is true that Captain Martello and Colonel Romanino feel alienated among the native population of the Libyan colony, then, after their "long descent to that Underworld" (*i.e.*, Africa seen from the Italian shores), they have also become "estranged" in their native Italy ([2], pp. 33, 37). Again, it is Signora Ferrara who perceptively uncovers Colonel Romanino's true emotional state: "he feels like a stranger here, as though . . . he too, like Captain Martello, had been subjected to unbearable apparitions that now make his sweet Lombardy as incoherent and random as a nightmare" ([2], p. 33). One even gets to wonder, again through an outsider's point of view, who is the colonized and who is the colonizer in this complex identity canopy—the Arab rebels who, "as nimble as acrobats", resist the foreigner's invasion; or the Italian soldiers, barricaded within the city walls of few, well-defended coast locations, too afraid to venture in that "vast, obscure country stretching out before [them]" ([2], p. 36)? Hajji himself feels estranged in his Cyrenaican exile so far away from his native Istanbul and lost paradise: "A guarded man, who spent many years in a faraway place and only partially belonged to the city, seeming to dwell in another place altogether" ([2], p. 64). Hajji's estrangement is reiterated further on: "He was living in a different dimension to Benghazi's other residents, and his detachment from them was thereby accentuated" ([2], p. 46). Although in different terms, even Zulfa, Hajji's child bride, experiences her share of estrangement the moment she is forced to leave her childhood behind and enter Hajji's homestead: "It was as though she had got lost in an unknown country, armed with a language known only to her" ([2], p. 40).

Only Emile, the young Maronite, seems to have found his peace and stability in an in-between and neutral cultural space of "unbelonging", of positive or wise estrangement in which even a felt sense of exclusion can be used in one's favor as a point of strength instead of as a weakness. This clarifies the rhetorical question Hajji asks himself while watching the confident and tranquil way in which Emile converses with his guests upon his return from a trip to Egypt: "He was a Christian, like the invaders, and yet spoke the Arabic like the Libyans. Both factions would consider him one of their own. Would he experience this duality as a mark of unassailable foreignness, or use it as a talisman, a source of strength?" ([2], p. 61) Emile's state of "unbelonging" opens up onto a privileged, perhaps already transcultural, intellectual and psychological dimension where one is able to feel quietly *in place*, rather than constantly *out of place*, and in which "numerous, and contradicting, possibilities [can] co-exist" ([2], p. 160). This individualized, possibly transcultural state allows to reconcile in oneself even the most ingrained binary group oppositions—foreigners *versus* natives, Christians *versus* Muslims, colonizers *versus* colonized.

5.4. A Complex Mix of Linguistic Codes and Narrative Genres

The *Young Maronite* is exemplary in showing to what extent Spina likes to mix and play with literary genres and stylistic registers, to the point that it is hard to define it as simply *a novel*. In it, Spina breezily mixes real facts with fictions, documentary data with the works of the imagination, the personal and the fantastic with modern Libyan history. The writer finds no problem in interspersing his fictionalized narrative with excerpts from articles published in Italian and French newspapers of the time; with official documents (proclaims, ordinances, royal decrees) released by the Italian Government; with accurate recounts of the Cyreneican colonial enterprise provided by British, French, or Italian historians; with the content of posters affixed by Arab insurgents on the walls of Libyan towns; or with *surahs* from the Koran. It must be noted, however, that André Naffis-Sahely, who did the English translation, omitted translating all the above-mentioned documents in order to give a smoother pace to the narrative and "keep the flow of Spina's prose unimpeded" [22]. This "fairly daring choice", as Naffis-Sahely himself described it, may be questionable but undoubtedly in its English amended translation *The Young Maronite* has acquired a new lightness and greater readability ([24], p. 367). Space and content restrictions do not allow a thorough discussion of the translator's choices, omissions and possible alterations in allowing Spina's voice to be heard in English. Due to its complexity and the ethical issues (in particular in regard to what Rodica Dimitriu calls "ethic ambivalence") it raises, this discussion requires further investigation [25].

Spina also likes to play with different registers. Occasionally, he construes his dialogues as if the characters were on stage, reciting lines in a play. In those instances, the language is dignified, solemn, as if the reader had been magically transposed in the midst of a Greek tragedy. At other times, the narration takes almost the form of a moral fable, even expressing a rule of behavior—in cases like these, the reference to *The One Thousand and One Nights* is almost formulaic. It happens for example when a wealthy merchant meets Emile to intercede on behalf of Armand, the young Maronite's brother. At the firm, with his careless and sometimes irresponsible attitude towards work, Armand had openly challenged Emile, thus embittering their relationship. After the merchant has successfully extracted a promise that Émile will forgive his brother and treat him more kindly in the future, he takes his leave with these words: "Criticise your own faults and weaknesses with the same vigor you apply to Armand's. One must measure oneself against perfection, not other people's mistakes" ([2], p. 107).

5.5. The Art of Unbelonging

Having made his home in an imaginary place at the intersection of Europe and the Middle East, Spina is hardly classifiable using traditional national or ethnic literary categories. He may thus better fit within that loose set of transcultural authors who wander across national and literary boundaries and whose identities cannot be reduced to nationalities. Let us just think, for example, of writers such as Paul Bowles, with his Moroccan acquired pedigree; of Marguerite Yourcenar, who devoted herself to spiritual and intellectual journeys across the Mediterranean; or of Jorge Luis Borges, who relished in his multifarious cultural vagrancies.

Spina was of Syrian descent but wrote and published in Italian. He was educated in Italy but spent most of his adult and professional life in Libya, speaking fluent Arabic and French while running the family textile business. While in Italy, he befriended Italian writers and poets (from Alberto Moravia to Cristina Campo), but his real writers of reference—from Proust to Joseph Conrad, from Thomas Mann to Robert Musil, from the medieval itinerant scholar Ibn Khaldun to the great Libyan writer Ibrahim al-Koni, from the fifth-century Greek philosopher-cum-bishop Synesius of Cyrene to Joseph Conrad—are to be found across many ages and many borders.

In his books Spina was not concerned with and did not delve into all those provincial lives and stories happening within the confines of the Italian peninsula. His scope was much wider and embraced the whole southern Mediterranean. Although writing in Italian, one senses he culturally and stylistically did not rely upon the limiting space of the Italian literary system.

All this partly explains why it was difficult for Spina to find proper recognition within the 20th century Italian literary canon. Whereas his complex sentence structure resonates with the 19th century German development of the philosophical novel, his choice of words seems to contain something of the poetic elements, elaborate forms, and layers of metaphor found in Arabic literature. Let us take, for example, the sentence *"come la caccia*, la strage passa leggera" ([13], p. 33)—in Italian it sounds beautifully lyrical (in this case, unfortunately, and in spite of Naffis-Saheli's refined ability with words, its English translation does not seem able to fully convey its poetic resonance: *"like hunting*—and massacres are taken lightly" ([2], p. 35).

In other instances, however, and despite the fact that "his sharp, poetic images lodge instantly in one's memory", Spina's way of conflating prose and poetry is not always that effective (at least in the Italian original text) [22]. For post-war Italian writers and readers, his writing style may be perceived as overtly elegiac and polished. Moreover, the conversations among merchants, married couples, Italian officers, or other representatives of the Italian community feel unconvincingly cerebral, stylized, and excessively eloquent. Above all, Spina's elliptical descriptions and dense, erudite sentences often prove hard to follow, "demanding to be reread" [22]. Nonetheless, as Ursula Lindsey states, "the originality of Spina's vision, the strength of his voice, compensates for the occasional longueur" [22]. Although stylistically Spina's work suffers from this fairly self-conscious, pre-meditated narrative and split literary register, its historical and cultural insightfulness makes up for it. Having a chance to explore how occupiers operated and conquered their territory, how they imposed rules or bent to local customs has much to teach us about the present day. In this regard, the 2015 English translation of the *Confines of the Shadow* seems particularly timely. As the writer Hisham Matar stated when asked about Spina's work, "What's happening in Libya is tragic but also baffling to a lot of people, not least of all Libyans. I think that returning to these works, returning to history as it were, and understanding that the present is very much a symptom of that past is very valuable and so, notwithstanding my literary criticism of some of [its] aspects, [Spina's work] does feel like a gift" [26].

In his youth and throughout his adult life, Spina underwent several transpatriation processes which led him to outgrow the culture in which he was raised, to embrace other cultures and, ultimately to transcend all of them. This made him simultaneously an insider and an outsider of the cultures in and with which he worked. Petra Rüdiger and Konrad Gross describe this position as the one of "an intimate insider and a determined outsider" ([27], p. xi), I prefer to describe this position as the one of the "outlier" rather than of the outsider—not of the one being (or willing to be) kept out of the group, but of the one who, having transcended various cultural, ethnic, religious, or territorial lines of demarcation ends up having a sense of "unbelonging" or of "belonging among the unbelonging", wherever he or she is. I open here a small parenthesis to elucidate my way of using the term "unbelonging". The writer Dubravka Ugresic has adopted the term unbelonging in her book *Europe in Sepia* when talking about "the intoxication of belonging (to a home, a homeland, a country, a faith) and the trauma of unbelonging" ([28], p. 204). In a personal email exchange, the writer Inez Baranay has provided a different nuance to the concept of unbelonging, which adheres to a transcultural viewpoint: "the transcultural is a theoretical arena, in which the company is fine with a sense of belonging among the unbelonging" [29].

By reading Spina's works, it seems impossible to fit him within a single, fixed national cartography and identify the cultural/national context he and most of his characters speak from. It is as if his novels were set in a metaphorical or mental transplace—a transcultural territory (or, perhaps, a dimension) which can still be the homeland, the adopted land, or one's country of residence, but where one nonetheless gets to feel a sort of intellectual or imaginary detachment from that well-known reality. Even when writing within an explicit Western canon, Spina still does it from a different perspective, as if he was thriving "on the fascination of the stranger's gaze" ([30], p. 248). This, it may be argued, is another reflection of the author's physical, cultural, and identity mobility, of his transient state of unbelonging—or belonging regardless.

As a result of all that has been said so far, *The Young Maronite* does not allow its readers to easily discern the author's nationality. At the most, Spina's readers may sense the author's underlying debt to an imagined (and possibly questionable) Western literary tradition but they would not be able to actually detect his ethnicity, nationality, cultural belonging(s), or religious view(s).

6. Conclusions

The Young Maronite clearly shows us to what extent Spina is willing—and able—to cross the fault-lines between cultures and societies—what Maurizio Ascari defines a "transcultural desire" ([31], pp. 3–4). Indeed, rooted in Spina's transcultural sensibility is a wish for and negotiation of difference. By acting as a "bridge writer", Spina is constantly operating in the mode of a cultural translator, going back and forth from one culture to the other, recognizing that each culture is the bearer of a cognitive and cultural tradition which has an effect on the other culture and vice versa, even in unbalanced power relations. As Anne Holden Rønning suggests: "No one can live in another country or culture, or read extensively about other cultures, without being influenced and affected by it" ([32], p. 5). This work of interpretation undeniably shows "the performative power of literature to cross cultural barriers and weave a network of connections, for in a way all good works of literature are transcultural" ([33], p. 6).

Reading and re-discovering Spina in a transcultural mode brings to light the striking newness of his literary efforts, in which lived transnational life, literary imagination, and transcultural sensibility are inextricably interlaced. The main element that characterizes Spina as a transcultural writer and distinguishes him from his "cousin species" (migrant/diasporic/exile/postcolonial writers) is his relaxed attitude when facing issues linked to identity, nationality, rootlessness and dislocation. It is an attitude acquired through a more or less (sub)conscious process of transpatriation, which reflects itself also in his narratives. Writers such as Spina can thus truly act as cultural mediators between otherness and identity, two terms that in transcultural terms should be intended as complementary rather than simply opposed. It is not only a question—or not any more—of how Westerners see Others, but also of how Others see Westerners and the rest of the world.

For this reason, Spina's works can unmistakably be inscribed within transcultural literature, a literature (part of the wider republic of world literature) able to transcend the borders of a single culture in its choice of topic, vision and scope. As humans, we are constantly in search of ways to relate to each Other and to constantly adapt to changing societal patterns. Stemming from and describing processes of cultural negotiation and translation, transcultural literature may contribute to an increased global awareness and a wider sense of solidarity, thus ensuring the continuity of societies, as it has done throughout time.

Conflicts of Interest: The author declares no conflict of interest.

References

1. Arianna Dagnino. *Transcultural Writers and Novels in the Age of Global Mobility.* West Lafayette: Purdue University Press, 2015.
2. Alessandro Spina. "The Young Maronite." In *The Confines of the Shadow. In Lands Overseas.* Translated by André Naffis-Sahely. London: Darf Publishers, 2015, pp. 21–221.
3. Fernando Ortiz. *Cuban Counterpoint: Tobacco and Sugar.* Translated by Harriet de Onís. New York: Knopf, 1947.
4. Mikhail N. Epstein. "The Unasked Question: What Would Bakhtin Say? " *Common Knowledge* 10 (2004): 42–60. [CrossRef]
5. Wolfgang Welsch. "Transculturality: The Puzzling Form of Cultures Today." In *Spaces of Culture: City-Nation-World.* Edited by Mike Featherstone and Scott Lash. London: Sage, 1999, pp. 194–213.
6. Sabrina Brancato. "Transculturalità e Transculturalismo. I Nuovi Orizzonti Dell'identità Culturale." *Le Simplegadi*, 2004. Available online: http://all.uniud.it/simplegadi/wp-content/uploads/2004/Brancato_Simplegadi_2.pdf (accessed on 13 January 2016).

7. Mikhail N. Epstein. "Transculture: A Broad Way between Globalism and Multiculturalism." *American Journal of Economics & Sociology* 68 (2009): 327–51. [CrossRef]
8. Edward W. Said. *Culture and Imperialism*. London: Vintage, 1993.
9. Ellen E. Berry, and Mikhail N. Epstein, eds. "In Place of a Conclusion: Transcultural Dialogue." In *Transcultural Experiments: Russian and American Models of Creative Communication*. New York: St. Martin's, 1999, pp. 302–22.
10. Rosi Braidotti. *Metamorphoses: Towards a Materialist Theory of Becoming*. Cambridge: Polity, 2002.
11. Graham Huggan. *The Postcolonial Exotic: Marketing the Margins*. London: Routledge, 2001.
12. Mark Stein. "The Location of Transculture." In *Transcultural English Studies: Theories, Fictions, Realities*. Edited by Frank Schulze-Engler and Sissy Helff. Amsterdam: Rodopi, 2009, pp. 251–66.
13. Alessandro Spina. *Il Giovane Maronita*. Milano: Rusconi, 1971.
14. Edward W. Said. *Representations of the Intellectual: The 1993 Reith Lectures*. London: Vintage, 1996.
15. Peter Burke. *Cultural Hybridity*. Cambridge: Polity, 2009.
16. Alessandro Spina. *I Confini Dell'ombra*. Brescia: Morcelliana, 2007.
17. David Damrosch. *What Is World Literature?* Princeton: Princeton University Press, 2003.
18. Debjani Ganguly. "Global Literary Refractions: Reading Pascale Casanova's The World Republic of Letters in the Post-Cold War Era." In *Literature for Our Times: Postcolonial Studies in the Twenty-First Century*. Edited by Bill Ashcroft, Ranjini Mendis, Julie McGonegal and Arun Mukherjee. Amsterdam: Rodopi, 2012, pp. 15–35.
19. Anna Baldinetti. *The Origins of the Libyan Nation: Colonial Legacy, Exile and the Emergence of a New Nation-State*. New York: Routledge, 2014.
20. Giovanna Tomasello. *L'Africa Fra Mito e Realtà. Storia Della Letteratura Coloniale Italiana*. Palermo: Sellerio, 2004.
21. Ali Mumin Ahad. "Towards a critical introduction to an Italian post-colonial literature." Paper presented at Conference Proceedings 31st AFSAAP Conference: Building a Common Future: Africa and Australasia, Melbourne, Australia, 26–28 November 2008. Available online: http://afsaap.org.au/conference/conference-2008/ (accessed on 3 March 2016).
22. Ursula Lindsey. "A Stage across the Sea. An Unjustly-Neglected Libyan Novelist Captured the Twisted Logic of Colonialism, Past and Present." *The Nation*, 19 October 2015. Available online: http://www.thenation.com/article/a-stage-across-the-sea/ (accessed on 15 January 2016).
23. Karen Barker. "Theory as Fireworks: An Interview with Brian Castro." *Australian Literary Studies* 20 (2002): 241–48.
24. André Naffis-Sahely. "Translator's Note." In *The Confines of the Shadow. In Lands Overseas*. Translated by André Naffis-Sahely. London: Darf Publishers, 2015, pp. 367–68.
25. Rodica Dimitriu. "Omission in Translation." *Perspectives* 12 (2004): 163–75. [CrossRef]
26. BBC. "Hisham Matar in Conversation with Presenter Mariella Frostrup." *BBC Radio*, 3 December 2015. Available online: http://www.bbc.co.uk/programmes/b06qgp5m#play (accessed on 5 February 2016).
27. Petra Rüdiger, and Konrad Gross, eds. *Translation of Cultures*. Amsterdam: Rodopi, 2009, pp. ix–xiv.
28. Dubravka Ugresic. *Europe in Sepia*. Translated by David Williams. Rochester: Open Letter, 2014.
29. Inez Baranay, e-mail message to Arianna Dagnino, 11 January 2016.
30. Mads Rosendahl Thomsen. "Migrant Writers and Cosmopolitan Readers." In *Studying Transcultural Literary History*. Edited by Gunilla Lindberg-Wada. Berlin: Walter de Gruyter, 2006, pp. 244–50.
31. Maurizio Ascari. "The Rise of the Grand Tour: Higher Education, Transcultural Desire and the Fear of Cultural Hybridisation." *Linguæ & Rivista di Lingue e Culture Modern* 14 (2015): 9–32. [CrossRef]
32. Anne Holden Rønning. "Literary Transculturations and Modernity: Some Reflections." *Transnational Literature* 4 (2011): 1–10.
33. Maurizio Ascari. *Literature of the Global Age: A Critical Study of Transcultural Narratives*. Jefferson: McFarland, 2011.

 *humanities*

Article

"I Felt Like My Life Had Been Given to Me to Start Over": Alice Kaplan's Language Memoir, *French Lessons*

Eleonora Rao

Department of Humanities, University of Salerno, Via Giovanni Paolo II, 132, Fisciano 84084, Italy; erao@unisa.it; Tel.: +39-089-943-7954

Academic Editor: Bernd Fisher
Received: 11 May 2016; Accepted: 14 June 2016; Published: 20 June 2016

Abstract: Alice Kaplan's memoir *French Lessons* (1993) is a story that deals as much with the issue of language learning as with that of cultural belonging(s). This "language memoir," as it is typical of this sub-genre, is an intimate tale of the transition between languages and cultures. *French Lessons* recounts her evolving relationship with French language and culture in various phases of her life: starting from childhood, continuing through her graduate student years at Yale and finally as professor of French at Duke. Soon, however, in this unconventional *Bildung*, the second language turns out to be a verbal safe-house, an instant refuge when her first language and culture happen to be too uncomfortable. Ultimately, French provides a psychic space and a hiding place. Ultimately, however, as Derrida has shown, we are alienated from both the first and the second; we find ourselves to be more comfortable in one than in the other. This essay will analyze such processes with special attention to the part played by the body in Kaplan's building as a student and eventually as a teacher. The analysis will be linked with the text's peculiar narrative style: fast-paced, with simple, concise sentences, nevertheless extremely effective and moving.

Keywords: autobiography; memoirs; language memoirs; foreigner language teaching/learning

---

1. Introduction

Alice Kaplan's *French Lessons: A Memoir*, published in 1993 [1], is a story that deals as much with the issue of language learning as with that of cultural belonging(s). This "language memoir" is an intimate tale of the transition between languages and cultures which falls into the subgenre of so-called autobiographical criticism, personal narrative or confessional criticism that has become quite widespread from the 1990s onward. It was Kaplan herself who coined the expression "language memoir" in an essay, "On Language Memoir," part of an excellent collection edited by Angelika Bammer, *Displacements: Cultural Identities in Question* [2]. The language memoir can be considered a new critical category of text, a genre whose generic frontier, as Brian Lennon observes, "is marked, possibly expanded, or otherwise modified by an encounter with language as a limit" ([3], p. 124). In *French Lessons* the narrator attempts to relate accounts of experience rather than expertise in language learning. Furthermore, in her dense essay "On Language Memoir," Kaplan reflects on multiple aspects of learning a second language. First of all, she does not believe that communication or the need to communicate is the principal driving force in the process. As will be discussed in the course of this article, Kaplan opens a radically new scenario on the process of foreigner language learning.

> I have always heard it said that people learn languages "in order to communicate" and "out of empathy for others." I never believed it, because it wasn't true of my own experience of learning French, and now that I am a French teacher, it isn't true of my students. "Communication" and "empathy"—such positive altruistic motives—cannot possibly take

into account the variety of contexts in which languages are learnt, the motivations, the emotional tenor of the new and old languages, the way language functions for each personality. Students learn out of desire and fear and greed and a need to escape as much as out of empathy. Language learning is clearly more interesting, and less innocent, that the truism would indicate ([2], p. 60).

In addition, in this essay Kaplan reflects on the arbitrariness of the linguistic sign and on the indissoluble rapport of language to culture. As the author notes,

> When I began, I read as many scholarly disquisitions as I could find on second language acquisition—linguistics, sociology, education—and I found methods and statistics and the occasional anecdote, but nothing, really, about what is going on inside the head of a person who suddenly finds herself passionately engaged in new sounds and a new voice, who discovers that "*chat*" is not a cat at all, but a new creature in new surroundings. I wanted to see the "cat," then the "*chat.*" I wanted the differences between languages to come alive in a dialogue and characterization ([2], p. 59).

French Lessons explores Kaplan's passion for, if not obsession with, another language and another way of life. In this unconventional *Bildung*, as Lennon has noted, the text presents and problematizes "the entry into the social order of a second, or third (*etc.*) self—of multiple selves, into potentially multiple and coexistent social orders" ([3], p. 126). To return to her essay "On Language Memoirs" where Kaplan looks into the psychological repercussions of living immersed in another language, she observes: "There is no language change without emotional consequences. Principally: loss. That language equals home, that language is a home, and that to be without a language, or to be between languages, is as miserable as to be without bread" ([2], p. 63). In this essay she also recounts her experience of sensing the birth of a new persona: "I hid in my second language, where I leaped out of myself" ([2], p. 60). To speak a foreign language is to depart from one's self. "Language memoirs are closest in genre to the classic *Bildungsroman*—the novel of education and development. The difference [here] is that it's not yourself you're growing into, but another self, perceived as better, more powerful, safer. The change in language is the emblem of a leap into a new persona" ([2], p. 69). In this laborious process of discovery and transformation writing plays a crucial part. Kaplan underscores that she has to find the right form for her memoir. Through the acts of memoir, memory can be rendered into what Kaplan calls "scenes of language" and into writing. This act of writing, Kaplan highlights in *French Lessons*, "isn't a straight line but a process where you have to get in trouble to get anywhere. Because I was disturbed, it was better writing than any I had done before" ([2], p. 194). She needs to regain contact with her emotions and the writing of the memoir—as it is usually the case with confessional narrative—provides a privileged access, as will be discussed in the course of this essay.

2. In Love with French

French Lessons recounts her evolving relationship with French language and culture in various phases of her life: as a child (after the sudden death of her father, she was sent to boarding school in Switzerland), then as a graduate student at Yale and eventually as professor of French at Duke. Soon, however, the second language turns out to be something more than a skill. It becomes, as John Sturrock notes, "a verbal safe-house, an instant refuge" when her first language and culture happen to be too uncomfortable ([4], p. 2). French provides a psychic space and a place to hide. As the author remarks in the "Afterwards": "When I was an adolescent, French was my storehouse language. I collected secrets in French; I spoke French to myself. I know now that my passion for French helped me to put off what I needed to say, in English, to the people around me" ([1], p. 214).

Needless to say, the second language learning here is not something undertaken to pass an exam or make sense of a tourist guide. It is a language that becomes second nature, an option or a substitute to the one we were born into. This carries many implications. We are free from clichés, for example, and we are free to express what we could only dream of saying in our native tongue [5]. Ultimately, however, as Derrida has shown, we are alienated from both the first and the second; we are just happier in one than in the other. According to Jacques Derrida, the only language we speak is not the one we know; instead it is a language of which we have been deprived. Derrida considers the rapport the subject can have with the first or second or third language to be one of "inalienable alienation" which "structures the peculiarity and property of language [...] I have only one language and it is not mine; my 'own' language is, for me, a language that cannot be assimilated. My language, the only one I hear myself speak and agree to speak, is the language of the other" ([6], p. 25). Our language is always the language of the other: "We only ever speak one language—and, since it returns to the other, it exists asymmetrically, always for the other, kept by the other. Coming from the other, remaining with the other, and returning to the other" ([6], p. 40). It could be added that for Derrida, the secret of a language is what interrupts it, rendering it a place of opening and reception, a place of an invention which comes from the other, rather than being the creation of a given subject.

Kaplan was born into a Jewish family in Minneapolis, middleclass and rich, although they were first-generation Americans. The father is a charismatic figure for the entire family. He was a successful lawyer involved in the Nuremberg trials of war criminals. Because of this appointment he spends most of his time at home listening to tapes, the relevance of which in relation to Alice the reader finds out towards the end of the text. The Kaplan family, as she says, "had made the transition from diaspora Yiddish to American English in a quick generation. You couldn't hear the shadow of an accent, unless my grandmother was around" ([1], p. 9).

> We spoke American in that house: I can't reproduce this language, but I know exactly what I mean by it. It was American more for what we talked about than how it sounded, although it is amazing to think that in one generation, a language can become so native, so comfortable, so normal, with no sense whatever of its relative newness: my parents were, after all, the first ones in their families to be born into English ([1], p. 7).

The only member of the family who was a witness of how widely the family had traveled linguistically was her Lithuanian grandmother. In fact, the grandmother in her later years had to be hospitalized, for she was in permanent psychological (and linguistic) confusion caused by the Babel of languages in which she had lived most of her life. The grandmother's terminally psychotic state is a terrifying prospect for young Alice. Later on, as an adult and professor of French, she surprises herself thinking in French about her nanny's "sliding from Hebrew to English to Yiddish. Sliding and pushing away bad memories" ([1], p. 13). Of course, she reflects, hers is a different case; nonetheless, Alice is worried by this switching of different languages which she herself does quite often. Therefore, she muses, it "feels disturbed, like hers. French, for me, is not just an accomplishment. It's a need. I wonder if I could end up like her?" ([1], p. 14).

Kaplan grew up in an America—the America of the 1950s—where the idea of foreignness was alien and remote in a way it will perhaps never be again. In retrospect she remarks: "We were so American" ([1], p. 7). "It seems now," she adds, "that no one will ever again have that sense of being American that we had then, in the time between the Second World War and Vietnam" ([1], p. 7). In dealing with cultural belonging and cultural differences, Kaplan's approach is two-fold: on the one hand, it preserves cultural difference; on the other, it points to culture's heterogeneity and therefore it forms a notion of "collective identity" as, to quote James Clifford, "a hybrid, often discontinuous inventive process" ([7], p. 10). It shows also that when it comes to "cultural difference [...] self-other relations are matters of power and rhetoric rather than essence" ([7], p. 14).

Kaplan only tells what we need to know about herself and her family for her purpose. I would like to highlight here the primary role the body and listening/hearing play in this complex and multipurpose memoir, which recounts the coming of age of an intellectual concerned with the nature and origin of knowledge. Kaplan's mastery of French will bring about what the narrator describes as an "awakening" which passes first and foremost through the body. At one point, for example, she goes through a kind of anorexic phase: "For each bar of chocolate I didn't eat I learned a verb/I grew thinner and thinner. I ate French" ([1], p. 53).During one of her visits to Minnesota she is so used to life outside the US that speaking English again brings about a sensation of disembodiment: "When I spoke I felt like I was outside my own body, listening to someone else, and translating" ([1], p. 70). Right from the start of *French Lessons* the narrator describes her obsession with French-language fluency as an "existential" experience. "I am not writing only about French anymore," she remarks, "French is the mark of something that has happened to me" ([1], p. 201).This something is a being divided into two languages—selves living two quite separate lives. In fact, from early on in her narrative, this split is staged as a split in the narrator's proper name itself. She describes the experience of a new self embodied in "my name pronounced French style with the accent on the second syllable, ah-LEASE" ([1], p. 52).

As soon as she lands in America something happens to her body: "I could feel the French sticking in my throat, the new muscles in my mouth" ([1], p. 70). During this stage she is working obsessively to reproduce the perfect French "r".

> It happened over months but it felt like it happened in one class [...] First feeling them wrong, like an impediment, feeling them again and again in their wrongness and then, one day, opening up and letting the right sound come. The "r" was the biggest hurdle: my system was now in place ([1], p. 55).

Mastering the "r" begets a physical and intellectual awakening: "I had found my ability to concentrate. I had woken up from the sleep I had lapsed into on my ninth-grade desk" ([1], p. 56). To her surprise she finds herself to be good at sports. Her body is no longer clumsy. In retrospect she acknowledges this turning point in her life and the salvific role French had assumed in the process:

> In February the whole school moved up to a ski town [...] We skied every day [...] We had a slalom race. The gym teacher took a picture of me coming down the course [...] I studied the picture and saw the angle of my skis, a perfect hockey-stop angle, sending up snow spray. At home I was the worst in sports; here miraculously, I was good. I felt like my life had been given to me to start over. French had saved me ([1], p. 57).

Eventually she will become very close to a French family in Bordeaux and will experience a life-long friendship with Micheline, a doctor who, interestingly, specializes in speech problems. "There in Bordeaux is where my mouth and my eyes and my ears for France started to work" ([1], p. 103).

3. The Years at Yale

Kaplan's description of her graduate studies at Yale in the 1970s is enlightening. Yale under its guiding light, the revered Paul de Man, was at the cutting edge of deconstructionism, which in its turn was the avant-garde of French literary studies. She recalls how De Man showed new ways of reading and how she learned that language can never be trusted with the whole truth. Despite the fascination for de Man, her research interests led her in another direction. In those years of pure textuality she decided to work on Fascist French writers; as she puts it: "I had chosen to work on material that made history impossible to ignore" ([1], p. 160).

There is another non-academic reason for this choice, and it relates to her deceased father, a presence/absence that haunts the text throughout. Kaplan Senior's involvement in "punishing war criminals" ([1], p. 160) surfaces at various points and Kaplan's relation to it is pulled together at the very end of the book. It is the absence of her father that she describes as the "force-field within which I had become an intellectual" ([1], p. 197). Her work, her dissertation on French literati who joined forces with the Nazis, permits her to share issues with her father that they were unable to share when he was alive: their Jewish heritage, the trauma of the Holocaust, the persistence of historical memory.

French Lessons can be read, on one level, as a belated elaboration of loss. This reading has been recently carried out by Ursula A. Kelly [8]. Suffice to say here that French can be seen as the language of denial: "I had learned a whole new language at boarding school but it was a language for covering pain, not expressing it" ([1], p. 58). Not only is she (self) exiled from her mother tongue, but Kaplan represents herself, figuratively, as an outsider from the very beginning, and later as a homeless person and an orphan: "I was afraid to go home, I was afraid of living alone in the big house with my mother who was sick and unhappy, I was dreading the charade of happiness" ([1], p. 58).

In *Losing North*, novelist Nancy Huston (born and educated in Calgary, Alberta, Canada, and then transplanted to France) speaks of foreigners in voluntary exile from their native land and language as people who are inevitably fated to wear a mask in their constant and unrelenting attempts to adapt. Therefore, they will be "involved in *theater, imitation, make-believe*" ([9], p. 19). In her French persona Kaplan feels safe and protected even from herself. She writes of her "desire to be accepted in France and of [her] need for camouflage" ([1], p. 196). On another occasion, on a return visit to the United States, her American self remains alien to her.

> In June I took the plane home [...] I had my ear open, on the plane, for the sounds of anyone speaking French, it was holding me up, running through me, a voice in my head, a tickle in my ear, likely to be set off at any moment. A counter language. When I got off the plane the American English sounded loud and thudding—like an insult or a lapse of faith. I would have to go hunting for French sounds, if I wanted to keep going ([1], p. 70).

In many other ways Kaplan describes her love affair with the French language. It is especially through French poetry that she realizes she "could lose [herself] in language" ([1], p. 76). From the academic point of view her results are, of course, excellent; she becomes a French major (beforehand she had chosen political sciences) and her French teacher sends her for a year to France. She stays at first in a small town, Pau, before settling down in Bordeaux. Despite her enthusiasm and her love for the French language, life at this time in France is far from easy. Like any other American student living immersed in another culture, this proves to be far from easy, as the narrator describes the difficulties she experiences during the first half of the year in Part Three: "*Getting It Right.*" But then it will be during the second part of that year in Bordeaux that she will meet Micheline and her family destined to become her lifelong French friends: "They became my French family and I their American friend" ([1], p. 97).

Towards the end of the text, in the "Afterwards," she admits to herself her necessity of wearing a mask: there she offers, however, more questions than answers:

> Why do people want to adopt another culture? Because there's something in their own they don't like, that doesn't *name them* [...] why have I confined myself to teach in this second language, this language which will never be as easy as the first one? Why have I chosen to live in not-quite-my-own-language in exile from myself, for so many years—why have I gone through school with a gag on, do I like not really being able to express myself? ([1], pp. 209–10, emphasis in the original).

It seems, nonetheless, that in and through the second language one can be freed of cliché, and perhaps more importantly, it is only in and through this second language that a moment of illumination may spur. This is Kaplan the professor in her French class:

> The simplicity of our communication moves us, we're outside of cliché, free of easy eloquence, some deeper ideas make it through the mistakes and shine all the more through them. / In French class I feel close, open, willing to risk a language that isn't the language of everyday life. A sacred language ([1], p. 210).

In class, the reading of Franz Fanon on Algerian women during the revolution creates moments that are "a chance for growth, for freedom, a liberation from the ugliness of our received ideas and mentalities" ([1], p. 211).

4. Scenes of Languages

No doubt, childhood is crucial in this memoir, as it is often the case in the genre. To quote Nancy Huston again: "*Expatriates are consciously (and often painfully) aware of* [...] the absolute unique nature of childhood, and the fact that it never leaves you" ([9], p. 9). Critics have stressed that the book begins with "scenes of languages" from her childhood. I would add, however, that in *French Lessons* the emphasis falls, first of all, on the act of listening: "Listening now to my childhood as the French Professor I've become, what I hear first are scenes of language" ([1], p. 5). Kaplan's very earliest memories are about her own entry into language, which happens of course through listening. She is three years old and, much to her father's delight, she parrots a funny sentence she does not comprehend: "Everything I like is illegal, immoral, or fattening" ([1], p. 3).

In earlier as well as in later years, hearing, listening and language will thus remain connected. In addition, hearing, according to Michel Foucault, is the only sense we cannot defend ourselves from [10]. Likewise, she cannot defend herself from an infection in her ear she gets from her French boyfriend when she is staying in Bordeaux. The trope of hearing surfaces in the text at many different levels, and first of all in the book's cover. It is a slightly faded photograph of three men sitting at a table, bending over it a little, in concentration: they are listening through headphones. The photo is from the Nuremberg trials—it belonged to her father, who was one of the prosecutors in those "trials of history" ([11], p. 17). Later on in the text Kaplan relates her father's act of listening to her own work. She describes him as "silent and distant with headphones over his ears, [it is] a founding image of my own work" ([1], p. 197). Helen Buss reads *French Lessons* as a trauma text: "Alice Kaplan does not call her book 'trauma' memoir, but I find that an understanding of trauma is essential to my understanding of the form of *French Lessons*" ([12], p. 160). Maybe it is worth stressing the fact that not only had eight-year-old Alice lost her father suddenly, but she also had to face her birthday cake and her father's funeral all in the same day. As Buss continues, "The French language comes along as an opportunity for Kaplan to get on with her life. Yet, given the ambiguity with which trauma acts itself out in a lifetime, the French language ultimately acts as a linguistic location for re-experiencing the trauma of a world in which her father, the man who persecuted evil, is no longer there" ([12], p. 146). According to research on the aftermath of trauma, something positive can be said of its consequences. As Helen Buss reflects, using experts on trauma, such as Kai Erikson, "While trauma is often written about as a site of debilitating illness, it can also be a source of great wisdom and a factor in great achievement. Kai Erikson views the person who has experienced trauma as having access to a special truth: 'Traumatized people calculate life's chances differently. They look at the world through a different lens...They evaluate the data of everyday life differently, read sing differently, see omens the rest of us are for the most part spared'" ([13], p. 194).

Looking back at her childhood in Minnesota, very early in the narrative, the narrating *I* locates herself outside mainstream North American culture and values. She chooses estrangement and exile from her mother country and mother tongue. In narratives of exile there is no *nostos*, no actual return is possible, though paradoxically these narratives are obsessed with 'home' and 'homecomings', elusive and ungraspable as they can be. Possibly writing is the only home there is.

The quality of her writing shares many aspects of diaspora autobiography, as has been argued by Susan Egan in her *Mirror Talk: Genres of Crisis in Contemporary Autobiography*. As Egan argues, one finds

> critics and analysts resistant to "pure culture". They move among genres with an imaginative ease that suggests all borders are permeable. Personal information and narrative as well as cultural history are embedded in the ironies of speculations and theory. Theory becomes autobiographical, as do political and cultural commentary, criticism, fiction, poetry, film ([14], p. 122).

Personal narrative, or rather personal criticism, as Mary Ann Caws puts it, "has to do with a willing, knowledgeable, outspoken involvement on the part of the critic with the subject matter, and an invitation extended to the potential reader to participate in the interweaving and construction of the ongoing conversation this criticism can be, even as it remains a text" ([15], p. 2). According to Nancy Miller, personal narratives function more like a relay between positions to create critical fluency: "These autobiographical acts may produce a new repertory for an enlivening cultural criticism" ([16], p. 25). Autobiographical criticism is able to open up a channel from mind to sensations, and it is valuable to intellectuals who are used to keep emotions to themselves. As Kaplan remarks, "I didn't realized until I tried to write [*French Lessons*] what an intellectual I had become and how unused I was to expressing emotions" ([17], p. 8). Autobiographical criticism may express "the deep desire of intellectuals not to be intellectual" ([18] p. 182). As Aran Veeser notes in his introduction to *Confessions of the Critics*, "Confessional criticism has the signal virtue of unsettling any certainty that the writer knows that s/he is evoking powerful emotions" ([19], p. xvii). Together with the releasing of emotions, another significant trait in confessional criticism is the importance of secrets. Alice Kaplan told her interviewer Scott Heller "that her book is all about secrets" ([17], p. 9). As the narrator remarks in the "Afterwards": "There are truths about the past but there is no authority, no policeman, ready and able to pin them down" ([1], p. 231). Besides, the recounting of the past is by necessity partial: the past "can't be erased" but is destined to remain "always incomplete" ([1], p. 213).

However, Kaplan's memoir shows also the difficulty in expressing emotions in writing. Kaplan asks interesting questions—"Why I am still fighting the battles of another time and place?" ([1], p. 199), for example—but seems to have little interest in trying to answer to her readers. As Vincent Pecora remarks, "How could she? Who, finally, ever writes the memoir that reveals what must remain hidden?" ([20], p. 79). Pecora continues, "In the end, Kaplan reveals personal feeling of any depth only when it comes to the French language [...] when Kaplan feels most deeply, what she feels most deeply about is French. And this is what is supposed to lend pathos to the final page of the memoir" ([20], p. 81; [21]). The question, however, is not as straightforward as Pecora maintains. Kaplan needs also to express her emotion in English and to issues pertaining to her life in America, in particular her professional life; she is, for example, emotional about her teaching to American students. Research in the experience of communication of emotion with special reference to bilingual subjects stresses what bilingual subjects have always insisted on, and that is the perception of different selves in different languages: in a bilingual subject each language has its own persona, with a different set of cultural norms: "The expression of emotions varies across cultures"([22], p. 357). There seems, however, to be a preference for a language over another depending on the context and the emotion in question, as research has shown [22]. For example, when Kaplan thinks about her Lithuanian grandmother, who fell into linguistic confusion and had a psychotic break, she is compelled to think about her in French. The narrator concludes that it may be an escamotage to exorcise suffering, to keep pain at bay, since one of her inmost fears is "to end up like her" ([1], p. 14).

It is paramount in this case to regain contact with the language of affect, with the mother tongue. Even though French had a salvific role in a phase of Kaplan's life, as it was responsible for her "resurrection," for her "new skin," ([23], p. 15), English remains the language of "the body's nocturnal memory," the language of "the bittersweet slumber of childhood" to quote Julia Kristeva ([23], p. 15).

In Kaplan's "Foreword" to a new edition of the experimental French author Nathalie Serraute's memoir *Childhood*, she stresses Serraute's ability to investigate "the kind of shimmering meaning that lay beneath the most ordinary communication, whether among literary snobs discussing poetry or women shopping" ([24], p. iv). Serraute's unconventional memoir, written in the form of an internal dialogue, "questions the validity of memoir and then questions that questioning" ([24], p. v). Sarraute does not offer any reassurance that what is in the book really happened. Indeed, in her 1956 collection of essays *The Age of Suspicion* [25], she theorizes on the incapacity of language "to reflect so troubled a universe" as the contemporary one ([24], p. vii). When it comes to language and intimate emotions Serraute, and Kaplan with her, ask the same question: "When you write, how do you capture in language, through language, what language doesn't want to tell you?" ([24], p. vi).

Kaplan's frequent return to the US on vacation makes her feel a stranger among her peers: "At a lawn party at Mary's I discovered that my classmates had new rituals: drinking from flasks, smoking pot in the bushes, talking about rock concerts. I felt formal in my tailored white shirt. I stood watching them" ([1], p. 72). Claire Kramsch in an article published in *Transit* reflects on the problematics of personal narratives in a plurilingual context. In "The Multilingual Experience: Insights from Language Memoirs", she notes: "Language memoirs bring back into public discussion the poetic dimension of

Humanities **2016**, *5*, 47

language—a dimension that is likely to better prepare learners to resist the (communicative) pressures of the market and the (cultural) seduction of national communities. What they model are narrators who have assumed their own diversity" ([26], p. 11). In other words, the narrators represent themselves as outsiders.

Starting from her early years in boarding school in Switzerland, and later on as a student of French language, culture and literature during her many long study sojourns in France, Kaplan represents herself as an orphan outsider, and at times an exile. Her return home, which will later result in an academic position as professor of French at a prestigious university, still leaves many questions unanswered. At the end of "On Language Memoir," she remarks "Why didn't I want to relax with my accent and my mistakes? What was at stake?" ([2], p. 70).

Here, as is often the case, the homecoming is the writing of the memoir itself. The whole text has a few references to its self-begetting, but happily no trace of deconstructionist jargon. Its peculiar narrative style is fast-paced, with simple, concise sentences, nevertheless extremely effective. The book's last two paragraphs are a moving and compelling testimony of an inner intimate need that paradoxically points both to the text's sincerity and to its fictive quality. But then, does it really matter? The passage is worth quoting almost in full:

> Why did I hide in French? If life got too messy, I could take off in my second world. Writing about it has made me air my suspicion, my anger, my longings, to people to whom it has come as a total surprise [...] Learning French did me some harm by giving me a place to hide. It's not as if there's a straightforward American self lurking under a devious French one, waiting to come out and be authentic. That's nostalgia—or fiction. French isn't just a metaphor, either—it's a skill. It buys my groceries and pays the mortgage. I'm grateful to French, beyond these material gains, for teaching me that there is more than one way to speak, for giving me a role, for being the home I've made from my own will and my own imagination.
>
> All my life, I've used and abused my gift for language. I'm tempted, down to the last page, to wrap things up too neatly in words ([1], p. 216).

Conflicts of Interest: The author declares no conflict of interest.

References

1. Kaplan, Alice. *French Lessons: A Memoir*. Chicago: The University of Chicago Press, 1993.
2. Kaplan, Alice. "On Language Memoir." In *Displacements: Cultural Identities in Question*. Edited by Angelika Bammer. Bloomington: Indiana University Press, 1994, pp. 59–70.
3. Lennon, Brian. *In Babel's Shadow: Multilingual Literatures, Monolingual States*. Minneapolis: University of Minnesota Press, 2010.
4. Sturrock, John. "Doing what does not come naturally." *London Review of Books* 15 (1993): 5–8.
5. Grosjean, Francois. *Bilingual: Life and Reality*. Cambridge: Harvard University Press, 2010.
6. Derrida, Jacques. *Monolingualism of the Other, or, the Prosthesis of Origin*. Stanford: Stanford University Press, 1998.
7. Clifford, James. *The Predicament of Culture: Twentieth-Century Ethnography, Literature, and Art*. Cambridge: Harvard University Press, 1988.
8. Kelly, Ursula A. "Inciting Teaching and Learning: Loss and Mourning in Alice Kaplan's *French Lessons*." *Biography* 33 (2010): 50–62.
9. Huston, Nancy. *Losing North: Essays on Cultural Exile*. Toronto: McArthur & Co., 2002.
10. Foucault, Michel. *The Hermeneutics of the Subject: Lectures at the Collège de France 1981–1982*. New York: Palgrave, 2005.
11. Felman, Shoshana. *The Juridical Unconscious: Trials and Traumas in the Twentieth Century*. Cambridge: Harvard University Press, 2002.
12. Buss, Helen. *Repossessing the World: Reading Memoirs by Contemporary Women*. Waterloo: Wilfrid Laurier University Press, 2002.

13. Erikson, Kai. *A New Species of Trouble: The Human Experience of Modern Disaster.* New York: Norton, 1994.

14. Egan, Susan. *Mirror Talk: Genres of Crisis in Contemporary Autobiography.* Chapel Hill: University of New Carolina Press, 1999.

15. Caws, Mary Ann. *Women of Bloomsbury: Virginia, Vanessa and Carrington.* New York: Routledge, 1990.

16. Miller, Nancy. *Getting Personal: Feminist Occasions and Other Autobiographical Acts.* New York and London: Routledge, 1991.

17. Kaplan, Alice. "A passion for French." *Chronicle of Higher Education* 40 (1994): 7–8.

18. Frith, Simon. "The cultural studies of popular music." In *Cultural Studies.* Edited by Laurence Grossberg, Cary Nelson and Paula A. Treichter. New York: Routledge, 1991, pp. 174–82.

19. Veeser, H. Aram. "Introduction: The Case for Confessional Criticism." In *Confessions of the Critics.* Edited by H. Aram Veeser. New York: Routledge, 1996, pp. ix–xxvii.

20. Pecora, Vincent. "Through the Academic Looking Glass." In *Confessions of the Critics.* New York: Routledge, 1996, pp. 76–81.

21. Franklin, Cynthia G. *Academic Lives: Memoir, Cultural Theory, and the University Today.* Athens and London: University of Georgia Press, 2009.

22. Dewaele, Jean-Marc. "Culture and emotional language." In *The Routledge Handbook of Language and Culture.* Edited by Farzad Sharifian. New York: Routledge, 2015, pp. 357–70.

23. Kristeva, Julia. *Strangers to Ourselves.* Translated by Leon S. Roudiez. New York: Columbia University Press, 1991, p. 15.

24. Kaplan, Alice. *Childhood.* Foreword by Nathalie Serraute. Translated by Barbara Wright in consultation with the author. Chicago: The University of Chicago Press, 2013.

25. Serraute, Nathalie. *The Age of Suspicion: Essays on the Novel.* New York: George Braziller, 1963.

26. Kramsch, Claire. "The multilingual experience: Insights from the language memoirs." *Transit* 1 (2004): 1–12.

 *humanities*

Article

The Transnational Turn in African Literature of French Expression: Imagining Other Utopic Spaces in the Globalized Age

Valérie K. Orlando

Department of French & Italian, School of Languages, Literatures, Cultures, University of Maryland, College Park, MD 20742, USA; vorlando@umd.edu; Tel.: +1-301-405-4027

Academic Editor: Bernd Fischer
Received: 9 February 2016; Accepted: 9 May 2016; Published: 18 May 2016

Abstract: This article focuses on African literature published since 2000 by authors of French expression. While contemporary authors' subjects are varied—ranging from climate change, human rights, to ethnic cleansing—they also imagine new "what ifs" and other utopic spaces and places that extend beyond postcolonial, Africa-as-victim paradigms. Literarily, authors such as Abdelaziz Belkhodja (Tunisia) and Abdourahman A. Waberi (Djibouti) have effectuated a transnational turn. In this literary transnational turn, Africa is open to new interpretations by the African author that are very different from the more essentialist-based, literary-philosophical movements such as Negritude and pan-Africanism; cornerstones of the postcolonial literary frameworks of the past. Belkhodja and Waberi offer original narratives for Africa that, while describing their countries as utopias, also traverse the very dystopic realities of our time.

Keywords: Afropolitanism; La littérature-monde; cosmopolitanism; transnational literature; African literature; Maghrebi; Francophone literature

---

1. Introduction

In the last decade, many contemporary African authors of French expression from both North and Sub-Saharan Africa posit perspectives in their novels that reveal a global cosmopolitanism that uniquely defines African literature in the 21st century. Authors writing in French, such as Salim Bachi (France/Algeria), Abdelaziz Belkhodja (Tunisia), Calixthe Beyala (Cameroon), Youssouf Amine Elalamy (Morocco), Fouad Laroui (Morocco), Alain Mabanchou (Congo), Marie Ndiaye (France/Senegal), and Abdourahman Waberi (Djibouti), among others,[1] promote a "way of being African in the world" that thematically exposes different attitudes about Africa and Africans remarkably unlike previous tropes ([1], pp. 13–22). Thematic shifts have broken with past scenarios that revolved around the angst of the postcolonial condition, the traumas rooted in tensions between modernity and traditionalism, the sociocultural and economic divisions between North and Sub-Saharan Africa, poverty and despair. Evan Maina Mwangi states that new, engaging 21st century African writing from the continent and the diaspora "is neither a 'writing back' to Europe nor an endorsement of Euro-American neocolonialism. It is first and foremost about self-perception" ([2], p. 4).

This article focuses on two African authors of French expression, Tunisian Abdelaziz Belkhodja and Djiboutian Abdourahman A. Waberi, who have published works since 2000. While in general contemporary writers' subjects are varied, ranging from climate change, immigration, human rights

---

1   The list is certainly not limited to those authors writing in French. Authors writing in English such as Nigerian Helon Habila, Kenyans M. G. Vassanji and Shailja Patel, Libyan Hisham Matar, and Zimbabwean Brian Chikwava equally can be classed in the Afropolitan camp.

Humanities **2016**, *5*, 30

abuse in the home country, socioeconomic challenges, and ethnic cleansing, they also imagine innovative "what ifs" that postulate new scripts for Africa. My core argument is that these hypothetical narratives from both North and Sub-Saharan Africa mark a "transnational turn" as articulated by Paul Jay, where the author creates and engages spaces that move away from "nation-state locations by focusing our attention on transnational spaces and regions" ([3], pp. 8–9). Specifically, Belkhodja's *Le Retour de l'éléphant* (The Return of the Elephant, 2003) and Waberi's *Aux Etats-Unis d'Afrique* (African USA, 2006)[2] offer exemplary cosmopolitan narratives that demonstrate this transnational turn.[3] Their themes extend beyond insular topics pertaining to the postcolonial nation state in order to explore the positive and negative realities of globalization, transnational migration, and the general planetary challenges of our age.

In the past, African nationalist novels contextualized the burgeoning nations emerging from the colonial moment, highlighting "commitment" and the "responsibility of writers to their societies" in order to evoke a renaissance of indigenous authenticity ([4], p. 248). At the outset of decolonization the role of the activist author (*l'écrivain engagé*) was, as Frantz Fanon proclaims in *Les Damnés de la terre*, to rally the people to the grand ideas of the newly formed nation. Authors and intellectuals would define the "cultural models" of postcolonial nations through their writings and "assert...liberation [in] a jagged style, full of imagery". The perfected image of the new nation was to be key to its people's liberated "consciousness" ([5], pp. 156–57). Authors rose to the challenges of nationalist commitment as prescribed by Fanon in the late 1950s and early 1960s.[4] Since the 1970s, however, their function as proponents of nationalist messages has waned as they have become disillusioned with state ideology and the failure of postcolonial institutions to meet the needs of their peoples.

Emerging from a literature of commitment (*la littérature de combat*) written in French, authors in the new millennium extend their themes beyond the boundaries of cultural and national specificity, embracing a more cosmopolitan transnational spirit that explores the world's others, and "obligations that stretch beyond those to whom we are related by the ties of kith and kind, or even the more formal ties of shared citizenship" ([6], p. xv). Although their cosmopolitanism and worldly engagement are evident, what is particularly interesting about these millennial narratives is that in order to explore the present, authors feel the need to tell their stories in the distant future. It is here where they create utopias to study the very real dystopic truths that Africa faces in its postcolonial reality. The utopias and dystopias, or what I suggest as being a combination of the two—a dystopic utopia—created by Belkhodja and Waberi allow for hopeful possibilities while also offering critical frameworks through which to articulate the universal shortcomings and challenges of the planet's modern societies.

The two novels discussed here, created within the dystopic utopia, imagine *other* and *othered* spaces and places possible for Africa and the West. Waberi turns the African continent into the powerful "United States of Africa" which dominates socio-politically and culturally the international landscape, leaving the impoverished West to fend for itself. The author's heroine, Maya (short for Malaïka), is white but grew up in Asmara, the capital of Eritrea in the Federation of African States,

---

2   All translations of these works are my own.
3   Aziz Belkhodja (b. 1962) is well known in Tunisia for his acerbic articles published in the 2000s in various Tunisian newspapers criticizing the first Gulf War as well as well-placed politicians in the Zine el-Abidine Ben Ali government. In 2002, he even dared to denounce in the press Ben Ali's dictatorial call to change the 1959 constitution, which would ultimately overturn many of the rights and liberties granted Tunisians in the early days of the nascent Tunisian republic. From the early 2000s up to the ouster of Ben Ali, Belkhodja was known for his activism on the Internet and particularly for his 2010 publication of a report entitled "The True Nature of the Ben Ali Regime" (*La Véritable nature du régime de Ben Ali*), in which the journalist called for a complete overhaul of the government and for Ben Ali to step down. Two days later, on 18 December 2010, Tunisia's "Arab Spring" unfolded.Novelist, essayist, and poet Abdourahman Waberi (b. 1965) is exemplary as a contemporary African transnational author. He has worked in positions in academia in Europe, the USA, and Canada and written widely in French and English. He studied English literature, worked as a literary consultant in Paris, and has lived his own transcontinental experiences since the publication of his first novel, *Le Pays Sans Ombre* (The Land Without Shadow, 1994).
4   As expressed in works such as *Peau noire, masques blancs* (Black Skin, White Masks, 1951) and *Les Damnés de la terre* (The Wretched of the Earth, 1961).

basking in the affection of her African father, "Docteur Papa", a humanitarian doctor who adopted her at birth. Waberi spins a tale that reverses history, making Africa an Eldorado recognized for the intellectuals, scientists, businessmen and women, and artists contributing to its greatness. A similar narrative, beginning on the back jacket cover of Belkhodja's *Le Retour de l'éléphant*, overturns the West's habitual, stereotypical view of the "Arab-East as a Depraved Society" to posit Arabs as "the fortunate of History" rich from oil revenues and investment in vast cultural enterprises. In the year 2103, world order has been turned upside down. It is now destitute Westerners (particularly Americans) like John who must immigrate to Carthage with one suitcase, seeking education and, hopefully, new fortunes in order to escape the socioeconomic poverty and decrepitude of his North American society. The great Roman city of the ancient past has been resurrected in the future as the grand Republic of Carthage. The gleaming city is a technologically advanced urban megatropolis, known throughout the world for its fortunes made through innovations in solar energy and reverse osmosis that have given it inexhaustible sources of electricity and clean water. Both novels present North and Sub-Saharan Africa as centers of civilization, culture, and economic stability. Africa is a continent on which, as Waberi writes, "l'homme d'Afrique s'est senti très vite, sûr de lui" (the African very quickly was sure of himself) ([7], p. 54).

2. The *Pensée-Autre* of the Afropolitan Novel in French

Waberi and Belkhodja cast their thematic nets wide to conceptualize the African subject as universally connected and committed to trying to solve, or at least better understand, the transnational challenges of our era. Their ideas about African *being* promote the conception of subjecthood as always evolving in a *becoming* that is "unlimited and unending" ([8], p. 33). The dystopic utopian spaces in which their narratives are cast provide the perfect window through which to explore the "what if" and what "could be" with respect to African postcolonial subjecthood. In order to scrutinize these potential spaces, I propose to engage two critical areas of postcolonial thought. The first draws on what Moroccan sociologist Abdelkébir Khatibi designates as *une pensée-autre* (an idea that embodies an "other way of thinking" or "thinking other") about the postcolonial subject's *being-in-the-world*. The second employs Cameroonian philosopher Achille Mbembe's theory of *Afropolitanism*, which promotes "a stylistic, an aesthetic and a certain poetics of the world" that argues for a *creolization*, or what Khatibi calls a *pluralization* of African modes of being-in-the-world. Mbembe's Afropolitanism envisions African authors as contributing to transnational connections that link the continent to other places. "Africans of the World", he notes, are "African immigrants, transnationals, émigrés and exiles, citizens of African nations living in the West as well as those living on the continent" who experience the intra- and extra-continental relationships taking place in transnational climates between self and other ([9], p. 16). Afropolitan authors strive to extend their ideas about what it means to be African beyond the borders of "nativist interpretations of culture and the claim to autochthonous cultures" as seen in earlier African national writing ([9], p. 18). Afropolitanism connotes, thus, movement forward and becoming something other than the stereotypes associated with the continent as defined by the West, while also defining identity not as insularly nationalist and tribal but rather global and transnational: "Afropolitanism is the spirit that espouses this paradigm of itinerancy, mobility and displacement" ([9], p. 19).

Khatibi's pensée-autre and Mbembe's Afropolitan worldview provide the means through which to explore the dystopic utopian worlds proposed by Belkhodja and Waberi. These thinkers and authors meld philosophies and ideologies, as well as aesthetic modes of African discourse and ways of looking at the globe from North and Sub-Saharan Africa with French and European philosophical frameworks, to offer readers an original conception of being-in-the world that is neither totally African nor European. Their conception draws on Heidegger's philosophy of selfhood promoting an understanding of the "being of all beings of a character other than its own" ([8], p. 33), Khatibi formulates his pensée-autre as a thought process that encapsulates the importance of understanding identity as "*being-already-alongside* with others". It is a conception of being that is derived through being "*fascinated by* the world with which it is concerned" (author's italics) ([8], p. 88). This fascination leads to intercultural scenarios in which two sign systems come into contact—African and Other—through which identity, history, culture, and language are parsed, fragmented, and then put back together again, allowing for a cultural mosaic to flourish. For Khatibi, who was particularly influenced by French phenomenologist philosophers such as Gilles Deleuze,[5] the conception of being as an ever-evolving becoming is also "always in between the past and the future [since] it moves in both directions at once" ([10], pp. 1–2). Therefore, being "is never fixed (even when it appears to be so) [it is] a continual process of change without destination" ([11], p. 41).

Both Khatibi and Mbembe contextualize how the African author has been influenced by the colonial imprints that have left indelible marks on his frames of reference; the most notable of which is the French language. For Khatibi, the pensée-autre is both acceptance of "cet heritage occidental" (this Western heritage) as well as "notre patrimoine" (our patrimony), which has often been limited by its postcolonial, nationalist failings ([12], p. 12). Khatibi's ideas about living in the postcolonial era, writing in the language of the former colonizer, but using this same language to critique the realities of Africa, efface binary thinking about Self as opposed to Other. For the Moroccan theorist and poet, the interweaving of West and African promotes thinking in a multiple way and thereby—"mettre au jour la pluralité"—(bringing to light plurality) ([12], p. 13). Within the plural, the African author's sense of identity is always enmeshed in the "bi-langue" (the bilingual) where "the 'maternal' language is at work in the foreign language", which then serves the writer by aiding in engaging with his environment, both locally and transnationally. Writing "bilinguistiquement" (bilingually) about the world in the language of the other ([12], pp. 13, 184), Belkhodja and Waberi, thus, "assume the French language" (its colonial past as well as the reality of its continued use in the postcolonial era) in order to negotiate all facets of their reality ([12], p. 179). Their utopias map a third space, as Khatibi outlines, which is at once Western and African, Self and Other:

> We want to uproot Western knowledge from its central place within ourselves, to decenter ourselves with respect to this center, to this original claimed by the West... The Occident is part of me, a part that I can only deny insofar as I resist all the Occidents and the Orients that oppress and disillusion me ([13], p. 106).

The dystopic utopias proposed by Waberi and Belkhodja are so significant because they explore African sociocultural and economic realities of the new millennium as well as the success and failures of the postcolonial nation. Afropolitanism and la pensée-autre are foundations for a literary and linguistically decentered space that transmits not only African-specific messages but also transnational humanist ones as well. Within the Afropolitan's scope, one finds in Africa the "history of the rest of the world of which we are a part" ([14], pp. 1–3) that represents a plurality of languages, migratory fluxes, and "comings and goings" between the continent and elsewhere ([14], p. 1).

3. Mapping Dystopic Utopias in Afropolitan Space

In their reconceptualization of Africa as a vibrant continent at the center of the world, Belkhodja and Waberi join sub-Saharan Africa and the Mediterranean Maghreb, thus disavowing the impossibility of harmony between the north and the south and refuting former colonial divisions that contributed to racial hierarchies. In these transnational texts of continental Africa, a universal African consciousness is promoted through continental universities (Waberi) and medical organizations such as "Toubib sans frontières" (Doctors without borders) that run refugee camps in Carthage and elsewhere for displaced Europeans ([15], p. 21). Young Africans, like Maya, are "talented" in their openness "to be nomads" where they often find their "tout" (all) "pas au centre de l'empire africain mais à sa périphérie" (not in the center of the African empire, but at its periphery) ([7], p. 163).

---

[5]   As well as linguists such as Jacques Derrida, philosophers Nietzsche, Foucault, and Blanchot.

Waberi's and Belkhodja's novels beseech readers to think about why the potential utopian space offers a compelling environment through which to explore the real, salient present challenges to African societies. "Utopianism is a deep and growing aspect of postcolonial literatures and it appears to trace a different trajectory from the Marxist utopianism that has dominated contemporary utopian theory [in the West]" ([16], pp. 8–14). Utopias usually posit hope, but as postcolonial literary theorist Bill Ashcroft suggests, in our modern world, when used as a trope to explore the non-Western context, "utopian achievement of postcolonial independent states becomes degenerate" subjected to "catastrophic failure...or outright swindles" ([16], p. 9). For the postcolonial nation, there is an "ambiguous relationship" between utopia and dystopia that arises because the "relation between memory and the future" are always at odds ([16], p. 9). These aspects are evident in the both novels. On the one hand, Waberi and Belkhodja project through their narratives what they want their countries and continent to be, yet on the other, these scenarios are only possible by making the rest of the world dystopic—a sort of Mad Max paradigm that opens up commentary on the state of Africa in the 21st century. Historic inversion allows for social criticism of the homeland's true realities in the present (but that are influenced by memory of the colonial past), expressed through the dystopic paradigms they portray. Their use of the West as a foil for reflecting the failed political arenas of their own nations is the most salient aspect of both works.

Examples of a satirical dystopic view are repeatedly noticeable in Belkhodja's *Le Retour de l'éléphant*. Although the context in his future place posits the West as despotic, the author is really referring to Tunisia in the present. The world has been turned inside-out, revealing the underbelly of capitalism run rampant, corruption and the overarching general malaise of humankind. John, who left behind the failed states of the USA in order to immigrate and benefit from the richness of the socioeconomic possibilities of Carthage, underscores throughout the novel the extent of American sociocultural failure. The northern hemisphere's downfall resembles Tunisia's postcolonial reality in the 2000s: "là où je viens, tout est faux. Tout est mensonge, bassesse...Les gens sont hypocrites, vils, faibles, prétentieux et profondément bêtes. Vivre dans un environnement pareil, ça te détruit le sens moral, le naturel, le vrai..." (there, from where I come, everything is false. Everything is a lie, baseless...The people are hypocrites, vile, weak, pretentious and profoundly stupid. Living in such an environment destroys a sense of morals, the natural and the true...) ([15], p. 139).

Waberi's and Belkhodja's dystopic utopian narratives describe the glistening cities of Carthage, Kinshasa, and Nairobi that signify "l'Afrique...au centre du monde" (Africa...at the world's center) ([7], p. 55), while they also explore "la misère de Manhattan ... la lagune paludéenne de Venise" (the misery of Manhattan...the malarial laguna of Venice) beyond the borders of the continent ([7], p. 89). In general, as Ashcroft suggests, the utopic-themed narrative is interesting to African authors because it allows for both use and subversion of this very recognizable Western literary motif. The glistening city of Aristotelian myth draws on "the long tradition of thinking about ideal cities" as including projections of beautiful, symmetrical, and harmonious designs for plazas, towers, and squares. These are conceived of on a dramatic scale, "sustaining ecological plans for self-sufficient environments, and so on" ([17], p. 150).

In Waberi's novel, these projections of the beautiful are reflected in the "progressive universities of certain African states such as Lubumbashi, in Ouagadougou or in certain remote ballet theatres of the savanna near Dar es-Salaam" ([7], p. 92). Luminous African cities are peopled with famous men and women of color from the continent and the diaspora, hailing from the real past and present: the tennis player Yannick Noah; authors Nuruddin Farah, Chinua Achebe, and Emmanuel Dongala; rappers King Caïn and Queen Sheba, all make appearances in Waberi's narrative. Universities across Africa are named after notables of the diaspora such as Langston Hughes, Angela Davis, and WEB Dubois, and streets for great artists and leaders, Ray-Charles, Habib-Bourguiba, and Abebe-Bikila ([7], p. 18). African places and institutions of higher learning are where "millions of white, Asian or American students...take long walks, books in hand" ([7], p. 179). The African utopian city in Waberi's novel exudes an intellectual cosmopolitanism that reflects a contemporaneous longing for a sustainable relationship in the present postcolonial era between "domestic governance and international politics" ([18], p. 453). The author thinks through transnational systems as they have impacted local societies both positively and negatively from the ancient, as well as more recent colonial past ([18], p. 453).

His "Fédération des Etas-Unis d'Afrique" is not just conceptualized in a new and unmapped utopia, it also has its roots entrenched in the "ancient Hamite kingdom of Chad", which now in the author's fictitious space is "rich in oil". In their futurist environment, "the golden boys of Tananarive" play on the shores of the island of Madagascar, a center for tourism from the continent ([7], p. 15). Waberi creates an Africa that is both capitalistic (touting its 1 percent of the very rich who hold power and money at every level) and moralistic, purporting ethical, universal understandings of human rights. The continent is also intellectually rich in scholarly institutions founded in countries like Kenya, where the *"The Kenyatta School of European and American Studies"* produces eminent specialists, and where the "vertus de la démocratie parlementaire" (virtues of parliamentary democracy) are practiced in Eritrea and Senegal alongside "on-line stock markets" that are the fruit of "the *high tech Keren Valley Project* and the military-industrial complexes of Assab" (author's italics) ([7], pp. 14–15).

These cosmopolitan establishments and institutions (which curiously continue in the future to remain tied to functioning in their former colonial languages, either English or French depending on the region) have all contributed to the continent's successes as well as failures. On the dark side of cosmopolitan largess, though, Africa has also been corrupted by its rampant, excessive capitalism. Thus, the utopic African world Waberi proposes is but an "imagined community" that cannot escape "the depravities of global capitalism and imperialism" as well as its inability to improve the human condition. His futurist Africa fails because it was unable to find solutions to real world crises ([18], p. 454). Utopian ideals are unable to come to fruition because, as Khatibi suggests, certain "values and hierarchies" must be overturned in order to "free ourselves from colonization" and "Western reasoning about the Third World" ([12], p. 50). Waberi's African world is stuck in the bogs of victimization and the usual cycles of capitalist exploitation that exist in the present as legacies of the colonial, imperial past.

In Belkhodja's novel, Carthage has prospered, its political machine founding universities in Tozeur and Tunis and remarkable "cités du désert" (desert cities) where "highways traverse the Sahara". The vast desert has been transformed into a green and fertile land by irrigation and amazing advances in ecological science ([15], p. 87). "In 2070, North Africa became an enormous garden. It was the end of plastic and pollution, where oil fields have been replaced by large solar energy panels which saved the Mediterranean Sea" ([15], p. 86). This fertile space is where "Le retour de l'éléphant" (the return of the elephant) has taken place. As a metaphor, Carthage, like the elephant, believed to be extinct, has now "come back to its home" ([15], p. 87). The Tunisian city's greatness, though, has only been able to be achieved at the expense of others. It is a "paradis" that promotes "une prospérité non seulement matérielle, mais intellectuelle, spirituelle et même environnementale" (a prosperity that is not only material, but also spiritual and environmental). However, at the same time, this status, notes Belkhodja, has been achieved by "superiority and coercion". The city and its society built by exploitation on the backs of others, like the lost city of Atlantis discovered to be underneath where Carthage now stands, will only know "une chute inévitable" (an inevitable fall) ([15], pp. 174–75). At the end of the novel, John's Tunisian friends Chams and Mouna tell him that morally and economically, "things have to change" ([15], p. 178), since Carthage has become too much of an exploitive bully, leading to failure in its humanist endeavors. Like the kingdoms of the past, in the modern age of 2103 this golden city is responsible for assuring the well-being of the less fortunate of the world, yet it has botched its mission ([15], p. 178).

Western utopian myths present a paradox for African authors. While the trope offers the possibility of liberation because it allows the writer to explore another way of being-in-the-world, utopias are also doomed to failure because they inherently always become "degenerate" ([16], p. 8). As much as the author is invested in creating a new possibility for his country and people, this space is inevitably haunted by the reality of the homeland's challenges. Attesting to this intrinsic quality of failure in his utopian ideal, Belkhodja notes in his novel's disclaimer, that the "book [is] pure fiction. The names, characters, places, organizations and described events are the products of the author's imagination, or are used in a fictional context" ([15], p. 12). He therefore places his novel in a context of impossibility before the reader even turns the first page. Through their works' fictionality, Waberi and Belkhodja reveal what Ashcroft notes is "increasingly obvious in postcolonial literatures" ([16], p. 8)—that utopias are myths that can never be fully realized.

Like Western authors who have drawn on the utopic space to explore alternative ways of being for contemporary humankind,[6] African writers are confronted with the fact that these very same utopias are fraught with contradictions that emerge when an author attempts to define what he wants his alternative space to be. The first lies in the inherent flawed meanings of utopia and utopianism, or in ideal versus practice. The very terms themselves create a binary stipulating that myth is one thing and reality is another. The second contradiction arises when authors attempt to negotiate their idealized worlds between their imagined futures and the real memories of their pasts. With respect to these narratives, the colonial past forever haunts the postcolonial present and thus cannot be dislodged. A third incongruity manifests in the tension between the individual's and the collective's aspirations and desires for a utopic world. These are at odds because a utopia can only be realized by the individual renouncing his individualism to adhere to the will of the collective majority. Despite these three contradictions faced by postcolonial authors, utopianism for Waberi and Belkhodja still manages to provide a means to explore a universal possibility that "lies deep in human consciousness" and remains a hopeful beacon countering tales of despair ([16], p. 9). Unfortunately, as both writers demonstrate, the actual utopia created within the pages of a text cannot be achieved through future hopes alone. Dislodging their narratives from the past is virtually impossible since, "in traditional post-colonial societies the radically new is always embedded in and transformed by the past" ([16], p. 9). Khatibi affirms this reality, stating that "the patriarchal, the tribal, the rural feudal" became in the postcolonial era the "instruments and techniques of a force left by imperialism" ([12], p. 52). Although the "nation is often conspicuously absent" in contemporary novels, the author is still haunted by residual colonization and later nationalist ideals that became broken promises ([16], p. 12). In the storylines of both novels, the disjunctive haunting that oscillates between residual colonialism and postcolonial disappointment is omnipresent. Waberi and Belkhodja fail to tell a different story other than the lived one in African reality. This is the danger of an alternative-history because, as a reversed image in the mirror, it still reflects back a certain truth. Khatibi underscores this conundrum, which he articulates as "the division of the world" marked by living "between the nostalgia of a totalizing identity", that of the colonizer, and "an unelaborated difference that informs what cannot be conceptualized"—an "au-délà" (a beyond), that is still unarticulated in the postcolonial era ([13], p. 14).

For the dejected immigrants from Europe and the North American continent described in both novels, coming to Africa to find work and a better life, "utopia may be...within the boundaries of the possible," but it remains "a wish-image", functioning as nothing more than "a fantastic longing or urge or desire that remains unknowable" ([17], pp. 148–50). In Waberi's novel, "les primitifs, les païens, presque toujours blancs, sont ravalés au rang de parias" (The primitives, the pagans, almost always white, are second-class to the rank of pariahs) ([7], p. 55). They will never enjoy, as Docteur Papa tells Maya, the satisfaction of building their utopia. Confirming this, Maya realizes that the evil-side of African greatness, the supposed perfect world in which she lives, has meant the "wiping away from the streets" all the undesirables; these immigrants from far off lands who are "les sous-développés [et les] miséreux" (the under-developed and the miserable) ([7], p. 55). This human dejection has been effaced by political machines making laws to keep Africa pristine ([7], p. 75). Waberi's utopia has

---

6   In the French context, Michel Houellebecq is the most well-known author writing today who repeatedly uses utopias and dystopias to explore contemporary humankind's sociocultural ennui in the age of rampant neoliberal capitalism and failed states.

fallen victim to the real scenarios of immigration, exile, poverty, and dehumanization we see daily on our television screens in our own real time.

Utopian spaces are dismantled when the individual seeks to challenge the monolithic collective whose power is integral to maintaining its vitality. Giving into the will of the collective is a caveat to the success of all utopian narratives because "while the equality of the individuals in the collective is a fundamental principle of utopian thought, the collective is always inimical to individual fulfillment". In general all members must buy into its ideology, and there is no room for dissent ([16], p. 11). This very salient fact links utopias to dystopias because for utopias to fulfill themselves, "the mobilization for the common good" must take place. Yet the price of total social cooperation means that individualism "is always denied as a condition of [fulfilling] a collective utopian dream" ([16], p. 11). In *Le Retour de l'éléphant*, when John reveals to his friend Chams that he is a member of the resistance movement in America striving to overthrow his repressive government, she responds enthusiastically, emphasizing that only the unity of the people will change the destiny of his despotic nation: "il faut sortir le peuple américain de sa peur, lui apprendre qu'il est seul maître de son destin" (it is necessary to bring the American people out of their fear, to teach them that they are the only master of their destiny) ([15], p. 179). John takes this to heart. He trades his own possibility of a better life in Carthage in order to return to the USA to cultivate the opposition that contains people "who are ready to die so that our children can live in a just and free world", a dream he knows is fraught with impossibilities ([15], p. 179). As a novel that predates the Arab Spring ignited in Tunis in December 2010, when another young man lit himself on fire in order to fight for a cause, this message takes on prominent meanings even in the pages of a novel of fiction.

Waberi's and Belkhodja's characters struggle to build the utopias of which they dream: "the mobilization of society for the betterment of all, for the common good." Ironically, though, how the common good is achieved "is virtually indistinguishable in utopias and dystopias", no matter if conceived of in a Western European or postcolonial African narrative ([16], p. 11). As explained above, both require individuals to make compromises for the larger collectives, which ultimately fail in their altruistic endeavors and hopes for a better society. The characters in both authors' novels ultimately realize that similarly to their writers' realities, collective unity and prosperity for all are virtually impossible to achieve. Ironically, though, they also send the message that hope rings eternal, particularly for younger generations on the African continent. Waberi concludes his novel through the voice of Docteur Papa, who assesses the life of his adopted daughter, Maya. She has traveled to France to look for her biological mother, whom she eventually finds trapped in destitution and poverty in the back alleys of a dingy and lawless France. Maya is resigned to return to Africa and make her fortune so that she can help her mother and other "whites" like Titus, her distant cousin. She will "use her influence" to help him enter a university in Africa. Docteur Papa wistfully tells her: "you will make everyone confident in the human race by your dedication. And you too will benefit from your dedication...this will help lift some of the burden of culpability. Ah! Culpability, my little Malaïka, this is what eats away at your guts, it sucks your blood" ([7], p. 180). Titus, like the few immigrants who make it to African shores, will "se cramponner" (climb) up the social ladder in his adopted land in order to "vaincre la chiennerie de la vie" (overcome the doggedness of life). He must realize his goals, or he will "glisser sous l'eau et se noyer pour toujours" (slip under water and drown forever) ([7], p. 180).

In both novels' reversed history, the African continent adheres to basic truths about capitalism and global markets which, in the end, are their utopias' downfalls. Greed and corruption are inevitable in the ultramodern societies these landscapes portray. Belkhodja and Waberi offer us a dark side to the fantastical, gleaming African world they create in order to bring to the fore some prominent messages about the human condition in the 2000s. These lead readers to ask, are we doomed forever to live in a world (even when fictionalized) where there will always be haves and have-nots? As in our geopolitical and economically strained global reality, their African utopias are tainted by what Mbembe stipulates is the antithesis of the Afropolitan ideal: "the violence and the victimization" meted out by the "torturers" of "so many countries—not only African". These negative forces "spur on the pulse of genocide…the incredible power of destruction" ([14], p. 2). Waberi's and Belkhodja's novels' utopic worlds fail because they are rooted in a one-model, capitalist system that does not allow for equality and equitable distribution of wealth. Their utopic fantasy-Africa can only project back a mirror image of the global realities in which we live. These authors' salient messages reflect the reality of the grave humanitarian crises of our era: the plagues of Ebola and dengue fever, poverty, urban blight, religious fanaticism, and environmental catastrophe that are destabilizing the continent.

The momentous African realities that haunt both narratives do, though, entreat thinking about the humanist stipulation that "one has obligations to others" ([6], p. xv) because s/he is "alongside others" in the world, and it is from this being with others that one fulfills his/her being-in-the-world. Although set in unreal spaces, both narratives are socioculturally and politically committed to educating their readers. They force us to think about possible solutions to the calamities raining down on humankind. For the well-being of the world's collective, we are all implicated in defining resolutions.

In Waberi's reversed history, something must be done to accommodate the Western-other who migrates to Africa to save himself. These poor and desperate "refugees" who make their way to Africa, primarily clandestinely, as "skeletal boat people", are part of the masses of "caucasiens d'ethnies diverses et variées (autrichienne, canadienne, américaine, norvégienne, belge, bulgare, britannique, islandaise, portugaise, hongroise, suédoise)" (whites of various and diverse ethnicities [Austrian, Canadian, American, Norwegian, Belgian, Bulgarian, British, Icelandic, Portuguese, Hungarian, Swedish]) for whom hope for a better life is elusive ([7], p. 12). In a continental effort to elicit aid, reports are written by scholars of migration at the University of Gao. In research groups, they publish papers such as "*Les Frontières invisibles ou le défi de l'immigration en provenance de l'Alaska*, Kigali, University Press of Rwanda/Free Press, 1994, 820 pages, 35 guinées)" in their efforts to document African aid work and its challenges ([7], p. 17). The shared citizenship of cosmopolitan communitarianism means finding ways, as revealed in Belkhodja's novel, of sharing wealth with poorer European and North American nations, ending the civil wars there, and "the corruption that ruled and caused an enormous proportion of the social problems until the middle of the 21st century" ([15], p. 78). While both utopias are founded on humanist principles that rely on sacrifice for the good of the collective whole, the characters realize that such martyrdom is unattainable. Africa has become the world's gate keeper, a beacon of light on a planet of civil strife yet, despite its socioeconomic strength, instability, and poverty elsewhere have slowly crept into its humanist ethos, forcing the continent into the same past cyclical failures with respect to helping others. In Belkhodja's novel, the technological advances Carthage has made could not keep the "affaissement des USA" (the wiping away of the USA) from happening in the 21st century. Victim of its lust for control, America and the greater "Occident…were unable to take the reins", which caused their "inevitable downfall". Such catastrophes as "les manipulations de virus, manipulations génétiques et frénésie du profit" (manipulation of viruses, genetic and frenzied manipulations for profit), as well as a politics that became increasingly "nationalist", even considered "fundamentalist", not to mention "racial and religious strife", allowed "Arabs to take up the challenge and to vanquish". However, Carthage's victory could not assure that its advances in technology would be able to "help the West, since its regimes were less and less democratic" ([15], pp. 89–90). By the end of the 20th century, the West was completely consumed by its backwardness.

4. The *Unheimlich* of Otherness

Mbembe suggests in his work that for the Afropolitan to realize a being-in-the-world that escapes insular thinking, "our activities" must "not be measured by the village next door, but rather by the extended world" ([14], p. 3). Both Belkhodja and Waberi compel readers to "know the other"—those of the extended world—by "putting oneself *in [the other's] place*" ([19], p. 25) (author's italics). Through these narratives we confront our fear and loathing, what Julia Kristeva names as the *unheimlich* (the uncanny and uncomfortable) space occupied by the "étranger" (foreigner) ([19], p. 282): "The uncanny strangeness allows for many variations: they all repeat the difficulty I have in situating myself with respect to the other" ([19], p. 187). Waberi's novel, in particular, engages with the fear and loathing that often manifests in the relationship between Self and Other: "La peur irrationnelle de l'autre, de l'indésirable, et qui continue à être la plus grande menace pour l'unité africaine" (the irrational fear of the other, the undesirable, and that continues to be the greatest menace to African unity) ([7], p. 16). This menace is encapsulated in Yacouba, a Swiss, white, illiterate, migrant worker who can only speak in his native "German patois" and who has clandestinely come to Africa, "fleeing violence and famine" hoping to find work in the fields of the continent ([7], p. 11). His story intertwines, yet never intersects, with the more dominant oppositional one of adopted, white Maya who has been saved from inevitable poverty by the powerful and well-off Docteur Papa. Yacouba is invisible, "unable to speak the language of the Federation of Africa" ([7], p. 39), forced to live in the shadows, on the borders of rich neighborhoods, victim to "alcohol made from khat that pollutes the body" ([7], p. 43). He finally dies in the street, dejected and unnoticed by the inhabitants of the rich high-rise apartments overhead. Where Yacouba and Maya share affinity is that their stories are told for them by Docteur Papa. He alone possesses the Master Narrative of Africa. Their deposed first-person narratives disrupt the European, logocentrality of white stories that have dominated Africa for centuries. Waberi displaces long-accepted "representations of whiteness in the black imagination" by displacing the history of the power of whiteness on the African continent. Embodied for centuries through a "critical ethnographic gaze", the narrative destabilizes the legacy of Western colonial ideals and neocolonial globalization that promote stereotypes about African inferiority woven into racial prejudice ([20], pp. 167–68).

Although he proposes a reversed history, throughout *Aux États-Unis d'Afrique* Waberi insists on engaging with Western conceptions of "Africa as an idea, a concept", which Mbembe affirms, "has historically served, and continues to serve, as a polemical argument for the West's desperate desire to assert its difference from the rest of the world" ([14], p. 2). In the novel's counter-narrative, European stereotypes of Africa haunt the mirror-image descriptions of decrepit Europe and the impoverished USA. These descriptions are meted out through dialogues among xenophobic African politicians and the interior monologue of Docteur Papa, who reflects on his society's failings as he expresses his concerns for the life choices his adopted daughter is making as she wanders across Africa and, later, to Europe in search of her birth mother. Many of these choices, and her general nomadic lifestyle, Docteur Papa attributes to her alterity: her difference embedded in her whiteness even though she has been separated her entire life from the Europe of her past. "Why, Maya, this hunger for difference, this constant availability, this sensibility that is so contrary to the haughty assurance of our African intellectuals who are nourished only with sarcastic force and disdain for their countries?" ([7], p. 162). Maya in her difference will always be marginalized in Africa.

Notwithstanding the subtexts of their novels, narrating very striking realities about the state of transnational, economic relationships between the West and Africa, Waberi and Belkhodja write new signs and signifiers that counter the standards of Western conceptions of Africa. These new signs challenge, as Mbembe notes, Africa as "one of the metaphors through which the West represents the origin of its own norms, develops a self-image, and integrates this image into the set of signifiers asserting what it supposes to be its identity" ([14], p. 2). Displacing these codified, spatial signifiers of African and Western realms in order to posit an alternative space that is not bound by racial or geographical binaries, Waberi uses Maya to create his "what if" and to make a point about the human condition in our modern world. Although she never speaks directly in the novel, the young woman metaphorically depicts the possible weaving of Self and Other, the fruition of Khatibi's pensée-autre. She is fluid, operating in a transnational realm where white and black skin, Europe and Africa, French and African could meld and shape a singular identity that is from everywhere and nowhere at the same time if only she were allowed to do so. Her essence evokes an Afropolitan being-in-the-world that represents shared citizenship with the world of others. This ideal remains, though, an unfulfilled reality for her. All the love and means given to her by her African parents cannot overcome the fact that she still feels and suffers from being "exiled" by her experience as a young woman "whose root is no longer anywhere" ([7], p. 168), as Docteur Papa remarks:

Tu es et tu restes une exilée, une exilée à la racine qui plus est. Tu aurais le choix, tu dirais aux os blanchis sous la dalle froide de tes ancêtres: "Levez-vous et suivez-moi sur les terres d'Afrique bénies par les Dieux et par le soleil douze mois sur douze"...Exilée à la racine, bannie dès l'origine...Tu seras une jeune pousse prête à avaler les nouvelles règles, les nouveaux labels et les plus récent poinçons. Tu seras une autre et toi-même à la fois ([7], p. 168).

(You are and you will remain exiled, an exiled woman whose root is no longer. You would say that you have the choice of whitened bones under the cold slab of your ancestors: "Get up and follow me on the African lands blessed by Gods and by the sun twelve months out of the year"...Exiled to the root, banned of origin...You will be a young shoot ready to swallow new rules, new labels and the most recent stamps. You will be an Other and yourself at the same time.)

Maya's transcultural ties as well as her exiled displacement compel her to crisscross continents in search of her mother and relearn "les rudiments de cette langue" (the rudiments of this language) of her childhood ([7], p. 151): a French that is "lacking...glosses, analyses...without an academy or a pantheon" ([7], p. 155). She is forced in this transcontinental space to engage with the "Other" that is really part of her Self, in a Europe that is both foreign and home. Even in Europe, though, she will not be able to claim her own narrative. Docteur Papa tells her, "tu as la couleur locale, tu le sais bien. Tant que tu n'ouvres pas la bouche, personne ne peut soupçonner ton statut d'étrangère" (you have the local color, you know this. As long as you don't open your mouth, no one will suspect that you are a foreigner) ([7], p. 150). In the end, despite her cosmopolitanism, her will to be a citizen of the world, and her attempts to bridge her African present with a decrepit European past, Maya remains alienated and alone, unable to articulate—to speak—her biculturalism. She is destined to wear her "origin like a wound and a defeat" ([7], p. 173). The trap of transnationalism, of being from "nowhere", Waberi warns, also assures a certain alienation of the subject: the potential failure to *be alongside others* that is unfortunately a reality of the postcolonial reality in which we live. Although perhaps liberating, Waberi warns that transnationalism, the presence of self and other in the same individual, also means inevitable disjunction from nation and tribe. Can the multicultural subject, then, really forsake "kith and kin", as Anthony Appiah would have her do, in order to embrace the cosmopolitanism for which she strives as a person who can live perpetually in the *elsewhere*? Utopic dreams of wholeness and Khatibi's "bringing to light" the plurality of a transnational existence that allows for *becoming something other* are still elusive in Waberi's and Belkhodja's narratives. They show what potentially could be but that is destined to exist only in the utopias of a future world.

5. Conclusions

The dystopic utopias proposed in *Le Retour de l'éléphant* and *Aux États-Unis d'Afrique* reveal that the postcolonial African author of French expression finds himself at odds, caught in a "double attachment", in the middle of what Khatibi defines as "the constantly reemerging world of the colonizer" and the "tribal, Makhzen [state power] of the postcolonial nation" ([12], p. 53). However, if we consider Waberi's and Belkhodja's novels as proposing alternative realities for Africa in order to study the challenges of contemporary issues that need to be addressed, then we can say they have met their goals as works that are universally humanist. Through these fictions, not only is Africa forced to confront its failings, the West, too, as it looks in the mirror and sees its image reflected back, is compelled to consider the potential that the African continent could offer if the tables were turned. Dystopic utopias compel us to think about colonial coercive pasts and the failures of postcolonial present. These 21st century Afropolitan novels written in French engage with transnational cosmopolitan ideals that ground Africans' being-in-the-world as multicultural, plural-lingual and open to a postcolonial world that is leaving the "post" behind. And while their novels are set in a distant future, they do not hide these authors' commitment to tackling the new challenges of our age that extend beyond the borders of nations and continents to embrace being a "citizen of the world".[7]

Conflicts of Interest: The author declares no conflict of interest.

References

1. Simon Gikandi. "On Afropolitanism." In *Negotiating Afropolitanism: Essays on Borders and Spaces in Contemporary African Literature and Folklore*. Edited by Jennifer Wawrzinek and J. K. S. Makokha. Amsterdam: Rodopi, 2011.
2. Evan M. Mwangi. *Africa Writes Back to Self: Metafiction, Gender, Sexuality*. Albany: SUNY Press, 2009.
3. Paul Jay. *Global Matters: The Transnational Turn in Literary Studies*. Ithaca: Cornell University Press, 2010.
4. Onwuchekwa Jemie Chinweizu, and Ihechukwu Madubuike. *Toward the Decolonization of African Literature*. Washington: Howard University Press, 1983.
5. Frantz Fanon. *The Wretched of the Earth*. Translated by Richard Philcox. New York: Grove Press, 2004.
6. Kwame Anthony Appiah. *Cosmopolitanism: Ethics in a World of Strangers*. New York: Norton, 2006.
7. Abdourahman Waberi. *Aux Etats-Unis d'Afrique*. Paris: Editions Jean-Claude Lattès, 2006.
8. Martin Heidegger. *Being and Time*. New York: HarperCollins, 1962.
9. K. S Makokha. *Negotiating Afropolitanism: Essays on Borders and Spaces in Contemporary African Literature and Folklore*. Amsterdam and New York: Rodopi, 2011.
10. Gilles Deleuze. *The Logic of Sense*. New York: Columbia, 1990.
11. Eugene Young, and Gary Genosko. *The Deleuze and Guattari Dictionary*. London: Bloomsbury, 2013.
12. Abdelkébir Khatibi. *Maghreb Pluriel*. Paris: Denoël, 1983.
13. Abdelkébir Khatibi. *La Mémoire Tatouée: Autobiographie d'un Décolonisé*. Paris: Denoël, 1971.
14. Achille Mbembe. "Afropolitanisme." *Africultures* 66 (2006): 1–3. Available online: http://www.africultures. com/ (accessed on 28 April 2016). [CrossRef]
15. Abdelaziz Belkhodja. *Le Retour de l'éléphant*. Tunis: Apollonia, 2003.
16. Bill Ashcroft. "The Ambiguous Necessity of Utopia: Post-Colonial Literatures and the Persistence of Hope." *Social Alternatives* 28 (2009): 8–14.
17. Gregory Claeys. "News from Somewhere: Enhanced Sociability and the Composite Definition of Utopia and Dystopia." *History: The Journal of the Historical Association* 98 (2013): 145–73. [CrossRef]
18. Tanya Agathocleous. "Cosmopolitanism and Literary Form." *Literature Compass* 7 (2010): 452–66. [CrossRef]
19. Julia Kristeva. *Strangers to Ourselves*. New York: Columbia University Press, 1991, p. 25.
20. Bell Hooks. "Whiteness in the Black Imagination." In *Displacing Whiteness: Essays in Social and Cultural Criticism*. Edited by Ruth Frankenberg. Durham: Duke University Press, 1997, pp. 164–79.

---

7 As promoted in Appiah's *Cosmopolitanism*.

MDPI

Article

Transculturalism and the Meaning of Life

James Tartaglia

School of Politics, Philosophy, International Relations and Environment, Keele University, Staffordshire ST5 5BG, UK; j.tartaglia@keele.ac.uk; Tel.: +44-178-273-4315

Academic Editor: Bernd Fischer
Received: 14 March 2016; Accepted: 22 April 2016; Published: 26 April 2016

Abstract: I begin by introducing the standoff between the transculturalist aim of moving beyond cultural inheritances, and the worry that this project is itself a product of cultural inheritances. I argue that this is rooted in concerns about the meaning of life, and in particular, the prospect of nihilism. I then distinguish two diametrically opposed humanistic responses to nihilism, post-Nietzschean rejections of objective truth, and the moral objectivism favoured by some analytic philosophers, claiming that both attempt, in different ways, to break down the distinction between description and evaluation. I argue that the evaluative sense of a "meaningful life" favoured by moral objectivists cannot track objective meaningfulness in human lives, and that there are manifest dangers to treating social meaning judgements as a secular substitute for the meaning of life. I then conclude that the problems of the post-Nietzscheans and moral objectivists can be avoided, and the transculturalist standoff alleviated, if we recognise that nihilism is descriptive, and maintain a principled distinction between description and evaluation.

Keywords: transculturalism; meaning of life; meaning in life; humanism; description and evaluation; moral objectivism; Nietzsche

1. The Transculturalist Standoff

Transculturalism is about looking for shared interests and beliefs, which extend across cultural, historically contingent boundaries [1]. To take a classic example, anyone likely to read this essay is unlikely to approve of the Samurai practice of "trying out one's new sword" on passing wayfarers [2]. If that seemed acceptable to the Samurai, we might say, then so much the worse for Samurai culture. If the aim of transculturalism is to transcend cultural baggage, which lands people with obnoxious practices such as these (and there are many contemporary examples, of course, such as female genital mutilation), then it might seem an uncontroversially good idea. But there is nothing uncontroversial about it, because from the perspective of historicist and relativist lines of thought, the natural response is that transculturalism is itself rooted in cultural baggage. In particular, it might be said, it is rooted in the European Enlightenment's ideal of universality, the paradigm of which is to be found in cultural practices such as natural science, mathematics and philosophy; but not all philosophy, because this objection itself comes out of a post-Nietzschean kind of philosophy that has been prominent since the 1960s. A strong conclusion you might draw from these lines of thought is that transculturalism is a project of cultural imperialism; an attempt to undermine the values of other cultures because we do not like them—and this because they do not cohere with our own. So perhaps transculturalism is not good after all, but rather bad. (Although the issue of which perspective this assessment is made from then naturally arises; I shall return to this).

This impasse starts to seem more tractable if we distinguish evaluations from descriptions. Judgements about morality or aesthetics are, on the face of it, evaluative; we evaluate a person's conduct or an artwork. Judgements about the circumference of our planet, what the square root of nine is, or whether the physical world is mind-independent, on the other hand, are, on the face of it, descriptive; our judgement is aimed at accurately describing an independent state of affairs. For evaluative disagreements to get off the ground, we must presuppose a description. We must agree about what the person did (smashed the vase, said "it's your fault"), before we can disagree about how to morally evaluate it; and there should be no problem agreeing about what the artwork consists in (how the paint is arranged on the canvas), even if we disagree about how to aesthetically evaluate it. In the case of descriptive disagreements, however, the description is exactly what is in dispute.

Only for evaluative judgements does the basic dispute about transculturalism sketched above seem reasonable. The defender of transculturalism might reasonably think that people's evaluations are sometimes rooted in regrettable cultural traditions, which prevent them from rationally evaluating their own best interests and those of others, and thus that we need to move beyond the problematic elements of our particular cultural inheritances. This need not mean abandoning our cultural roots, of course, simply looking beyond them. The detractor of transculturalism, on the other hand, might reasonably think that since *all* values emerge from a culture, this is a sly attempt to give one set of evaluative judgements the upper hand.

If we turn to descriptive judgements, however, the dispute immediately looks more dubious. If your cultural background inclines you to disagree when those of another culture proclaim that an abstract expressionist painting is great art, or that an act of "ethnic cleansing" is a moral abomination, then trying to find any mutual ground on which the matter might be resolved does indeed seem problematic; appeals to a shared humanity are likely to fall on deaf ears when dealing with people who evaluate only from the perspective of their own ethnic group, for instance. You can tell them they should not do this, but that is just another evaluation. However if your cultural background inclines you to think the world is flat, or that your traditional medicines are more effective than contemporary medical science, then since this is at root a descriptive disagreement, the world can intervene to settle the matter. Those with such beliefs will find that no matter how hard they try, they cannot reach the edge of the world; and that if they take the right drugs they will get well.

To think culture has any relevance to this, I think, is to confuse the fact that the views came out of a culture, as well as the cultural significance they have, with what the views actually *are*, and hence what they tell us about the world. If you start talking about how flat-Earth belief might serve the cultural purpose of maintaining a theological perspective best suited to a certain group's way of life, or how a traditional medicine, however "ineffectual" by Western standards, nevertheless serves other, more important cultural purposes, then you are in the grip of that very confusion. The flat-Earth people may never *try* to reach the edge, and may be better off because of that; and you might even argue that it is better, from their perspective, to stick to their own medicinal practices, even if this leads to avoidable death. However, if they did look for the edge, they would not find it; and if they took the drugs, they would survive. A reality indifferent to our cultures upholds these conditionals. We may not want to evaluate more accurate descriptions as better descriptions. However, you cannot evaluate without describing, and to evaluate inaccurate descriptions as better, perhaps because they are more useful to us, is to implicitly describe them as not describing how the world actually is (and then commend the useful consequences of this). Either way, our non-evaluative, descriptive notion of description remains. Evaluation does not go all the way down because it rests upon description; but description bottoms out.

Now the "post-Nietzschean" philosophers, as I have labelled them, would not accept this distinction. Rorty, the clearest writer from this tradition, vehemently rejected the idea that there is a "way the world is" which can validate our descriptions, for he held that aesthetic, moral, political, scientific and mathematic statements are all on a par ([3], pp. 315–56). To think that when evaluations are accepted, this is simply due to their fit with a contingent social consensus, whereas descriptions can be made true by the objective facts, irrespective of what any society thinks about it, is in his view to confuse the greater consensus found in some areas of culture (natural science; maths) with the dictates of an independent world. Politics and art could achieve just as much consensus, he thinks, and have done at certain periods in history ([3], pp. 321–22). The notion of an objectively spherical

Earth which falsifies flat-Earth theory is, for Rorty, a pernicious, quasi-religious idea that infantilises us; it stems from a desire to have our beliefs pressed upon us by a greater power, so that we do not have to take responsibility for what we think. For the world cannot *justify* our beliefs; it can *cause* us to hold beliefs, but only once cultural evolution has embedded an interpretation of the world within us, through collective negotiation, extended discussion, and no little happenstance. Additionally, since the driver of this cultural evolution is the pragmatic one of meeting the needs of the community, such interpretations are always, in effect, evaluations. So there is no pure description, any more than there is an independent, objective "way the world is" to describe.[1]

"Post-Nietzschean" is an apt label for this kind of view, because it originates in Nietzsche's conception of truth as "the last form of nihilism" ([6], p. 13). Nietzsche's nihilist is someone who condemns the world from the perspective of historically inculcated values, which place all worth in another world beyond this one; such as the Christian heaven. By the time the nihilist's understanding has ascended to this "last form", they realise that this supposedly better world was simply a product of human psychological needs, such as the need to be vindicated and to overcome fear of death. As such they deny the existence of the other world—they declare that religious beliefs are *not true*—but still retaining values formed in accordance with its concept, they find themselves condemning the real world; it does not live up to their otherworldly ideals, so they evaluate it negatively. For Nietzsche, this renders the notion of truth a life-denying fabrication, which leaves us reaching for "nothingness" (which is all the nihilist finds when looking for a God to vindicate us) in order to condemn "*this* state of being" ([6], p. 253). The nihilist realises that human life will never be vindicated by a meaning of life, since there is none, so because they conceive life's potential for value as residing solely with the supernatural, they consequently regard the meaninglessness of life which they have now discovered as a truth which condemns life; the only pertinent truth as regards the value of human life seems to them that of our contingent and arbitrary existence within an indifferent physical universe. The deepest root of this nihilism, which Nietzsche thinks we must learn to overcome, is our notion of truth; the objective kind, indifferent to human interests, which I endorsed above in my commonsensical distinction between evaluation and description.[2]

I think that this worry about the meaning of life remains at the basis of post-Nietzschean rejections of the notion of objective truth; rejections which are, on the face of it, as implausible as anything to be found in the history of philosophy. I also think that the worry is unfounded. For the claim that reality is meaningless, and consequently that there is no meaning of life (which is what I call "nihilism", in contrast to Nietzsche's more loaded usage), is not an evaluation; and hence it is not a negative (or indeed, positive) evaluation. It is a description. I shall not make this case here (but see [8]); although the basic idea is that human life as a whole could only be meaningful if it existed within a context that transcends the physical universe, and whether or not there is such a context is a factual matter.[3] Neither will I evaluate the positive arguments behind denials of objective truth (but see [5]). My concern in this paper is rather to reveal common ground between this post-Nietzschean reaction to nihilism, and the very different reaction of analytic, naturalist philosophers; and to bring this to bear on the transculturalist standoff.

Suppose, then, that we grant my distinction between evaluation and description, and put the post-Nietzscheans to one side for now. In that case, we can dismiss the standoff about transculturalism as applied to descriptions. If cultural inheritance ever gets in the way of accepting non-evaluative, purportedly (and we hope, actually) objective descriptions of the world, then we do indeed need to

---

1 For a full account of Rorty's story, see [4]; for a shorter account with more critical intent, see [5].
2 My interpretation of Nietzsche broadly follows Reginster [7].
3 If this is right, then there is no prospect of collapsing the distinction between evaluation and description by arguing, as was suggested by a reviewer of this paper, that the meaning of life is to perpetuate life: that the physical universe has hard-wired into us a desire to survive, such that an "ought" is a disguised biological "is". For if the physical universe has no intrinsic meaning or purpose, which explains why it exists, then there can be no intrinsic meaning or purpose to human beings surviving within that context; so this cannot be the meaning of life (see [8], esp. p. 48ff.).

look beyond that cultural inheritance, *if*—and the "if" is important—we want our descriptions to match up with the world. We might not want this, because we might consider the maintenance of other descriptions of greater cultural importance. But this would of course be an evaluation. It would not be cultural imperialism for another culture to point out that our descriptions are, in fact, false; but it would be if they insisted that we ought not, in an absolute sense, endorse them. We ought not to if we want to endorse the truth, but the hypothesis is that we are prioritising other needs.

So that just leaves the evaluative standoff. On the one hand, it seems like a good idea to look beyond cultural baggage that leads people to endorse practices like "trying out one's new sword". But on the other, it seems as if condemnation of such practices itself reflects cultural baggage, and hence that recommending another culture to change, on the basis of principles we can purportedly all agree on, smacks of cultural imperialism.

It is not clear to me that this standoff needs to be resolved in order for recognisably transculturalist results to be achieved. If we think there are universal principles, or at least principles wide enough to apply both to us and the other culture, then there is no cultural imperialism involved in recommending them; because we do not think the principles we are recommending *are* simply our own cultural baggage. Moreover, it is only a recommendation, which the other culture is free to consider, while perhaps suggesting their own take on what the universal principles are. We may of course want to undermine some of their values; but then, they may well want to undermine some of ours too, and starting a conversation is a far cry from imposing our values by means of force, which is what "imperialism" suggests. Perhaps those at the receiving end of the practice (the innocent wayfarers) have no freedom to appeal to transcultural principles to those in power (the Samurai), but this is not a theoretical difficulty with transculturalism; only its political practicality. On the other hand, if we do not think there are any such principles, then we could adopt Rorty's "ethnocentric" proposal of advertising the benefits of our way of doing things, in the hope that our culture is attractive enough to inspire others to join it; or at least adopt some of its features [9]. The hope is that the values of the others are such that these benefits can be recognised; or that new generations will discover the new options we have presented when developing their values. Again, we can assume it will work both ways, so the result is more readily conceived as free conversation than forced imposition.

On either approach, the anticipated results are recognisably transculturalist, in that we are not reconciling ourselves and others to the cultural practices history delivered, just because they were so delivered, but are rather looking beyond them in the hope of finding—or in Rorty's case, trying to create—mutual ground. Thus, we do not need to resolve the standoff in order to endorse the manifest benefits of transculturalism, then, since we can approach its aims from the basis of either theoretical commitment; in reality, both kinds of approach will probably take place when we strongly disapprove of a practice.[4] It only becomes important if we hold that cultural practices should only be evaluated from the perspective of their own culture, and hence that we should keep our evaluations to ourselves. However, the problem with this line, alluded to in parenthesis when I originally set things up, is that the evaluative "should"s then immediately come into question. For either they refer to a universal stance the evaluation itself rules out, or else they refer to the standards of the culture from which they emerge. It must be the latter, on pain of incoherence; but since most people would not share this evaluation when confronted with an abhorrent practice, it can at most amount to a recommendation for cultural change. One which is very unlikely to be adopted in our rapidly shrinking world, and, by its own standards, is unable to provide stronger grounds for its adoption than that such an evaluative practice is possible. Strong relativist positions have faced this kind of intractable self-referential difficulty ever since Protagoras.

My primary concern in this paper lies with a philosophical issue which I think lies at the root of the standoff: Namely the meaning of life. In particular, my concern is with the interest recently taken in it by

---

[4] As I think they are in the current debate about attitudes to sexuality between different cultures within the Christian faith.

philosophers at the opposite end of the spectrum from the post-Nietzscheans. For these philosophers, operating within the analytic tradition, and with at least a presumption of naturalism—though sometimes explicit commitment to metaphysical physicalism—hold that there can be objective truths even in evaluative matters.[5] This statement requires qualification, because not all the philosophers within the "meaning in life" paradigm I have in mind are open about this. Some are; Thaddeus Metz, the most prolific writer in the area, is a physicalist who believes there are objective moral truths ([10], pp. 91–92, 171–72).[6] However, the majority show little or no concern for the metaphysical foundations of their position.

It seems to me, however, that the paradigm requires objective truths of this kind in order to make sense. For the aim is to discover the criteria human beings must fulfil in order to live an objectively meaningful life; without appealing to God, or anything else beyond the physical universe. If there are such criteria—which are supposed to be objective and universal rather than relative to any particular culture—then they must at the very least supervene upon the facts about the physical world. Cultural relativity never comes into these debates, so I can only assume that when these philosophers focus their attention exclusively on intuitions about which kind of lives count as meaningful, in order to generate a formula for a "meaningful life", most are either unaware of the naturalistic, objective backdrop presupposed by their work, or else are simply too focused on the matter in hand to find the metaphysics worth mentioning; thus leaving it as a matter for others. Analytic philosophy is typically conceived as a piece-meal, collaborative effort, so perhaps such a division of labour makes sense.

I do not think so, however, because according to the argument I shall present in the next section, reflection on the naturalistic metaphysical backdrop of this debate puts it into a whole new light; and not a good one. Moreover, I think that the problem I will bring out bears fruitful comparison with that averred in connection with the post-Nietzscheans, namely that they make the mistake of thinking that nihilism is a negative evaluation. Now of course, to hold that there are objective moral facts is not necessarily to reject the distinction between evaluation and description. For you could accept the distinction while still holding that both evaluative and descriptive judgements are ultimately settled by objective facts. These could just be different kinds of facts; for instance, physical facts in descriptive cases, and moral facts, which supervene on the physical facts, in the evaluative cases. However although the distinction is not explicitly rejected simply in virtue of commitment to moral objectivism, it is still significantly diluted, such that evaluation and description turn out to be much more similar than they first seemed.

2. An Objectively Meaningful Life

There is a natural, important, but apparently very easy-to-miss distinction to be made between the meaning *of* life and meaning *in* life. The meaning *of* life would be the reason we are here, which could make all our lives intrinsically meaningful. It could, but might not, because human beings may have no essential role in the cosmic plan; or maybe just some do. However, nevertheless, this is the meaning issue that has vexed religions, philosophies and innumerable ordinary people since time immemorial; it is a dominant theme in the earliest substantially extant work of Western literature, to take just one evocative example [11]. However, whether or not there is a meaning of life, we sometimes make judgements about the social meaning of each other's lives; we might judge that Gandhi had a particularly meaningful life, for instance. Judgements about social meaning concern the meaning individual lives build up within the context of human society, and take a number of different forms, as will be discussed below. Clarifying such judgements is the meaning *in* life issue, which has preoccupied analytic philosophers in recent times. Its origins are far more recent than those of the meaning *of*

---

5   I understand naturalism as the view that the nature of reality is best investigated through the methods of natural science, and physicalism as the view that fundamental physics provides our best answer to the metaphysical question of what exists.

6   Although Metz uses "naturalist" rather than "physicalist" to describe himself, these cited passages (among many others) leave little doubt as to his metaphysical intent; and he describes himself as defending a "realist metaphysic" ([10], p. 7).

life question; they lie predominantly, in so far as I am able to ascertain, in 19th century reactions to atheism [8].

The distinction is natural because we often distinguish between the meaning *in* and *of* a phenomenon. For instance, we distinguish the meaning in an artwork, such as the classical themes it alludes to or the emotions it portrays, from the meaning of the artwork, such as the significance it was invested with in the cultural milieu of its times. Additionally, the distinction is philosophically important, because the meaning of life and judgements about social meaningfulness may or may not be connected. If there is a meaning of life, there may be a strong connection, because the meaning of life may dictate that we must live in certain ways; which is of course what innumerable religious believers have supposed. To live meaningful lives, in that case, we must aim to make our judgements about social meaning track the meaning of life; we must live in accordance with the reason for which we were put here. However, there may not be any such connection, because what we do with our lives may be irrelevant to the intrinsic meaning they possess. In addition, if we do not know the meaning of life, we are not in a position to try to align our lives with it anyway.[7] Nevertheless, if there is a meaning of life, it *might* have important connections to our judgements about social meaning. If there is not, however, then it is far from obvious that the issues are connected. For if reality is meaningless, and I am right that this is not an evaluation, but rather just a description of a neutral fact, then arguably there is *no* connection between the issues, except for an historical one concerning how interest in meaning *in* life arose ([8], pp. 1–11). Reality as a whole is meaningless, and hence so is human life; but within life there is social meaning, generated relationally by our interactions. Social meaning is something we make judgements about.

Natural and important as it may be, however, within the recent debate in analytic philosophy, the distinction is routinely trivialised, conflated, or simply missed. One popular tactic (e.g., [13]) is to mention and dismiss the question of the meaning *of* life as if it were a trivial addendum to the real issue, namely social meaning judgements; which in terms of cultural significance and the history of philosophy, is to get things precisely the wrong way around. Metz, for instance, casually dismisses "cosmic" issues (*i.e.*, the meaning *of* life) as a minority interest, and resolves to talk exclusively about social meaning in his book *Meaning in Life*—as would be expected from the title—but then informs the reader that he will use the labels "meaning in life" and "the meaning of life" interchangeably ([10], p. 3ff.).[8] Another tactic is to start out with the question of the meaning of life, and claim to answer it with an account of social meaning. Robert Nozick [15] and Todd May [16] take this approach. However, most philosophers, especially those within the thought-experiment riddled paradigm which Susan Wolf [17] initiated in the late 1990s, seem oblivious to the distinction, and hence tend to change the subject without realising; most typically by engaging the reader's interest with the question of the meaning of life, and then proceeding to talk about social meaning.

I have grave reservations about the "meaning in life" project, quite apart from my overarching concern that it neglects, and encourages neglect of, the far more philosophically interesting issue of the meaning of life. Three main themes to these reservations, which I have developed before ([8], pp. 12–19; [18,19]), are as follows. The first is that judgements about social meaning take a number of different forms; four stand out. Sometimes they simply concern the social significance of a life, irrespective of its moral dimension; such that it might be said that Hitler had a particularly meaningful life. Sometimes they concern what a person valued about their life, such that we might say of someone who loved stamp collecting, that the hobby "gave meaning to his/her life". Sometimes

---

[7] Philosophers sometimes try to overcome this epistemic obstacle by positing intimations of transcendent reality within ordinary life; e.g., ([12], p. 100).

[8] Metz now recognises the distinction, because he explicitly states it at the beginning of his review of Todd May's *A Significant Life* [14]; a book which Metz says provides a theory of meaning *in* life only. He is right about that, but somehow manages to miss the fact that May evidently takes himself to be addressing the meaning *of* life. The level of confusion this apparently simple distinction generates never ceases to amaze me.

they simply concern what a person did with their life, such that we might say that the meaning of a medieval peasant's life was determined by his or her farming activities. Sometimes they are used as a term of approbation; as in the case of Gandhi, or perhaps that of a great artist or scientist. It is this final, approving sense which the debate overwhelmingly fixates upon. Nevertheless, some philosophers instead opt for the "what the person valued" sense [20,21], leading to arguments at cross-purposes. Others, like Wolf [17], try to combine the two, leading to an incoherent "subjective and objective" account.[9]

The reason the approving sense is privileged within these debates, I think, is that its participants think they are providing a naturalistic account of the meaning *of* life. However—and this is my second theme of reservation—this particular sense is *obviously* culturally relative, in that which culture you were born into will obviously affect your judgements about which lives have good social meaning. A Samurai could hardly be expected to agree with the Pope on such matters. Yet the methodology of this debate is simply to think hard about various imaginative test-cases, in order to see if the feature the test-case shines a spotlight on would make a person's life more or less meaningful; according to the intuitions of individual contemporary western analytic philosophers, who as a group tend not to share many intuitions on these matters, judging from the disagreements that ensue. Perhaps such a methodology is apt when debating about perception or the problem of universals, for instance, where on the face of it, cultural background is of little or no relevance. But "socially meaningful in a good way" was hardly going to belong in that bracket.

My third source of reservation is ethical. For if you focus exclusively on the approving sense, as most do—with paradigmatic great men like Gandhi as your starting point—then the result will almost inevitably be a formula for meaningfulness which the vast majority of human beings will fall short of, and thereby be condemned as living more or less meaningless lives.[10] For what is admired about lives of great moral, aesthetic or intellectual significance is little in evidence in the lives of people just trying to make ends meet. Even if it were an objective fact about the world that most ordinary lives are practically meaningless (in a negative sense), the enormity of this would still call for serious reflection about whether to reveal it; and if this was decided upon, then at least a little sensitivity would be apt. Instead, we find Metz, for instance, blithely recording the degree to which prostitution removes meaning from a life, perhaps to the point at which the life has negative value; that is, becomes worse than meaningless.[11] However, although the participants in these debates do not reflect on their motivation for looking into these matters, I think it is clear. It is to produce a theory of "the meaning of life" capable of offering the same kind of reassurance to dissatisfied atheists, which belief in a meaning of life (properly so-called) offers to religious believers. Their atheism persuades them that there is no meaning of life, this perceived absence leads to existential dissatisfaction, and so they turn to meaning *in* life for comfort. All they really do, however, is produce highly dubious theories of one particular type of social meaning judgement, with the added result—more often than not—of revealing their elitist prejudices.

I am no fan of the meaning *in* life debate, then. Yet, rather than further rake over old ground, I now want to ask a foundational question about it, with an eye to acquiring more insight into the transculturalist standoff concerning evaluative judgements. This foundational question should have been settled before the debate ever got underway, but was not in fact addressed. It is the question of whether there really is one type of social meaning judgement which has priority over the others, such that if there is such a thing as an objectively meaningful life, in the social sense, then this is the kind of

---

[9] For the argument that this is incoherent, see ([8], pp. 14–15); also [19].

[10] I have added the word "almost" to this sentence in response to a reviewer who pointed out, quite rightly, that the formula need not have this result if the exemplary cases are just used to make vivid what the meaningful features are; ordinary lives might exhibit these features to a strong, if not exemplary, degree. Nevertheless, this has been exactly the result in every case I have seen, and given my views on the underlying motivation for this project, I think this is almost inevitable.

[11] The prostitution example recurs throughout Metz's book [10].

judgement we need to employ to detect its presence. The debate was able to get off the ground because there were plenty of philosophers keen to talk about an issue of as general interest as the meaning of life (as they saw it), who belonged to a generation for which logical positivism was a distant enough memory for them to be unconcerned by its faded strictures on what a philosopher may legitimately discuss. Since the foundational question was never asked, however, the vindicating connotations of the question of the meaning of life carried over into the meaning *in* life debate, and the approving sense of "socially meaningful" became the *de facto* focus.

What I shall conclude is that three out of four of the different types of social meaning judgement I distinguished could refer to an objectively meaning life. The only one that could not is the approving one which the debate has fixated upon. The argument is as follows.

Evidently, the criteria for an objectively meaningful life cannot have pre-dated the evolution of human beings. For our topic is social meaning, not the meaning of life, for which, to state the obvious, the possibility of some kind of human social interaction is required. In any case, the notion of such criteria pre-dating our appearance on Earth is alien to naturalism. In a universe of physical particles and forces, there simply cannot have been candidates for objective criteria dictating how humans must live in order to live meaningfully; not at a time when humans did not yet exist. Our existence was not preordained, so no prior arrangements were made. Rather, if there are such criteria, they must have been generated by our social interactions. We must have moved in such a way that certain of our movements laid down objective criteria for certain other movements to count as meaningful. More precisely, our linguistic behaviour of describing the movements of certain lives as "meaningful", or other cognates which amount to the same thing, must have set up the criteria for those movements, as a matter of fact, to be what count as objectively meaningful lives. Of course, talk of "describing" and "setting up criteria" raises the thorny issue of intentionality. However, since we are presupposing a naturalistic framework, let us assume this amounts to something like causal covariation. Thus, the linguistic behaviour covaried with certain patterns of behaviour, and those objective patterns are the meaningful ones. An objective pattern developed and we labelled it as "meaningful"; the latter amounting to another objective pattern.

So far so good, in that I doubt I have said anything a naturalist would seriously quibble about, at least in the sense that if there are objectively meaningful human lives, then within a naturalistic framework, they would have to have come about in something like the above fashion. However, now consider the type of social meaning judgement which is of primary concern in the meaning *in* life debate, namely the kind used as a term of approbation. This is an evaluative kind of judgement; we evaluate Gandhi's life positively, for instance, by saying that it was meaningful. The fact that this is an evaluation need not be a concern for the objective aspirations of the naturalist, since we are, for the sake of argument, supposing that there are moral (and other higher-order) facts to ground these evaluations; facts that supervene on the physical facts. As such, evaluations can be construed as a kind of description; in evaluating Gandhi's life as meaningful, we are describing the objective moral (or other non-fundamental) facts that the physical movements of his life, as embedded in his environment, instantiated.

This is not to say that the story so far bodes well for the meaning *in* life debate; in fact I think enough has already been said to show that it is completely untenable. For if philosophers are to isolate the meaningful patterns through *a priori* analysis, they need good reason to believe that there is some unitary, ahistorical pattern that such judgements have always co-varied with. But there is extremely good reason to think there is not. If the Samurai evaluated a life as meaningful in this sense, there seems little doubt that their judgements would not coincide with ours. So I cannot see how these philosophers expect to isolate a physical pattern, which amounts to anything more than: what I, and contemporary like-minded people, call "meaningful". Hardly an appropriate substitute for the meaning of life! But even if you did think that there is some pattern, which people would always have recognised as meaningful, the methodology of the debate is clearly inappropriate. For to isolate such a pattern, you would need to do considerable historical research, while also gathering extensive empirical evidence about contemporary meaningfulness-judgements; it would be quite a project, and imaginative thought-experiments would have little, if any, role to play in it. You might perhaps think the pattern has always been there, but many cultures have missed it; and perhaps continue to do so. However, we need only appeal to counterfactuals—"what would they have judged?"—for the question to arise of why we should trust *our* judgements about which patterns count as the meaningful ones, rather than others that differ.

This is orthogonal to my main point, however, since I am giving the project the maximum benefit of the doubt to see where it leads. My main point is as follows. Evaluations can always go either way: good or bad. If judgements about the objective patterns of meaningfulness are evaluative, then, these judgements must be able to go either way, even if they ultimately reduce to descriptive judgements about moral (or other non-fundamental) facts. Thus, since "meaningful" as a term of approbation is evaluative, it must be shorthand for meaningful-in-a-good-way; "good" may mean morally, aesthetically, conducive to the spread of knowledge, or whatever. But in that case, the pattern we are detecting must be that of a *good* meaningful life. There must also be a pattern for a *bad* meaningful life. All the philosophers in this debate—except for one—skirt around this consequence by simply talking about more or less meaningful lives, with the presupposed limit being a complete absence of meaning; by which they mean an absence of *good* meaning.

The exception is Metz, whose notion of negative meaning (which he calls "anti-matter" ([10], p. 64), shows recognition of this consequence of the naturalistic framework of the debate. For when we get down to very small amounts of meaning, our evaluation cannot be positive; we do not praise somebody for living an almost meaningless life, and certainly not a completely meaningless one. We are condemning them. Thus, at some point, the target of our judgements must switch from the pattern for good meaning to the pattern for bad meaning.[12] Metz shows insight, which I previously missed, in recognising that once the bad meaning pattern becomes the focus, there is no reason that incrementally more of that pattern should not continue to be recognised, even after the good meaning pattern has completely disappeared. Hence a life could count as having a worse meaning than one that is simply completely lacking in good meaning. Bad meaning, like good meaning, has no obvious limits; there may be some kind of physical constraint on the patterns, but if so, this is hidden from our ability to imagine lives accruing more and more meaning (positive or negative) without limit.

The important consequence of this is that the patterns tracked by the approving type of judgements about meaningfulness cannot be the patterns for an objectively meaningful life. They track the patterns for a *good* meaningful life, but that is just one type of meaningful life. Since good and bad meaningful lives must have something in common, if we are correctly labelling an objective pattern, there must be a third kind of pattern underlying both—and *that* is the pattern for an objectively meaningful life. *A fortiori*, no kind of evaluative judgement can track this pattern, since then the same issues will arise; there will be a good/bad split, and the pattern we are looking for must be common to both sides.

This means that the meaning *in* life project has focused on the wrong sense of "meaningful". Particularly if, as I think is clear, it was looking for a secular substitute for the meaning *of* life. For the attraction of the meaning of life is that it might provide guidance on how we should live, such that if we live in that way, then our lives are vindicated; we have not simply been "burning" our days, as May puts it ([16], p. vii). If our social interactions create objective meaning in life, however, then it is of a kind which is completely unsuited to this role. We can live in such a way as to acquire large quantities of it—we can amplify the pattern all we like—and yet the result may be worthy of universal condemnation.

Which, if any, of the other three "meaningful" judgement-types, which we considered, does track the relevant pattern? They are all candidates, because they are all descriptive. I think the answer must

---

12 The issue of vagueness, concerning what happens in the vicinity of the "switch", is not relevant here; though naturalists might find an epistemic view on these matters conducive (e.g., [22]).

be that they all track patterns which have an equal right to be called a life's objective meaningfulness; but none of them provide anything worthy for us to aim for. That said, if we think of "meaningful" as an incremental term, and as something we *could* aim to get maximal amounts of—as philosophers typically do—then there are only two options.

The flat sense, in which we might say that agriculture determined the meaning of a peasant's life, is neither incremental nor a possible goal. The meaning of a person's life, in this sense, is simply determined by what they do with it; so everyone has an objectively meaningful life. A human life creates a physical pattern and part of that pattern is its meaning. We make this kind of judgement for the purpose of drawing attention to the dominant feature of that meaning-pattern—the farming activities, in my example—but the rest has an equal claim. The peasant no doubt did other things which generated social meaning, but we are interested in the dominant factor.

The sense in which our lives are meaningful when they subjectively engage us, which has attracted attention from philosophers, albeit nowhere near as much as the evaluative one, is both incremental and a possible goal; but it is not a worthy one. It might at first glance seem evaluative, but it is not, since it depends on what subjectively engages you. To say that a project really engaged somebody, and hence, in this sense, added meaning to their life, is not necessarily to positively evaluate it; for the project may have been utterly trivial or even evil. It is just to describe how the person engaged with it, which the naturalist might construe in terms of the presence of a certain kind of brain activity. It is incremental, however, and we could aim to maximise the meaningfulness of our lives in this sense. But the aim itself would not be worthy. Villains tend to be highly engaged people, which is something philosophers overlook when they commend to us "intensity" ([16], p. 75) or phenomenological "whooshing up" ([23], p. 200) as routes to a meaningful life.

The final sense, that of sheer social significance, is certainly incremental and also a possible goal. But it is a terrible goal. For if that is the objective meaning you are trying to acquire for your life, then you could hardly do better than by spreading a disease that eradicates human life; perhaps slowly and painfully, since that would be bound to increase the meaning-patterns. By contrast, doing something so wonderful that the whole world sings your praises, would be an immeasurably more difficult route to take to the same outcome.

Any of these three descriptive senses could track the objective meaning at the root of evaluative judgements of meaningfulness; any or all. The second and third are disturbing, however, because they can be goals. This is not just a theoretical consideration. People do, in fact, abandon their ordinary lives for the thrills (intense subjective engagement) of crime. Shows like *Breaking Bad* teach us to admire this. Moreover, achieving objective significance (a synonym for "meaning") is a motivation for high-school massacres. A culture in which fame is not necessarily linked to merit actively encourages this. If that is what the aim of achieving objective meaning in life can lead to, then it is not just an aim best forgotten, but one which should be actively resisted. Aiming for a good meaningful life is to be commended, of course; but you are really just aiming for "good" and hoping to maximise its effects (or the pleasure you will realise in it; or both). Objectified and isolated, however, meaning *in* life—the supposed secular alternative to the meaning *of* life—is an utter disaster. Philosophers, of all people, should wake up to this.

3. Description and Evaluation

Both post-Nietzscheans and moral objectivists attempt to dilute the distinction between description and evaluation; but from opposite directions. The post-Nietzscheans do so by rejecting the notion of objective truth, thereby making all statements about the world a kind of culturally rooted evaluation. The moral objectivists do so by positing objective moral facts, thereby making all statements about the world a kind of description. I think both are reactions to the waning of the firm hold over intellectual life that religions once enjoyed; a process which began in earnest in the nineteenth century and has accelerated ever since. With a meaning of life assured to us by religion, evaluation stood on just as firm metaphysical ground as description. The epistemic ground for this evaluation was not so good—the observable physical world had the advantage on that count—which is one major reason why religious influence began to fade; but nevertheless, so long as we trusted the religion, the metaphysic which evaluation rested upon was assured. As science increasingly took over our intellectual aspirations, however, the situation changed.

Science presents us with an objective physical universe in which human life blindly evolved; in that universe there is no place for a meaning of life. Given the residual influence of religion on how we thought about this, the resultant nihilism seemed like a negative evaluation of all our efforts. Ultimately, we were worthless. This situation led to the post-Nietzschean and moral objectivist reactions. The post-Nietzscheans, like Nietzsche himself, coupled the meaning of life with objective truth: both had to go in a world where there was no greater authority than the human. This immediately removed the sting from nihilism, because it now emerged as simply an optional interpretation of our situation; and conceived as the ultimate negative evaluation, nihilism was plainly not an attractive interpretation. With the newfound freedom to put it aside in favour of others, a freedom purchased by the rejection of truth, nihilism could thereby be overcome.

Naturalists of a more metaphysical bent did not see the cold, uncaring physical universe in which nihilism holds sway as simply an optional interpretation, however; but they still conceived nihilism as a negative evaluation. So they developed a different humanist response which seemed more in keeping with science and its ideal of objectivity; and one which allowed them to avoid the unpalatable Protagoran tensions of the post-Nietzscheans. Their tactic was to replace the meaning *of* life with a humanistic and naturalistic substitute: meaning *in* life. Humans make their own meaning, and this, they thought, could do all the work of the older idea; but without the religious and metaphysically untenable baggage. They thought of this meaning as objective, as everything must be in a purely physical universe, and since they thought of meaning *in* life—just like the meaning *of* life it had replaced—as essentially evaluative, they thereby came to endorse forms of moral objectivism.

Both responses produced equally unattractive results. The post-Nietzscheans, over and above the conceptual tangles and manifest implausibility they embroiled themselves in, ended up promoting a cultural insularity that was squeamish about looking for transcultural common ground, and consequently, progress. The moral objectivists, on the other hand, building upon patently shaky philosophical foundations with earnest and supposedly scientific seriousness, ended up promoting the goals of *making your mark* and *loving what you do*; no matter what that mark is, and no matter what it is that you love. The moral or otherwise praiseworthy element they tried to build into these goals, was always destined to appear as a preachy and expendable addendum to the main message, *i.e.*, make your life objectively meaningful, any way you like. The "any way you like" was meant to be redacted, but once convinced that you can secure objective meaning for yourself, who cares what some theorists (who cannot agree with each other in any case) say about how you ought to do it? Who cares what anyone thinks, in fact, so long as your life is *meaningful*. The meaning *of* life was conceived as the be-all-and-end-all, and conceived as its secular replacement, so is meaning *in* life. This priority was desirable in a religious context, since the meaning *of* life was bound up with moral precepts. But outside that context it is not, because theoretically, the goal of an objectively meaningful life cannot be moral in and of itself, and practically, the goal is highly unlikely to be taken that way within a secular context; where scientific realism dominates, and the view of some philosophers that objective morality resides in the atoms is little known.

All this can be avoided. First, we need to realise that nihilism is not an evaluation but rather a description. If there is no meaning of life, then human beings do not exist for a reason; there is no purpose to human existence, and this is simply a fact about the reality we are describing. Outside of a religious context in which living a meaningless life contravenes an imperative to live in accordance with the meaning of life, this is not an evaluative condemnation. Second, we must keep description and evaluation distinct; which is easy to do in a refreshingly meaningless reality. Description concerns working out what reality amounts to. Evaluation concerns the value we invest in it. Evaluation is guided by description, but is ultimately a matter of collective and personal action. Our aspiration for objectivity is to have as little role in description as possible and instead let the world guide us. But in the case of evaluation, our input is not an obstacle, but rather the whole point of the exercise. We *do* value things, and can come to value new things; but our evaluations can only change rationally when we know what is available to value. Understanding our cultural history can reveal things of value to us that others might overlook; but transcultural considerations can show us new things to value, which we might find that we value more—and have good reason to.

4. Conclusions

Returning to the transculturalist standoff, then, the worry is that some cultures have evolved practices that seem abhorrent to us, but that our desire to help reveals cultural prejudices of our own, which we could never persuade them of, only force upon them. Underlying that worry is a conflict between two humanistic thoughts. The first is that such practices reveal that these cultures are not pursuing meaning *in* life in the right way; the second is that they should be free to pursue it however they like. However, if we reject meaning *in* life as a goal, since it has nothing to do with "the right way", the first thought is divested of metaphysical significance; we are left with an evaluative disagreement, to be resolved as best we can. In addition, if we accept that life is metaphysically meaningless without collapsing the distinction between evaluation and description, then the second thought is also divested of metaphysical significance; for we still have a common descriptive background against which our evaluative disagreement can take place. The conflict is no longer metaphysically principled, and we can return to the particularities of the case in hand. If we find some of their practices abhorrent, and think we have good reason to do so, then we try to persuade them of our evaluations while advertising their benefits. They can do the same with us. In the end, we hope, a rational, well-informed equilibrium will emerge. The concern that we could never find common ground fades against a common descriptive backdrop for our conflicting evaluations; there is a point of entry for debate, at the very least in physiological facts like pleasure and pain. The more niggling concern is that without firm foundations of the kind provided by the meaning of life, this process might go the wrong way, such that we end up in a Naziesque world. However, if we no longer believe in a meaning of life, there is not much we can do about that. After all, the meaning of life has hardly proved a recipe for peace throughout the ages, and continues, in the hands of religious fanatics, to generate much of the trouble we find ourselves in today. The remedy is not to try to drag the meaning *of* life into the secular world as the humanistic doctrine of meaning *in* life. For it cannot do the same theoretical work; and its practical implications are considerably more worrying than the lack of guidance it seeks to remedy.

Conflicts of Interest: The author declares no conflict of interest.

References and Notes

1. Richard Slimbach. "The Transcultural Journey." *Frontiers: The Interdisciplinary Journal of Study Abroad* 11 (2005): 1–26.
2. Mary Midgley. *Heart and Mind: The Varieties of Moral Experience*. Hemel Hempstead: Harvester Press, 1981, pp. 80–87.
3. Richard Rorty. *Philosophy and the Mirror of Nature*. Princeton: Princeton University Press, 1979.
4. James Tartaglia. *Rorty and the Mirror of Nature*. London: Routledge, 2007.
5. James Tartaglia. "Philosophy and the Mirror of Nature." In *A Companion to Rorty*. Edited by Alan Malachowski. Oxford: Wiley-Blackwell, 2016.
6. Friedrich Nietzsche. *The Will to Power*. Edited by Walter Kaufmann. Translated by Walter Kaufmann and R. J. Hollingdale. New York: Random House, 1967.
7. Bernard Reginster. *The Affirmation of Life: Nietzsche on Overcoming Nihilism*. Cambridge: Harvard University Press, 2006.
8. James Tartaglia. *Philosophy in a Meaningless Life*. London: Bloomsbury, 2016.
9. Richard Rorty. *Contingency, Irony, and Solidarity*. Cambridge: Cambridge University Press, 1989.
10. Thaddeus Metz. *Meaning in Life*. Oxford: Oxford University Press, 2013.

11. Andrew George. *The Epic of Gilgamesh*. London: Penguin Books, 1999.

12. John Cottingham. *The Meaning of Life*. London: Routledge, 2003.

13. Antti Kauppinen. "Meaningfulness and Time." *Philosophy and Phenomenological Research* 84 (2012): 345–77. [CrossRef]

14. Thaddeus Metz. "Review of Todd May, A Significant Life: Human Meaning in a Silent Universe." *Notre Dame Philosophical Reviews*, 2015. Available online: https://ndpr.nd.edu/news/59870-a-significant-life-human-meaning-in-a-silent-universe/ (accessed on 25 April 2016).

15. Robert Nozick. *Philosophical Explanations*. Oxford: Clarendon Press, 1981.

16. Todd May. *A Significant Life: Human Meaning in a Silent Universe*. Chicago: University of Chicago Press, 2015.

17. Susan Wolf. "Meaning in Life." In *The Meaning of Life: A Reader*. Edited by E. D. Klemke and Steven M. Cahn. Oxford: Oxford University Press, 2008.

18. James Tartaglia. "Metz's Quest for the Holy Grail." *Journal of Philosophy of Life* 5 (2015): 90–111.

19. James Tartaglia. "Why Save the World?" Review of *A Significant Life* by Todd May. *TLS: The Times Literary Supplement*, 26 February 2016, p. 22.

20. Harry Frankfurt. "Reply to Susan Wolf." In *The Contours of Agency: Essays on Themes from Harry Frankfurt*. Edited by Sarah Buss and Lee Overton. Cambridge: MIT Press, 2002.

21. John Kekes. "The Meaning of Life." *Midwest Studies in Philosophy* 24 (2000): 17–34. [CrossRef]

22. Timothy Williamson. *Vagueness*. London: Routledge, 1994.

23. Hubert Dreyfus, and Sean Dorrance Kelly. *All Things Shining*. New York: Free Press, 2011.

 *humanities*

Essay

Transcultural Space and the Writer

Inez Baranay

Department of Western Languages and Literature, Canakkale Onsekiz Mart University, Kepez 17100, Turkey; inezbaranay@comu.edu.tr; Tel.: +90-531-884-4071

Academic Editor: Bernd Fischer
Received: 15 February 2016; Accepted: 25 April 2016; Published: 5 May 2016

Abstract: (1) As a long time writer, I always found, even before I began to publish, that my work was difficult to categorise, even while categories seemed essential for publication, reception and visibility. (2) In this personal essay, I apply the notion of the transcultural to a short writing [auto]biography. The methodology adopted for this purpose is a form of autoethnography: "a form of self-reflection and writing that explores the researcher's personal experience and connects this autobiographical story to wider cultural, political, and social meanings and understandings"[1] to explore how my immigrant background and transcultural lived experience is reflected in my creative writing, and to give an account of how my literary output has been placed in various but always restrictive pre-existing categories. I am also encouraged by Mikhail Epstein's proposed "scriptorics", the study of the one who writes Each section of the essay is divided into two: the first sections provide a succinct version of the issues in a developing writer's life, framed by the need for the practice and production to "belong" somewhere; the second sections take them to a posited "Transcultural Space" where the work seems more authentically to have originated and in which it seems to be more perceptively read. (3) The result is not so much a conventional academic article as a fiction writer's reflection on her work in the embrace of an inclusive and meaning-making realm.

Keywords: transcultural space; transculturalism; fiction and transculture; scriptorics and transculture; experimental writing; feminism and transculture

---

1. Introduction

In *Transformative Humanities: a Manifesto*, Mikhail Epstein proposes what he calls *scriptorics*: A discipline dedicated to the writing human: "those for whom the very act of writing constitutes their way of life and worldview"; its key tenets are questions like "who writes? For whom?" [2]. Epstein's proposal encourages the present writer, author mostly of novels and short fiction, to offer an overview of her writing biography as most productively framed by the concepts and sympathies embraced by the transcultural, in a context where identity is increasingly understood as labile, subject to alteration, to situational definition. It is as if the transcultural were always the destination, though it remains to be seen if it proves to be another transitional space or one that is so comprehensively inclusive that it has no limits. This essay may be useful to literary critics and researchers interested in exploring the effects of physical, cultural and psychological mobility on creative literary productions.

2. The World of Englishes

2.1. It Starts with Language, with Reading

She first heard stories and songs and verses and sayings and prayers in Hungarian, and there were French verses, as her mother and grandmother spoke French as well. But when Inez began

---

[1] I take this definition from Carolyn Ellis [1].

reading, it was in English, and once she began she never stopped. She read everything she could get her hands on; she was allowed to take books from the adults' library once she had exhausted the children's. It must have begun with fairy tales from Europe and the Bible (magisterial King James version of course) and Australian children's stories: Gumnut babies, the kangaroo, the magic pudding. Inevitably, Enid Blyton adventures gave way to Dumas and Verne and then Flaubert and the books on psychology and theology in her father's study, the odd racy bestseller, comic books too somehow. From the start an eclectic reader, she looked for books mentioned in books; always she would seek the writers other writers mentioned. She couldn't tell you which of those she read in what order, or recall all of it.

Is it the medium itself that creates the addiction? Or is it the way reading brings your thoughts alive, makes you wonder and wonder, about words, about sentences, about language, about how you could put anything into words, about how there is more to life than being stuck where you are. (Reading makes you feel both less so and more so.) As an immigrant child she was always aware there could have been another, a different, life, and maybe that is what she was looking for, to know what might have been, how she might one day find it. Later, after most of the reading of her early life had made its unrepeatable impact—surely no writings affect you as much as the first ones you read, the ones you read over and over—eventually she learned about the kinds of distinctions that should be made: the respected and the disreputable, literature and trash, high art and mere popularity. The unease over such distinctions was encouraged by their bombardment by a new popular culture movement.

What intrigued her from the start was the variations in the English language. Who's to say what's proper and correct in the English language? There were so many Englishes—this is something she's writing and talking about a lot these days [3].

She had been noticing this from the very start of using language: there was but one name for the language and yet there were so many variations. Different schools, different districts, different kinds of people, different kinds among the ones who are meant to be one kind. What she's listening to is English spoken in Australia at a range of schools—state, selective, private; English spoken by those whose mother tongue it was, and there were variations among them; English spoken by adults who had learned English late in life, nothing having prepared them for being migrants in Australia and having to learn the lingo.

2.2. Trans-Cultural Space: Entering the World of Englishes

In the present, Inez enters Transcultural Space. Enters, is entered by: it's a space in alien and Dreamtime dimensions. In here, all other categories have been made redundant, outmoded or spurious. Yet it's above all an inclusive space, so you can even bring your previous categories with you, and see what happens to them in here.

The space has been described in her invaluable work by Dagnino [4] thus:

> *transcultural continuum/transpace/transplace.* An all-inclusive space of subjective consciousness and cultural possibilities which does not deny the formative importance of native cultures (and, to some extent, their accompanying worldviews) but at the same time allows an openness to the reception, integration, negotiation, and permeation of other cultures, languages, worldview *transpace/transplace.* Another way of defning the transcultural continuum. Transpace/transplace is the transcultural dimension that lies beyond the divides, often commercially or ideologically emphasized, of cultures. It represents a nonoppositional point of confluence or overlapping of cultures that in many ways expands Bhabha's notion of the third space, the in-between space where hybridization occurs.

Come inside, let's look around, listen, feel.

Listen, there are so many languages in here, people speak what they feel like speaking. You may come across conversations about the value or utility of a particular language for particular purposes. But everyone in here knows some version of the world language; it's English now and the word has but a historical connection to the people of England; the language is not defined by, not authorised by, the England where it purportedly originated, at first spread by former forms of imperialism. In here, we speak English. Not England language. (Yes, let's use England as the adjective for "from England". As in cricket: "the England team".)

English has increasingly been altered and hybridised and simplified and complexified, it takes on sayings from wherever it is employed, it inflects its local versions with local vocabulary and references. Listen to all the accents, all the rhythms and registers. Evolution, mutation, mixed marriages, selections natural and un: all happened to English, and it never stops. The way writing in English might be evaluated is transformed by the recognition of such phenomena. Traditional correctitude is not always apt. Those whose business is evaluation need to consider this.

No-one is monolingual in here. Some speak several languages fluently; some speak a couple, some many. Some speak smatterings of various languages. Everyone knows words, phrases, expressions, from various languages, people naturally blend them into the language they're speaking. Hybrid languages proliferate. No one's concerned to separate a language from a dialect.

The idea of a single kind of "correctness" in the English language is a dodo.

> There are ever more young authors writing in the languages of their host countries. ... Some write in the language of their host countries while retaining the mental blueprint of their mother tongue, giving rise to surprising linguistic mélanges; others create defamiliarising effects by mixing the vocabulary of two or sometimes multiple languages [5].

3. Outsiderness Becomes Insiderness

3.1. It Always Starts with Being an Outsider; Being from "Over There"

When the others played sports she kept reading. When television arrived in Australia she kept reading. A kid who'd always rather be reading becomes a teenager, an adult, who would always rather be reading. Not truly always, she's always going to be curious about life and living, experiment and experience, but she will always need frequent time alone, time to immerse in reading.

So that's one kind of outsider she was.

"They're all coming here, we're not going over there" grumbled a man at a bus stop wanting everyone to hear, grumbled loudly his observation which simply proved that Australia was better than anywhere in the world. Also proved that no-one from *over there*, those migrants and refugees, those foreigners with their distasteful smells and sounds, would ever be anything *but* "from over there"; they never will be From Here.

Nationalism comes a lot more sophisticated and pussy-footy than that too.

In the 1970s Australians asserted their right to their own accents, motifs and stories: cultural nationalism swept in, actors' characters and radio announcers began to speak in broad Australian accents rather than try to sound British, designers exuberantly employed the shapes of gum leaves, Aboriginal motifs and the Sydney Opera House, writers told stories heralded as "about us, about Australia, showing us who we are".

But it was still only ever the Australia of people From Here.

Inez couldn't tell Australia about itself, but she wanted to write even before she knew it was possible.

She wrote in secret, she still had no context she could name.

3.2. Transcultural Space: Outsiderness Is Insiderness; Not the End of Difference

Everyone's here in Transcultural Space because of some kind of non-belonging outside of here; in here everyone belongs because of their non-belonging. Their outside non-belonging was thrust upon them or claimed or realised, it was clearly evident or it was subtle and subdued; in any case it bestowed its gifts or ambiguous gifts.

> In order to understand, it is immensely important for the person who understands to be *located outside* the object of his or her creative understanding—in time, in space, in culture... In the realm of culture, outsideness is a most powerful factor in understanding [6].

But know this: it is not the end of difference. There's space for a melting pot, there are countless versions of hybridisation and fusion (cultural, personal) and there is endless difference, and it does not even need the "celebrating" called for outside.

> The differences complement each other and create a new interpersonal transcultural community to which we belong, not because we are similar but because we are different [7].

The belongers might also choose to be in here. (Everyone has belonged somewhere sometime to some degree.)

4. Experiments Never End

4.1. It Was Called Experimental Writing

The secret writings of her secret beginnings were poetry but no-one ever saw it, and one day she no longer had any copies of what she used to write. You have to be precise in poetry, also suggestive; you have to use the right word also the startling word. You have to examine your experience, you have to let your experience reveal itself to you with all its clear truth and teasing mystery. You are allowed to use language as it comes to you, you're allowed to make it yours. Poetry taught her to write prose; she spent hours at her notebooks. No-one should see her writing, not for a very long time, and then, slowly and tentatively, she admitted her secret practice and intentions. Eventually she went to a women writer's group (Sydney, 1981) and read her work to others for the first time (pieces about travels) and also she recognised something in *their* work, the work of people who wrote seriously and well, that told her that what she wrote was actually writing not only a preparation for writing. I came out of the closet, she would say, that's when she came out as a writer.

The work was categorised as "experimental writing".

Experimental, because forget about neat plots, twists, closure. They wrote "pieces" rather than "stories". It was all about finding a voice, trying things out: capturing the voice of the moment, saying it your own way. It was about speaking out of sub-cultures and margins, getting published in small press anthologies, with covers designs from the counter-cultural printing presses that ran off posters for new bands, anarchist street parties, demonstrations.

4.2. Transcultural Space: An Ongoing Experiment

To experiment is constantly to interrogate and test what you think you know, to be open to new ways of considering, to break structures apart and find new patterns in the pieces. This is the essence of existence in Transcultural Space. The experimental mind set applies to both the production and the reception of literary works.

We might ask, is Transcultural Space itself an experiment?

Isn't any space? But in here we know it, we rejoice in it, we delight in discovering any received assumptions so that they may be exuberantly interrogated.

5. From Feminism To Gender Fluidity

5.1. It Was Called Feminist Writing

She was categorised as a feminist writer also, often in the same place (anthologies of "experimental feminist writing"). Because so often you had to say whether or not you were. Because if the question had to be asked, the only answer could be yes.

If it remains at all remarkable, worthy of being remarked, that you believe in the self-determination of women, and in the need for the end of patriarchal structures and biases, you must still be called a feminist writer.

Once upon a future time no-one has to ask. Inez wrote stories of single women striving for independence in settings where usual normalities did not apply.

In the 1970s and 1980s, living in Sydney, when she was starting to publish, all kinds of queer cultures—*avant la lettre* or never claiming that *lettre*—made their mark on inner city culture and also that of the suburbs, small towns and so on. Cultural gayness, now considered apart from homosexuality, and more broadly cultural queerness changed the contextual culture. The culture of her city was immensely influenced by queer arts practitioners, and knew it. Inner-city cultures were international; inner-city denizens had more in common with each other than with the small towns of their nations. The understanding of "culture" was separated from the national looking-glass.

5.2. In Transcultural Space: Where Gender Is Fluid

In Transcultural Space, you can take for granted that gender is fluid and everything that follows. Feminist, camp, gay, queer, trans...it all became part of the transcultural, it all formed, to the extent there is one, the common sensibility.

Everyone in Transcultural Space has a sexuality and a gender of their own, not necessarily named. There are overlapping categories of gender. Gender and sexuality each are on a spectrum and you can move along it, you can even be in more than one place on the spectrum.

Maybe the binary might occasionally be convenient. There might even be room in here for die-hard fixed-in-place heterosexuality; Inez doesn't see it, but maybe first you have to believe in it. What there isn't is heteronormativity.

This is evident in the writing that comes from here, it speaks to and from this space, the sensibility informs the work and does not require explanation.

None of this might have the slightest apparent relevance to some of the conversations and activities in here.

6. From The Multi-Cultural to Real Diversity

6.1. The Multi-Cultural Writer

Along with "experimental" and "feminist" the anthologies that first published her work were subtitled with the term "multicultural".

At first it seemed that at last there was a recognition of a sensibility formed by the experience of an immigrant identity.

Among her earliest published work, Inez supplied her version of growing up migrant in a very British-colonial 1950s Australia [8]. But the Anglo hegemony was nothing like over, in fact it strengthened itself by adopting an Australian version of multiculturalism it called the "mosaic".

The mosaic model was chosen, in Inez's considered opinion, and she'd tell you this any chance once she figured this out, so that each colour in the mosaic, representing a separate ethnic, national or linguistic entity, remained separate and identifiable by its signature colour while there would be a principal colour in this mosaic, that of the Anglo-origin hegemony, which remained dominant in public life, media and the arts. The ideal of the "melting pot", a kind of ideal of a society, was eschewed, for the hegemony does not want to melt.

Everyone proclaimed that they adored "diversity" but a "multicultural" writer was meant to write only about being "between two cultures" and the dear diversity remained extrinsic to the dominant, and treated as if is primary purpose was to enrich and validate the mainstream. Post-graduate thesis-writers contacted Inez to ask her about the discrimination she had faced and the "Hungarian community" she had (they told her) grown up in; multicultural was also a name for victim, and people who'd grown up with a language other than English at home were known to live in ghettos, were expected to be very angry or very proud or possibly both. They were considered liable to wear some peasant clothing from the place of their ethnic lineage. Multicultural writers were meant to be loyal to their origins or maybe in anguish about them and the multicultural communities were ever so much appreciated for the wonderful cuisines they brought to the mainstream.

Australia declared itself a multicultural nation and arts bodies (publishers, grants-givers, curators, *etc.*) made sure that in no time one had to tick a box for being of multicultural background.

Where was the multi in multiculturalism? Only in the number of so-called cultures contributing to the whole, each of them remaining, indeed encouraged to remain, as separately mono-cultural, each remaining, as Amartya Sen says, "enclosed in separate identities pens" [9].

There was a quite a sense of self-congratulation from the hegemony whenever they nodded and pointed at the "multicultural" nature of Australia, while anyone who could claim, or was landed with, this identity category tried to make the most of it, but soon came to that wall between themselves and mainstream culture, that which considered itself normal, average and above all able to tell the only stories that were for everyone.

6.2. Transcultural Space: Taking up the Torch from Multiculturalism

The best use of multiculturalism was that, as Mikhael Epstein says, it paved the way from the dominance of one canon to the diversity of cultures:

> Transculturalism moves further, from the diversity of cultures to the even greater diversity of individuals, transcending their rigid cultural identities. The vision of nonviolent and nonuniform globalization coincides with the transcultural perspective in which more and more individuals find themselves "outside" of any particular culture, "outside" of its national, racial, sexual, ideological, and other divisions. The global society can be viewed as the space of ultimate diversity: diversity of free individuals [7].

In Transcultural Space, diversity is untrammelled and difference untroubled. No-one is assigned a rigid cultural identity: there is no such idea in here. Individuals are assumed all to be different from each other to some degree; they are as various and diverse as they can be, want to be. Hence they find like-minded people and soul mates according to whatever aspects of their ever-altering self finds itself alight with recognition, empathy, fascination. The writer needs no permissions or directions to write from here.

7. The Global Foreign

7.1. From Travel Writer to Global Soul

Where is home? Inez is asked. Wherever I'm sleeping tonight, she says, wherever I'm headed when I say, going home now. Once long ago she wrote "I'll always be homesick wherever I am" and later she wrote "that never stopped being true".

She wrote about sojourns and explorations in open-ended early travels in Asia and Europe. Calling upon a famous, indeed clichéd distinction that ceased to have much meaning around the time it was coined, a critic categorised Inez, or a narrating voice Inez used, as "not quite tourist not quite traveler".

There were already many other Western people disturbing those categories, with unconfirmed return tickets, smatterings of local expressions, insistence on local food, local markets, local manners. Inez traveled among them and away from them; she observed them and she observed herself, writing in local cafes, learning a bit of a local language and noting the language of exchange: local waiters talking with travelers, travelers of various origins comparing notes. Neither tourist nor traveler fit the category of people who increasingly decided to come back for longer, do something here, a business a job a project, retirement. Buy some property, live here some of the time. There were precedents, even a long tradition, of such decisions but now the scale was epoch-making.

She did not think of herself as a travel writer, particularly; least of all when anyone suggested she could supply newspapers and magazines with her accounts. She did not write the way the weekend Travel Section required.

Inez was described in a book called *The Global Soul* [10] when its author who met her in Toronto reported that she was born in Italy of Hungarian parents, grew up in Australia, had lived in SE Asia, was on her way to a writing residency in USA and had just spent some months researching in India. The book was full of such exultant examples, people who could not be confined to a single national identity and kept on moving.

So she was a global soul, ok, nice, but it wasn't a publishing category.

It was a good notion, though, the description of a massive phenomenon, suggesting we need a better first question for people we meet than "where are you from?"

As a traveler you can return; you can not return from your soul going global.

7.2. Transcultural Space: Feeling Foreign Everywhere

The traveling person knows how much parts of you are not where you are, that is, are not where your body is. She knows the feeling of having bodily arrived while the soul tears itself away and follows more slowly. The feeling of being in transit becomes familiar.

The feeling of getting lost in strange cites.

You have to be infinitely adaptable, and that includes when you haven't prepared to be.

It's like that in Transcultural Space.

The feeling of being "at home" does not attach to a country or even a city entirely; it can be found in a kind of cafe or bar, a kind of conversation, the ambience of someone's house. It's where you experience yourself as authentic without having to think about it. It's where you find a transcultural space within some other space. In physical space, the feeling is temporary. More lastingly, it's where constant foreignness becomes familiar.

So, the writer thinks, one might choose not to claim, or aspire to, being "at home everywhere" but, instead, the more desirable condition of being a foreigner everywhere.

Refugees, forced migrations, displacement and trauma are reasons some have no return; some have a new nation in Diaspora.

For Inez who took off in a more willful (if seeming imperative) way, the difficulty of return is more about not having property, a home, nor a living family in her first and dearest city; there are the oldest friends but it's not as if she can turn up and say she will live with them. The city has changed, the gap she made by leaving has been filled. It's a place in *time* she left.

Once you've lived the neo-nomad life, or the life of a multiple migrant, then you will also feel a touch of foreignness returning to places you ought to feel you belong to. No matter how often you have seen it or how well you once knew it, everything you notice has a tinge of the exotic, the foreign, the remarkable; the sense that what you find non-ordinary is ordinary if you're from here.

As Helene Cixous wrote about dreams, "foreignness is a fantastic nationality" [11]. In Transcultural Space foreignness is the way to feel at home, foreignness is your nationality.

8. Beyond The Post-Colonial Binaries

8.1. The Post-Colonial Margin

How are you going to define post colonial? It can't be everything that comes out of a nation that once was officially a colony. There is a politics and a sensibility essential to the post-colonial; colonial history and the way it never ends inform the subject material whatever it is, the characters whoever they are; this is at best recognised implicitly or explicitly in the text. But is that all, or, is that enough? Is it in the intention or in the reading? In this case it's not up to the writer to fit the category.

Her book about tourists in Bali had the word *edge* in its title [12]. The narrative agent deliberately placed itself and the main characters as outsiders on the island; they are not short-holiday tourists, for each has a personal mission, but in relation to Balinese culture they are strangers, spectators, no matter how much they reach realms unavailable to the more casual tourist. The culture of tourism itself is the novel's subject; the simulacrum becomes the real; beneficial and destructive effects of tourism are not easily separated, the exchanges and encounters between people demolish notions of borders or affinities being a matter of national, ethnic or historical inheritance.

The next book, a non-fiction, a memoir of a challenging year as a volunteer worker in Papua New Guinea, questioned the philosophies, the ideals, the assumptions—conscious and un—in the development industry, considered as a kind of colonialism; notions of progress and evolution discomfited the memoirist. Its tone of grim revelations and willingness to criticise the host national culture as well as her own made the book spectacularly unwelcome at a time when shocking revelations of viciously racist policies of the past in Australia were in the air, and a tone of New Age-y romanticism about the lives of tribal black-skinned people was a fashion even among intellectuals [13].

The most complex fiction she wrote [14], based on several lengthy travels in India, channeling Indian voices and events, thematically about the relationship between tradition and globalization, considering whether globalisation was Westernisation, and exploring the strife over intellectual property and the politics of knowledge, was turned down by Australian publishers ("I've been to India and it wasn't like that") but published to acclaim in India. This edged her even more to the outer margins of the category Australian writer and but of course she isn't an Indian writer.

It was a curious position to be in, and it was in the aftermath of that publication that Inez left her last home in Australia, to move around the world for years, to develop a screenplay adaptation of the Indian novel at a film school in Amsterdam, a transcultural space where people from a range of national and language backgrounds worked together on their creative projects.

In recent fiction Inez sent an Australian character to Amsterdam to become a vampire [15] and placed another in Berlin there to join forces with some ghosts [16].

As Dubravka Ugresic says:

> That is why I have passionately propagated the notion of transnational literature, which could be a new cultural platform, a literary territory for those writers who refuse to belong to their national literatures, or to belong to their national literatures only. I think that establishing a theoretical ground for transnational literature and opening other options than national culture and literature is an extremely important cultural job [17].

It isn't even always a matter of a deliberate refusal, it's more a matter of impossibility.

8.2. Transcultural Space: The Energetic Co-Existence and Dissolution of Binaries

Post-colonialism's vocabulary does not fit, it is transcended by, the transcultural; categories of dominant and subordinate, coloniser and colonised, subalterns and superiors, orientalists and occidentalists. Their usefulness, the discourses they engendered, are not the air of Transcultural Space.

Wait, you might ask, but what about the realities of a world where one is categorized by others and treated accordingly; where you yourself might dismiss their categories but cannot thereby prevent their perceptions and their prejudice, discrimination, violence? Look, I answer, when we enter Transcultural Space we are in a space where such phenomena cannot exist. It's a notional space, an ideal, and we can decide how it feels to live there. Everyone and everything is subject to, altered by, absorbed by, integrated with its energies.

In Transcultural Space, the energies—in the form of ideas, sympathies, artworks—circulate, taking and giving aspects of all they touch, thereby dissolving hierarchies and binaries of identity. In Transcultural Space every difference co-exists.

And all of this *matters* in a world that needs ideals to be articulated:

> Once again, a rule of thumb for transcultural diversity: *oppose yourself to nobody, identify yourself with nothing.* No identities and no oppositions—only concrete and multiple differences. The deeper is differentiation, the better is the prospect for universal peace [7].

Humanities **2016**, *5*, 28

Conflicts of Interest: The author declares no conflict of interest.

References

1. Carolyn Ellis. *The Ethnographic I: A Methodological Novel about Autoethnography.* Walnut Creek: AltaMira Press, 2004.
2. Mikhail Epstein. *The Transformative Humanities: A Manifesto.* London: Bloomsbury, 2012. Available online: https://books.google.com.tr/books?id=rYnFAgAAQBAJ&printsec=frontcover&dq=mikhail+epstein+manifesto&hl=en&sa=X&redir_esc=y#v=onepage&q=mikhail%20epstein%20manifesto&f=false (accessed on 5 January 2016).
3. Inez Baranay. "Questions of Identity." *Journal of the European Association for Studies of Australia (JEASA)*, 2015. Available online: http://www.easa-australianstudies.net/node/399 (accessed on 5 January 2016).
4. Arianna Dagnino. *Transcultural Writers and Novels in the Age of Global Mobility.* West Lafayette: Purdue UP, 2015, pp. 201–2.
5. Dubravka Ugresic. *Europe in Sepia.* Edited by David Williams. Translated by Rochester. New York: Open Letter, 2014.
6. Richard Taruskin. *Defining Russia Musically: Historical and Hermeneutical Essays.* Princeton: Princeton University Press, 2000, p. xxiii.
7. Mikhail Epstein. "Transculture: A Broad Way between Globalism and Multiculturalism." *American Journal of Economics and Sociology* 68 (2009): 327–51. [CrossRef]
8. Inez Baranay. "You Don't Whinge." In *Beyond the Echo: Multicultural Women's Writing.* Edited by Gunew and Mahyuddin. Brisbane: University of Queensland Press, 1988.
9. Malik Kenan. "Review of 'Amartya Sen *Identity and Violence*'." *Prospect*, August 2006. Available online: http://www.kenanmalik.com/reviews/sen_illusions.html (accessed on 5 January 2016).
10. Pico Iyer. *The Global Soul: Jet Lag, Shopping Malls, and the Search for Home.* New York: Knopf, 2001.
11. Helene Cixous. *Three Steps on the Ladder of Writing.* Translated by Sarah Cornell and Susan Sellers. New York: Columbia University Press, 1994.
12. Inez Baranay. *The Edge of Bali.* Sydney: HarperCollins/A&R Imprint, 1992.
13. Inez Baranay. *Rascal Rain: A Year in Papua New Guinea.* Sydney: A&R Imprint, 1994.
14. Inez Baranay. *Neem Dreams.* Delhi: Rupa & Co., 2003.
15. Inez Baranay. *Always Hungry.* Melbourne: Arcadia/Press On, 2011.
16. Inez Baranay. *Ghosts Like Us.* Raleigh: Local Time Publishing, 2015.
17. Daniel Medin. "A Conversation with Dubravka Ugresic." *Music and Literature*, 18 May 2015. Available online: http://www.musicandliterature.org/features/2015/5/12/a-conversation-with-dubravka-ugresic (accessed on 5 January 2016).

MDPI AG

St. Alban-Anlage 66

4052 Basel, Switzerland

Tel. +41 61 683 77 34

Fax +41 61 302 89 18

http://www.mdpi.com

Humanities Editorial Office

E-mail: humanities@mdpi.com

http://www.mdpi.com/journal/humanities